LIVING THE WORD

Scripture Reflections and Commentaries for Sundays and Holy Days

Msgr. Ralph Kuehner
and
Rev. Joseph J. Juknialis

LIVING THE WORD

Scripture Reflections and Commentaries for Sundays and Holy Days

Vol. 22 December 3, 2006—November 25, 2007

Published annually
Individual copy: $12.95
(2-9 copies: $9.95 per copy;
10-24 copies: $8.95 per copy;
25-99 copies: $7.95 per copy;
100 or more copies: $5.95 per copy)

Editor: Michael E. Novak
Copy Editor: Marcia T. Lucey
Typesetter: Tejal Patel
Cover Design: Paula Wendland and Tejal Patel
Editorial Director: Mary Beth Kunde-Anderson

Published with ecclesiastical approval

3708 River Road, Suite 400, Franklin Park, IL 60131-2158
800 566-6150 • Fax 888 957-3291
E-mail orders: wlpcs@jspaluch.com
Web address: www.wlpmusic.com

Printed in the United States of America
(ISSN) 1079-4670
(ISBN) 978-1-58459-354-6

Our renewed liturgy has generated a great deal of interest in sacred Scripture. In turn, a richer appreciation of the readings for Mass has done much for participation in our liturgical celebrations. It is this twofold deepening of the Christian life that *Living the Word* is intended to facilitate. It is our hope that individuals, homilists, catechumens, candidates, discussion groups, religious education classes, and similar gatherings will all benefit from the commentaries and reflections found on these pages.

The readings for each Sunday, holy day, and major celebration from December 2006 through November 2007, Year C of the liturgical cycle, are presented here, along with a brief passage intended to suggest a focus or approach to consider while reading them. Following the readings is a commentary that provides a context for understanding them, incorporating both biblical scholarship and the Church's age-old wisdom. A reflection section develops the initial focus and ties it together with the commentary. The discussion questions and suggestions for responses that follow offer help in moving from reflection to action, inviting those who use this volume to go about truly "Living the Word."

Whether reflecting on the scriptures in a group setting or individually, it is best to do so in the context of prayer. Consider creating an atmosphere that will foster prayerful reflection when you are using this book. In a quiet space, perhaps with lit candles and simple seasonal decoration (incense or soft music may also be appropriate), begin with a prayer and read aloud the scriptures for that day, even if you are alone. Groups can encourage members to focus on one word or idea that speaks to them from each reading. Participants might want to share these ideas with one another before continuing.

After listening to the readings, ask yourself how they have changed you, enlightened you, moved you. Proceed to the commentary, reflection, and response. Use the discussion questions to shape your conversation or as a springboard for your own questions. How does the brief "Responding to the Word" reflection invite you to "live the Word" in your relationship with God, with family and friends, at work, school, or church, or in the broader community?

Having started with prayer, perhaps once you have spent time in reflection or discussion it will be appropriate to lift up someone or something in a prayer that is related to the readings or your reflections. Pray spontaneously as you think about the texts' meaning for you or invite people in the group to offer prayers informally.

Finally, what action will you take this week that grows out of your prayerful reflection on this week's Scriptures? You may propose your own prayer for help to do something in response to the readings or simply stand and pray the Lord's Prayer. If you are in a group, offer one another a sign of peace before departing. If alone, extend yourself to another in a gesture of peace later in the day or week, in person, by phone, or by offering a simple prayer.

Repeating this pattern over time can help your prayerful reflection to deepen your appreciation for and commitment to God's Word every day of your life.

Table of Contents

Prayers Before Reading Scripture

Lord Jesus,
we give you praise.
Speak to us as we read your word,
and send your Spirit into our hearts.
Guide us today and each day in your service,
for you are our way, our truth, our life.

Lord Jesus, we love you:
keep us in your love for ever and ever. A*men*!

or

Blessed are you, Lord God,
king of all creation:
you have taught us by your word.
Open our hearts to your Spirit,
and lead us on the paths of Christ your Son.

All praise and glory be yours for ever. A*men*!

or

Lord, open our hearts:
let your Spirit speak to us
as we read your word. A*men*!

or

Lord Jesus,
to whom shall we go?
You have the words of eternal life.

Speak, Lord,
your servants are listening:
here we are, Lord,
ready to do your will. A*men*!

Prayers After Reading Scripture

Blessed are you, Lord God,
maker of heaven and earth,
ruler of the universe:
you have sent your Holy Spirit
to teach your truth to your holy people.
We praise you for letting us read your word today.

Grant that we may continue to think and pray
over the words we have read,
and to share your thoughts with others
throughout this day.

Loving God, we praise you
and thank you in Jesus' name. A*men*!

or

God of all graciousness, we thank you
for speaking to us today
through your holy word. A*men*!

Introduction to Advent/Christmas

Year C of the Church's liturgical cycle begins with some of the Gospel of Luke's best-known material, the Infancy Narratives. The author manages to weave his principal teachings into these accounts of the announcement and the birth of both John the Baptist and Jesus.

Throughout this liturgical year the Gospel of Luke will stress as the most important teaching that the Son of God came into the world to be the savior of all, especially the poor and sinners. Key verses, therefore, are Luke 2:10–11: "The angel said to them [the shepherds], 'Do not be afraid; for behold, I proclaim to you good news of great joy that will be for all the people. For today in the city of David a savior has been born for you who is Christ and Lord.' "

The concept of universal salvation is seen clearly in the angels' proclamation, "Glory to God in the highest / and on earth peace to those on whom his favor rests" (Luke 2:14). Luke is telling the reader that with the birth of Jesus there is now true glory to God in the highest and peace on earth to all since all enjoy God's favor. Jesus often makes the point in his public life that God has love for all of creation's children. "For he makes his sun rise on the bad and the good, and causes rain to fall on the just and the unjust" (Matthew 5:45).

Before the liturgy deals with these meaningful events in the life of Jesus, it introduces throughout Advent significant figures from salvation history. Jeremiah, the prophet of the New Covenant (31:31–34), tells the Israelites that God "will raise up for David a just shoot; he shall do what is right and just in the land" (33:15). Baruch, influenced by the writings of Jeremiah, tells his contemporaries that "God is leading Israel in joy / by the light of his glory, / with his mercy and justice for company" (5:9). Zephaniah has comforting words for the remnant that will survive the destruction of Jerusalem: "Shout for joy, O daughter Zion! / Sing joyfully, O Israel. / . . . The King of Israel, the LORD, is in your midst" (3:14, 15). Micah, a great advocate for social justice, is best known for this verse, "You, Bethlehem-Ephrathah, / too small to be among the clans of Judah, / from you shall come forth for me / the one who is to be ruler in Israel" (5:1). These Old Testament insights prepare Christians for the realization at Christmas of what these prophets had foretold.

As the Old Testament is coming to an end, Zechariah and Elizabeth, the parents of John the Baptist, are introduced. They insist on the name John ("God has shown favor"), a name given to them by God for their child. He is the outstanding figure of Advent, fulfilling his role in salvation history. He will "go before the Lord to prepare his way" (Luke 1:76).

Luke divides salvation history into three periods—the Period of Israel, the Period of Jesus, and the Period of the Church. The Church recalls the Period of Israel by the Advent season and begins the Period of Jesus on Christmas Day.

December 3, 2006

FIRST SUNDAY OF ADVENT

Today's Focus: Echoes of a New Creation

All life has been made new in Christ Jesus. Advent shoots of that new life break out as one world collapses and another is being breathed forth by our God. Indeed, nothing will ever be the same again.

FIRST READING
Jeremiah 33: 14–16

The days are coming, says the LORD, when I will fulfill the promise I made to the house of Israel and Judah. In those days, in that time, I will raise up for David a just shoot; he shall do what is right and just in the land. In those days Judah shall be safe and Jerusalem shall dwell secure; this is what they shall call her: "The LORD our justice."

PSALM RESPONSE
Psalm 25:1b

To you, O Lord, I lift my soul.

SECOND READING
1 Thessalonians 3:12 — 4:2

Brothers and sisters: May the Lord make you increase and abound in love for one another and for all, just as we have for you, so as to strengthen your hearts, to be blameless in holiness before our God and Father at the coming of our Lord Jesus with all his holy ones. Amen.

Finally, brothers and sisters, we earnestly ask and exhort you in the Lord Jesus that, as you received from us how you should conduct yourselves to please God—and as you are conducting yourselves—you do so even more. For you know what instructions we gave you through the Lord Jesus.

GOSPEL
Luke 21:25–28, 34–36

Jesus said to his disciples: "There will be signs in the sun, the moon, and the stars, and on earth nations will be in dismay, perplexed by the roaring of the sea and the waves. People will die of fright in anticipation of what is coming upon the world, for the powers of the heavens will be shaken. And then they will see the Son of Man coming in a cloud with power and great glory. But when these signs begin to happen, stand erect and raise your heads because your redemption is at hand.

"Beware that your hearts do not become drowsy from carousing and drunkenness and the anxieties of daily life, and that day catch you by surprise like a trap. For that day will assault everyone who lives on the face of the earth. Be vigilant at all times and pray that you have the strength to escape the tribulations that are imminent and to stand before the Son of Man."

Understanding the Word

In today's liturgy Luke begins the season of Advent with a strong stress on the Second Coming of Christ. This Gospel provides the final goal for every believer—to be with Jesus at his majestic appearance at the end of time. What Advent begins, the Second Coming concludes.

At this point in the Gospel of Luke Jesus had been speaking of the end of Jerusalem. Now he teaches about the end of the world. His second coming at that time is highlighted in terms borrowed from the prophet Daniel (7:13), "And then they will see the Son of Man coming in a cloud with power and great glory" (Luke 21:27).

Luke's advice to his readers is still useful to all followers of Christ. Christians are to be prepared for Christ's second coming at the end of time. They are not to become "drowsy from carousing and drunkenness and the anxieties of daily life" (21:34). Rather, they are to be vigilant and prayerful. Vigilance is the quality regularly required of Christians as they await the fulfillment of salvation history at the end of time. Vigilance and prayer will enable the followers of Christ to stand at the final judgment before the Son of Man.

Already in this first of the Gospels for this year Luke presents his favorite theme, namely that Jesus came into the world to save all. This concern for universal salvation and also universal judgment is reflected in his admonition that the day of his coming "will assault everyone who lives on the face of the earth" (21:35).

On this First Sunday of Advent Luke is asking all Christians to read the signs of the times, not to be frightened, but to stand joyfully with deep faith, aware that redemption is at hand at the Second Coming of Christ.

Reflecting on the Word

Advent no longer awaits the birth of an infant. Instead, we scan the horizons of our lives for the Son of Man who rides the cosmic winds of undreamed worlds being born. And every once in a while our hearts skip a beat as we recognize his coming made flesh. Then we stand up straight and raise our heads to welcome him yet one more time.

All is in the process of becoming. Within the brief span of two hundred years the American experiment has caught on, and the cry for democracy is heard on every continent in such a way that nothing will ever be the same again.

Knowledge and thought processes and attitudes and identity, once shaped predominantly by the printing press, are now molded through electronic circuitry, and nothing will ever be the same again.

A world economy is evolving while a nation-based industrial infrastructure is beginning to rust away, and nothing will ever be the same again.

And Church in the image of a pyramid has been challenged to ripple forth as a community of concentric circles instead, and nothing will ever be the same again.

Some would wonder whether all the change that is taking place is of God. But the believer puts faith in a God who is integral to all of life's events, a God who has not abandoned us, a God who makes all things work for good.

"The days are coming, says the LORD, when I will fulfill the promise I made" (Jeremiah 33:14). *Marana tha!* Come, Lord Jesus!

CONSIDER/ DISCUSS:

- As you look back upon your life, what was an unexpected "coming of God"?
- Of all that is taking place in today's world, what challenges you the most to trust that it could work to God's advantage?

Responding to the Word

God has been made flesh, eternally so, and as a result we who are believers are able to hear the faintly audible echoes of a new world being born in our midst. Nothing will ever be the same again.

Spend a few minutes in quiet prayer. Ask God to show you one (or more) ways that you may be called to respond to this week's scriptures—

- in your relationship with God
- with family and friends
- at work, school, or church
- in the broader community

December 8, 2006

THE IMMACULATE CONCEPTION OF THE BLESSED VIRGIN MARY

Today's Focus: Center of the Universe

Mary is a symbol of the Church. She represents all that we are called to be. Her willing response to God's invitation is a model for us when we, too, are invited to acknowledge God as the center of our universe.

FIRST READING
Genesis 3: 9–15, 20

After the man, Adam, had eaten of the tree, the LORD God called to the man and asked him, "Where are you?" He answered, "I heard you in the garden; but I was afraid, because I was naked, so I hid myself." Then he asked, "Who told you that you were naked? You have eaten, then, from the tree of which I had forbidden you to eat!" The man replied, "The woman whom you put here with me—she gave me fruit from the tree, and so I ate it." The LORD God then asked the woman, "Why did you do such a thing?" The woman answered, "The serpent tricked me into it, so I ate it."

Then the LORD God said to the serpent:
"Because you have done this, you shall be banned
from all the animals
and from all the wild creatures;
on your belly shall you crawl,
and dirt shall you eat
all the days of your life.
I will put enmity between you and the woman,
and between your offspring and hers;
he will strike at your head,
while you strike at his heel."
The man called his wife Eve, because she became the mother of all the living.

PSALM RESPONSE
Psalm 98:1a

Sing to the Lord a new song, for he has done marvelous deeds.

SECOND READING *Ephesians 1: 3–6, 11–12*

Brothers and sisters: Blessed be the God and Father of our Lord Jesus Christ, who has blessed us in Christ with every spiritual blessing in the heavens, as he chose us in him, before the foundation of the world, to be holy and without blemish before him. In love he destined us for adoption to himself through Jesus Christ, in accord with the favor of his will, for the praise of the glory of his grace that he granted us in the beloved.

In him we were also chosen, destined in accord with the purpose of the One who accomplishes all things according to the intention of his will, so that we might exist for the praise of his glory, we who first hoped in Christ.

GOSPEL *Luke 1:26–38*

The angel Gabriel was sent from God to a town of Galilee called Nazareth, to a virgin betrothed to a man named Joseph, of the house of David, and the virgin's name was Mary. And coming to her, he said, "Hail, full of grace! The Lord is with you." But she was greatly troubled at what was said and pondered what sort of greeting this might be. Then the angel said to her, "Do not be afraid, Mary, for you have found favor with God. Behold, you will conceive in your womb and bear a son, and you shall name him Jesus. He will be great and will be called Son of the Most High, and the Lord God will give him the throne of David his father, and he will rule over the house of Jacob forever, and of his kingdom there will be no end."

But Mary said to the angel, "How can this be, since I have no relations with a man?" And the angel said to her in reply, "The Holy Spirit will come upon you, and the power of the Most High will overshadow you. Therefore the child to be born will be called holy, the Son of God. And behold, Elizabeth, your relative, has also conceived a son in her old age, and this is the sixth month for her who was called barren; for nothing will be impossible for God."

Mary said, "Behold, I am the handmaid of the Lord. May it be done to me according to your word." Then the angel departed from her.

Understanding the Word

The Immaculate Conception is a defined teaching of the Catholic Church. The words themselves are negative, indicating that Mary was conceived without the stain of original sin. But the feast has the very positive aspect of the graces, the holiness of the virgin of Nazareth. This richness of her spiritual life is strongly highlighted in today's Gospel.

The very greeting of the angel Gabriel is most meaningful, "Hail, full of grace! The Lord is with you" (Luke 1:28). "Full of grace" translates a Greek verbal form that says that Mary has been favored by God and therefore now enjoys God's continuing favor. "The Lord is with you" follows naturally for one who is favored by God. With that favor, many graces, many blessings become part of her life.

Understandably the humble maiden is "greatly troubled" at this unusual greeting. The angel calms Mary's fear by reminding her again that she has won God's favor. She will experience the conception and birth of a wonderful child, the Son of God. She is to name the child Jesus, which means savior. This child will inherit the throne of David and will have an everlasting kingdom. The theologians and saints indicate that one's role in salvation history determines God's gifts to a person. Clearly then, Mary is very blessed by God as she is asked to become the mother of God's Son.

Mary has a problem. In a simple, straightforward way she points out that she "[has] no relations with a man" (1:34). Again she is the recipient of an amazing promise: "The Holy Spirit will come upon you, and the power of the Most High will overshadow you" (1:35). Mary's child will therefore be the Son of God.

God respects free will here as always with God's children, and awaits Mary's response. Importantly for all humankind she says, "I am the handmaid of the Lord. May it be done to me according to your word" (1:38). This response to God's will becomes the theme of Mary's entire life, constantly increasing her holiness.

Reflecting on the Word

From the very beginning we want what we want as soon as we want it. When the "terrible twos" come upon the scene our egos rise to a new level as we learn the power of no. By the time we reach the age of three, we've begun to develop the skill and learn the wisdom of subtlety, of having our way without making it so obvious. Unfortunately the temptation to assert ourselves as the center of the universe continues throughout all our days. We want our unfolding lives to mirror our dreams, our spouses to love in our ways of love, our children to choose our plans for them, our politics to be the politics of the nation, and our church to preach our understanding of faith.

The consequence of succumbing to that endless desire seems to be the source of evil in the world. In the end it becomes a choice contrary to St. Paul's counsel that "In him we were also chosen, destined in accord with the purpose of the One who accomplishes all things according to the intention of his will" (Ephesians 1:11). To live as if we are the center of the universe then becomes the ultimate clash of wills.

If it is true that God's love is greater than our sin, then the undoing of evil takes place in our mirroring Mary's yes, even when doing so baffles and mystifies and frightens. Then the power of original sin is undone. Or to turn the equation around, if evil withers and goodness blossoms when we willingly mold our choices to God's ways, rather than rigidly persisting in our own paths, then it must be true. Then the center of the universe is not us but God.

CONSIDER/ DISCUSS:

- How have you experienced God's will in your life? Has it been fruitful or a bitter pill to swallow?
- How do you sort out God's will for you? How do you know what it is to which you should say yes?

Responding to the Word

The mythical tale of good and evil is retold in every age. It is the story of Luke Skywalker and Darth Vader, of Frodo and Sauron, of Harry Potter and Lord Voldemort. In the end it is the story of grace and sin in each of our lives, a battle of wills over control of the center of the universe. When we follow Mary's example we end the battle and recognize that God's rule is supreme.

Spend a few minutes in quiet prayer. Ask God to show you one (or more) ways that you may be called to respond to this week's scriptures—

- in your relationship with God
- with family and friends
- at work, school, or church
- in the broader community

December 10, 2006

SECOND SUNDAY OF ADVENT

Today's Focus: The Sugarplums of Advent

It may be that liturgically these days are Advent preparing us to celebrate the birth of Jesus. Humanly, however, these days are already Christmas simply because all of life has been made new. All of life has become the Word made flesh.

FIRST READING
Baruch 5:1–9

Jerusalem, take off your robe of mourning and misery;
put on the splendor of glory from God forever:
wrapped in the cloak of justice from God,
bear on your head the mitre
that displays the glory of the eternal name.
For God will show all the earth your splendor:
you will be named by God forever
the peace of justice, the glory of God's worship.

Up, Jerusalem! stand upon the heights;
look to the east and see your children
gathered from the east and the west
at the word of the Holy One,
rejoicing that they are remembered by God.
Led away on foot by their enemies they left you:
but God will bring them back to you
borne aloft in glory as on royal thrones.
For God has commanded
that every lofty mountain be made low,
and that the age-old depths and gorges
be filled to level ground,
that Israel may advance secure in the glory of God.
The forests and every fragrant kind of tree
have overshadowed Israel at God's command;
for God is leading Israel in joy
by the light of his glory,
with his mercy and justice for company.

PSALM RESPONSE
Psalm 126:3

The Lord has done great things for us; we are filled with joy.

SECOND READING *Philippians 1: 4–6, 8–11*

Brothers and sisters: I pray always with joy in my every prayer for all of you, because of your partnership for the gospel from the first day until now. I am confident of this, that the one who began a good work in you will continue to complete it until the day of Christ Jesus. God is my witness, how I long for all of you with the affection of Christ Jesus. And this is my prayer: that your love may increase ever more and more in knowledge and every kind of perception, to discern what is of value, so that you may be pure and blameless for the day of Christ, filled with the fruit of righteousness that comes through Jesus Christ for the glory and praise of God.

GOSPEL *Luke 3:1–6*

In the fifteenth year of the reign of Tiberius Caesar, when Pontius Pilate was governor of Judea, and Herod was tetrarch of Galilee, and his brother Philip tetrarch of the region of Ituraea and Trachonitis, and Lysanias was tetrarch of Abilene, during the high priesthood of Annas and Caiaphas, the word of God came to John the son of Zechariah in the desert. John went throughout the whole region of the Jordan, proclaiming a baptism of repentance for the forgiveness of sins, as it is written in the book of the words of the prophet Isaiah:

A *voice of one crying out in the desert:*
"Prepare the way of the Lord,
make straight his paths.
Every valley shall be filled
and every mountain and hill shall be made low.
The winding roads shall be made straight,
and the rough ways made smooth,
and all flesh shall see the salvation of God.'"

Understanding the Word

"Prepare the way of the Lord" is clearly the theme of all the readings on this Second Sunday of Advent, reminding the Christian to prepare for the coming of Jesus on Christmas Day. The prophet Baruch strongly encourages Jerusalem to ascend the heights to prepare the way of the Lord who is bringing the exiles home. "God is leading Israel in joy / by the light of his glory, / with his mercy and justice for company" (Baruch 5:9).

In his letter to the Philippians Saint Paul encourages his favorite community to "prepare the way of the Lord" by an increase in love and knowledge so that they "may be pure and blameless for the day of Christ" (Philippians 1:10), the day of his Second Coming. He assures them and all followers of the Savior that "the one who began a good work in you will continue to complete it until the day of Christ Jesus" (1:6).

The Gospel reminds us that "preparing the way of the Lord" was the purpose given to John for his ministry, for his key role in salvation history. Luke applies the text from Isaiah (40:3–5) to the Baptist. The importance of this role of John is seen in the fact that the same words of Isaiah are also applied to him in the Gospels of Matthew and Mark. In the Gospel of John, the Baptist applies these word of Isaiah to himself and goes on to say, "the reason why I came baptizing with water was that he might be made known to Israel" (John 1:23, 31).

Luke takes the quotation from Isaiah further than the other evangelists in order to highlight these words, "all flesh shall see the salvation of God" (Luke 3:6). The reader is reminded of Luke's principal theme, namely that Jesus has come to be the savior of all. John the Baptist is indeed "preparing the way of the Lord," a Lord who will give his life for the salvation of each and every human being.

Reflecting on the Word

On most days since early October the students in the college residence in which I live have been eagerly and insistently bouncing Christmas carols off walls and into hallways. It began with occasional songs on the piano. Soon after, the Christmas CDs were brought out, and a week later one of them came upon an old turntable and some Sinatra Christmas LPs. As they left for Thanksgiving vacation, they each reminded me that the radio would begin playing Christmas music all day long on the day after Thanksgiving. As a result of all this I've found myself wondering what it is that's driven these twenty-year-olds toward such early visions of Christmas sugarplums.

I've come to believe that beneath all the glitter draped and swagged with ribbons and bows over these days, deeper longings are at play, longings beyond desire for the newest iPod or the latest cell phone, longings for community or healed relationships, longings, too, for peace among nations and for some sort of equality among people.

Curiously, such deepened longings are never marketed by any hype. Yet like Christmas spirit, they just seem to sprout wherever the human spirit finds a niche. I suppose one could make the observation that a twenty-year-old's longing for Christmas is little more than leftover nostalgia for childhood Santas and once-upon-a-time daydreams. Maybe so. Yet Paul once wrote to the Philippian community that such urgings for goodness all begin with God and that ultimately "the one who began a good work in you will continue to complete it until the day of Christ Jesus" (Philippians 1:6). In other words, these deeper longings, they seem to be God's doing, and who are we to put them on a timetable?

CONSIDER/ DISCUSS:

- What valleys in your life have most recently been filled? What mountains have you seen brought low?
- What is the current longing with which you live? What is God's role in its fulfillment for you?

Responding to the Word

Advent is about the very place from which all of our dreams begin—in God. It's where age-old gorges of human pain and suffering begin to be filled and where mountains of injustice are eventually brought low. It's the way God begins to lead the people home to where it all began.

Spend a few minutes in quiet prayer. Ask God to show you one (or more) ways that you may be called to respond to this week's scriptures—

- in your relationship with God
- with family and friends
- at work, school, or church
- in the broader community

December 17, 2006

THIRD SUNDAY OF ADVENT

Today's Focus: Wandering Hearts

Hearts wander, sometimes against our best efforts and sometimes without our even realizing it or intending it. Sometimes it's to another heart that they wander, and sometimes they just wander on and on. If we could guard against that wanderlust, well, we'd just be better off.

FIRST READING
Zephaniah 3: 14–18a

Shout for joy, O daughter Zion!
  Sing joyfully, O Israel!
Be glad and exult with all your heart,
  O daughter Jerusalem!
The LORD has removed the judgment against you
  he has turned away your enemies;
the King of Israel, the LORD, is in your midst,
  you have no further misfortune to fear.
On that day, it shall be said to Jerusalem:
  Fear not, O Zion, be not discouraged!
The LORD, your God, is in your midst,
  a mighty savior;
he will rejoice over you with gladness,
  and renew you in his love,
he will sing joyfully because of you,
  as one sings at festivals.

PSALM RESPONSE
Isaiah 12:6

Cry out with joy and gladness: for among you is the great and Holy One of Israel.

SECOND READING
Philippians 4: 4–7

Brothers and sisters: Rejoice in the Lord always. I shall say it again: rejoice! Your kindness should be known to all. The Lord is near. Have no anxiety at all, but in everything, by prayer and petition, with thanksgiving, make your requests known to God. Then the peace of God that surpasses all understanding will guard your hearts and minds in Christ Jesus.

GOSPEL
Luke 3:10–18

The crowds asked John the Baptist, "What should we do?" He said to them in reply, "Whoever has two cloaks should share with the person who has none. And whoever has food should do likewise." Even tax collectors came to be baptized and they said to him, "Teacher, what should we do?" He answered them, "Stop collecting more than what is prescribed." Soldiers also asked him, "And what is it that we should do?" He told them, "Do not practice extortion, do not falsely accuse anyone, and be satisfied with your wages."

Now the people were filled with expectation, and all were asking in their hearts whether John might be the Christ. John answered them all, saying, "I am baptizing you with water, but one mightier than I is coming. I am not worthy to loosen the thongs of his sandals. He will baptize you with the Holy Spirit and fire. His winnowing fan is in his hand to clear his threshing floor and to gather the wheat into his barn, but the chaff he will burn with unquenchable fire." Exhorting them in many other ways, he preached good news to the people.

Understanding the Word

"Gaudete Sunday" is a traditional name given to this Third Sunday of Advent. *Gaudete* is the Latin word for "Rejoice!" The joy comes from the realization that we are approaching the wonderful event of the birth of the Messiah. The prophet Zephaniah, confident of the future, calls out, "Shout for joy, O daughter Zion! / Sing joyfully, O Israel! . . . The LORD, your God, is in your midst, / a mighty savior" (3:14, 17). Saint Paul continues the joyful note: "Rejoice in the Lord always. I shall say it again: rejoice!" (Philippians 4:4).

John the Baptist gives many reasons for rejoicing. In the first part of today's Gospel an example of the Baptist's moral preaching (Luke 3:10–14) reaches out to the people with practical guides for social conduct. The crowds are asked to show loving concern for their neighbors; the tax collectors are asked to be honest; the soldiers are not to use their power to intimidate people in order to get money. John does not ask anything heroic, just essentially good conduct.

The special cause for joy, however, is the messianic preaching of the Baptist (3:15–18). The Jewish people were waiting for the Messiah, an anointed agent of God. The belief started with God's promise to David that his royal family would last forever (2 Samuel 7:13). At the time of Christ the expectation was for an ideal David, the Messiah. In fact, the most popular title for the Messiah was "Son of David." This promise is fulfilled in Jesus: "The Lord God will give him the throne of David his father" (Luke 1:32).

While insisting that he is not the Messiah, John promises that one mightier than he is coming. "The coming one" was also a Messianic title. "He will baptize you with the Holy Spirit and fire" (Luke 3:16). Christians would tend to see "the Holy Spirit and fire" in connection with the Spirit's descent with tongues of fire on Pentecost. The Baptist saw "the holy spirit and fire" as purifying and refining qualities of the Messiah's baptism, a baptism that would purify, refine, and unite one with Jesus.

Reflecting on the Word

When hearts wander it can happen that they stop by woods dark and deep on some snowy night, as the poet Robert Frost once happened to notice. At such times we can find ourselves daydreaming of some other life, of one that lives only in our wishfulness. And then if we're lucky the jingling bells on the horse's reins call our hearts back to the waiting sleigh so we can make our way home to where our true love lives.

Sometimes our hearts wander to times ago, to the way we once knew life long past, when we were children living in a gingerbread home with candy cane doorframes and love that seemed so customary that we never even knew its absences.

In these Advent days we talk much about waiting—waiting for the coming of the Lord and for the Lord's return and for the Lord's being enfleshed in our lives anew. It may be more the case, however, that our God is waiting for us. Scattered amid our own wanderings, amid our own comings and goings, it is God who waits for us to come on home. In the meantime, St. Paul says, that same God guards our hearts.

How so, you ask? The very fact that we wonder why we cannot live the entire year through in the same fashion that we do in this season suggests that we are being guarded from total indifference. And the hint of a different sort of joy we experience these days—that, too, says much about realizing where our hearts belong. And the generosity as well. And the forgiveness and tolerance. They all say something about the fact that our hearts are guarded all year long, even amid our wanderings.

CONSIDER/ DISCUSS:

- Where is your heart inclined to wander?
- What is best for you about these days of Advent and Christmas? Does that say something to you about what your heart tends to wander from?

Responding to the Word

Because hearts do wander, John the Baptist reminds the people to stay grounded, sometimes by sharing what they have, sometimes by being content with what is, sometimes by not taking advantage of a lost soul. They are all ways of keeping our hearts from wandering off.

Spend a few minutes in quiet prayer. Ask God to show you one (or more) ways that you may be called to respond to this week's scriptures—

- in your relationship with God
- with family and friends
- at work, school, or church
- in the broader community

December 24, 2006

FOURTH SUNDAY OF ADVENT

Today's Focus: Nooks and Crannies of Bethlehem

Sometimes we forget to treasure the small and seemingly discarded jewels of life, quiet moments of peace and joy and the presence of one another. As we negotiate the transition to adulthood we seem to quit giving them as much attention. As with Bethlehem, it is in small places that great treasures are found.

FIRST READING
Micah 5:1–4a

Thus says the LORD:
You, Bethlehem-Ephrathah,
too small to be among the clans of Judah,
from you shall come forth for me
one who is to be ruler in Israel;
whose origin is from of old,
from ancient times.
Therefore the Lord will give them up, until the time
when she who is to give birth has borne,
and the rest of his kindred shall return
to the children of Israel.
He shall stand firm and shepherd his flock
by the strength of the LORD,
in the majestic name of the LORD, his God;
and they shall remain, for now his greatness
shall reach to the ends of the earth;
he shall be peace.

PSALM RESPONSE
Psalm 80:4

Lord, make us turn to you; let us see your face and we shall be saved.

SECOND READING
Hebrews 10: 5–10

Brothers and sisters: When Christ came into the world, he said:
"Sacrifice and offering you did not desire,
but a body you prepared for me;
in holocausts and sin offerings you took no delight.
Then I said, 'As is written of me in the scroll,
behold, I come to do your will, O God.'"

First he says,
"Sacrifices and offerings, holocausts and sin offerings,
you neither desired nor delighted in."
These are offered according to the law. Then he says,
"Behold, I come to do your will."

He takes away the first to establish the second.
By this "will," we have been consecrated through the offering of the body of Jesus Christ once for all.

GOSPEL *Luke 1:39–45*

Mary set out and traveled to the hill country in haste to a town of Judah, where she entered the house of Zechariah and greeted Elizabeth. When Elizabeth heard Mary's greeting, the infant leaped in her womb, and Elizabeth, filled with the Holy Spirit, cried out in a loud voice and said, "Blessed are you among women, and blessed is the fruit of your womb. And how does this happen to me, that the mother of my Lord should come to me? For at the moment the sound of your greeting reached my ears, the infant in my womb leaped for joy. Blessed are you who believed that what was spoken to you by the Lord would be fulfilled."

Understanding the Word

Mary's visit to Elizabeth was an example of concern for her cousin, but became the occasion of important religious teaching.

The Gospel of Luke highlights the key role of the Holy Spirit in the life of Jesus. The Spirit appears prominently in today's Gospel of the Visitation. The angel Gabriel had already promised Zechariah that his son "will be filled with the holy Spirit even from his mother's womb" (Luke 1:15). As Mary arrives, the Spirit causes John to leap for joy in the presence of the Messiah in the womb of Mary. The stage is now set for the culmination of salvation history. The one who is to prepare the way has met the Lord.

Elizabeth, filled with the Holy Spirit, greets her cousin with words of great importance for the role of Mary. "Blessed are you among women, and blessed is the fruit of your womb" (1:42). Clearly it is the fruit of Mary's womb, the incarnate Son of God, who is uniquely blessed and brings blessings to his mother. Father Joseph Fitzmyer explains, "Since according to contemporary Jewish ideas a woman's greatness was measured by the children that she bore, the mother of the *kyrios* (Lord) would naturally be said to surpass all others" (*The Anchor Bible*, vol. 28, p. 364). Elizabeth referred to Mary as the "mother of my Lord" (Luke 1:43). "LORD" is used to translate Yahweh in the Greek version of the Old Testament. Elizabeth is recognizing her cousin as the mother of the Messiah, and Luke in the light of Resurrection faith proclaims her the mother of God (LORD).

Elizabeth has further words of praise for Mary, "Blessed are you who believed that what was spoken to you by the Lord would be fulfilled" (1:45). In the public life of Jesus a woman will remind the reader of Elizabeth as she calls out, "Blessed is the womb that carried you and the breasts at which you nursed" (11:27). But Jesus' response reminds one of Elizabeth's final words praising the faith of Mary. Jesus says, "Rather, blessed are those who hear the word of God and observe it" (11:28). Mary is the prime example of the disciple who hears the word of God and observes it.

Reflecting on the Word

Faith seems to begin in obscure and tiny Bethlehem nooks of daily living that not only make us human but in time believers as well. In the beginning such moments take the shape of learning to say "Thank you" and "I'm sorry" and of being told that we must share. It's also about a large adult hand taking our tiny three-year-old hand and dipping it in the holy water as we walk into church and then in tandem awkwardly making the sign of the cross.

Much later in life there are other small Bethlehems where life and faith are discovered and rediscovered. Sometimes they are the quiet that nuzzles its way into a portion of our day. Sometimes a knowing smile that says it was all worthwhile. Sometimes it's the shoots of goodness and compassion and tenderness that spring up in an adolescent's life when you thought it was way too late for the seeds to sprout now. And sometimes it's unexpected justice in the workplace.

It's also true that sometimes such moments are so small that we're not sure they really took place. Maybe we just imagined it, or wanted it all too much and made it happen in our daydreams. Sometimes. But then something else happens in our hearts, or maybe in the womb of our spirits. Something happens in that place where faith and hope and love are born. Something dances and leaps for joy, and we begin to believe that somehow what was spoken by the Lord is being fulfilled in our own lives. We begin to think that maybe we understand a little bit better what it means to believe that the Word became flesh. And then beyond the twinkling lights and sparkling glitter and wafting carols, Christmas happens.

CONSIDER/ DISCUSS:

- Take time to remember the tiny fields of Bethlehem where your faith began. Treasure them. Look for an opportunity to give them birth in someone else's life.
- Where do you find faith nurtured in these days? Are there still tiny fields of Bethlehem in your life?

Responding to the Word

We presume that real life happens amid all the great and grand schemes, that what makes a difference takes place outside our own lives. Still, the moments we remember, the times that shaped us into who were are today, were often small Bethlehems hardly noticed at the time.

Spend a few minutes in quiet prayer. Ask God to show you one (or more) ways that you may be called to respond to this week's scriptures—

- in your relationship with God
- with family and friends
- at work, school, or church
- in the broader community

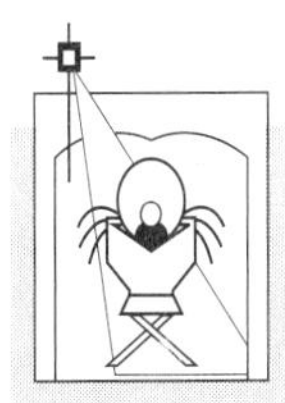

December 25, 2006

THE NATIVITY OF THE LORD CHRISTMAS MASS DURING THE DAY

Today's Focus: Saved Inside Out

The Incarnation attests to God being one with all that is. All creation has been made good. Still the most recent dazzling technology does not save us from boredom, and new clothes do not save us from the reality that we are as ordinary as the person next to us. Despite wonderful Christmas gifts, we still find ourselves yearning for more.

FIRST READING *Isaiah 52:7-10*

How beautiful upon the mountains
are the feet of him who brings glad tidings,
announcing peace, bearing good news,
announcing salvation, and saying to Zion,
"Your God is King!"

Hark! Your sentinels raise a cry,
together they shout for joy,
for they see directly, before their eyes,
the LORD restoring Zion.
Break out together in song,
O ruins of Jerusalem!
For the LORD comforts his people,
he redeems Jerusalem.
The LORD has bared his holy arm
in the sight of all the nations;
all the ends of the earth will behold
the salvation of our God.

PSALM RESPONSE *Psalm 98:3c*

All the ends of the earth have seen the saving power of God.

SECOND READING *Hebrews 1:1-6*

Brothers and sisters: In times past, God spoke in partial and various ways to our ancestors through the prophets; in these last days, he has spoken to us through the Son, whom he made heir of all things and through whom he created the universe, who is the refulgence of his glory, the very imprint of his being, and who sustains all things by his mighty word. When he had accomplished purification from sins, he took his seat at the right hand of the Majesty on high, as far superior to the angels as the name he has inherited is more excellent than theirs.

For to which of the angels did God ever say:
You are my son; this day I have begotten you?
Or again:
I will be a father to him, and he shall be a son to me?
And again, when he leads the firstborn into the world, he says:
Let all the angels of God worship him.

In the shorter form of the reading, the passages in brackets are omitted.

GOSPEL
John 1:1-18

In the beginning was the Word,
and the Word was with God,
and the Word was God.
He was in the beginning with God.
All things came to be through him,
and without him nothing came to be.

What came to be through him was life,
and this life was the light of the human race;
the light shines in the darkness,
and the darkness has not overcome it.

[A man named John was sent from God. He came for testimony, to testify to the light, so that all might believe through him. He was not the light, but came to testify to the light.] The true light, which enlightens everyone, was coming into the world.

He was in the world,
and the world came to be through him,
but the world did not know him.
He came to what was his own,
but his own people did not accept him.

But to those who did accept him he gave power to become children of God, to those who believe in his name, who were born not by natural generation nor by human choice nor by a man's decision but of God.

And the Word became flesh
and made his dwelling among us,
and we saw his glory,
the glory as of the Father's only Son,
full of grace and truth.

[John testified to him and cried out, saying, "This was he of whom I said, 'The one who is coming after me ranks ahead of me because he existed before me.'" From his fullness we have all received, grace in place of grace, because while the law was given through Moses, grace and truth came through Jesus Christ. No one has ever seen God. The only Son, God, who is at the Father's side, has revealed him.] What came to be through him was life,

and this life was the light of the human race;
the light shines in the darkness,
and the darkness has not overcome it.

[A man named John was sent from God. He came for testimony, to testify to the light, so that all might believe through him.
He was not the light, but came to testify to the light.] The true light, which enlightens everyone, was coming into the world.

He was in the world,
and the world came to be through him,
but the world did not know him.

He came to what was his own,
  but his own people did not accept him.

But to those who did accept him he gave power to become children of God, to those who believe in his name, who were born not by natural generation nor by human choice nor by a man's decision but of God.

And the Word became flesh
  and made his dwelling among us,
  and we saw his glory,
  the glory as of the Father's only Son,
  full of grace and truth.

[John testified to him and cried out, saying, "This was he of whom I said, 'The one who is coming after me ranks ahead of me because he existed before me.'" From his fullness we have all received, grace in place of grace, because while the law was given through Moses, grace and truth came through Jesus Christ. No one has ever seen God. The only Son, God, who is at the Father's side, has revealed him.]

Understanding the Word

The Prologue is a magnificent beginning to the Gospel of John. As a reading for Christmas Day, it can truly be seen as John's infancy narrative. "The Word became flesh / and made his dwelling among us" (John 1:14) reminds the reader of that first Christmas when Jesus was born at Bethlehem. What precedes this verse and what follows gives a great understanding of who this child truly is. The Prologue begins as Genesis does, "In the beginning," and adds, "was the Word, / and the Word was with God, / and the Word was God" (1:1). These words from Genesis remind us of the effective word of God at creation, " 'Let there be light,' and there was light" (Genesis 1:3). This creative word of God together with texts dealing with divine Wisdom may have suggested using "Word" for the Second Person of the Trinity. The following verses in John stress the role of the Word in creation and suggest texts such as this from the Book of Wisdom: "Now with you is Wisdom, who knows your works / and was present when you made the world" (Wisdom 9:9).

The Prologue also has much to say about the Baptist. He is principally portrayed as a witness to the true light, the Word coming into the world on Christmas Day. John the Baptist and John the Evangelist are clear that though the Baptist is important in salvation history, the Baptist is a human being whereas the "Word is God."

The Prologue foretells the reaction that Jesus, the incarnate Word, will receive. His own will reject him (John 1:10–11) as the first half of John's Gospel makes clear. But some will receive him and become children of God, not by any human initiative, but by the grace of God (1:12–13). This is the message of the second half of the John's Gospel.

The two great qualities of God in the Old Testament were loving mercy and fidelity. John stresses that those same qualities are seen in the glory of the Father's only Son (1:14). Also, this only Son, God, will start a new covenant, replacing the covenant of Moses. We receive this loving mercy and fidelity from Jesus Christ. He alone knows the Father and reveals the Father to everyone (1:16–18).

Reflecting on the Word

New billion-dollar levees will not guarantee New Orleans or any other city safety from the ravages of nature. More efficient weapons will not save us from terrorists. Botox will not save us from growing old. The real question is who or what will save us from ourselves?

What we celebrate on the solemnity of the birth of Jesus is the fact that God saves us from within, that the Word did become flesh. Once upon a time God chose to get inside our skin, and ever since then God has not abandoned this human condition. In Jesus Christ God became light amid so much human darkness. In so doing, God saves us from endless groping for life by revealing through Jesus how we are able to find real life—in our love for one another.

None of us love as well as we'd hope, but it does seem that we as a people do love one another a bit better during this season than we do during the rest of the year. It's the Godly spark we've picked up from Jesus that enables us to tolerate one another a bit more willingly, to greet strangers with a smile more readily, to give more generously without assessing the cost or the need. We do so, and if our enthusiasm for it wanes during the rest of the year, at least during these days we are willing to give way and let Christ save us from within by fostering our love for one another.

CONSIDER/ DISCUSS:

- Why do you do things for strangers or those on the periphery of your life?
- What "works" in giving your life meaning? What seems to fall short?
- Personally, are you more likely to find God deep within or in wonder and awe of that which is beyond?

Responding to the Word

We can wish Christmas would last all year long, or we can choose to live it personally and so find that Christmas can indeed live all year long, not because of what others do for us but because of what we do for one another.

Spend a few minutes in quiet prayer. Ask God to show you one (or more) ways that you may be called to respond to this week's scriptures—

- in your relationship with God
- with family and friends
- at work, school, or church
- in the broader community

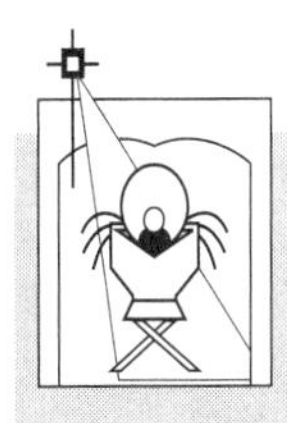

December 31, 2006

THE HOLY FAMILY OF JESUS, MARY, AND JOSEPH

Today's Focus: Family Instincts

In some ways we might say that family happens by instinct; but then there is another part of us that believes just as surely that that instinct is none other than the very grace of God within each of us, refusing to abandon a soul-deep longing that this crippled world of ours be made whole.

FIRST READING
1 Samuel 1: 20–22, 24–28

In those days Hannah conceived, and at the end of her term bore a son whom she called Samuel, since she had asked the LORD for him. The next time her husband Elkanah was going up with the rest of his household to offer the customary sacrifice to the LORD and to fulfill his vows, Hannah did not go, explaining to her husband, "Once the child is weaned, I will take him to appear before the LORD and to remain there forever; I will offer him as a perpetual nazirite."

Once Samuel was weaned, Hannah brought him up with her, along with a three-year-old bull, an ephah of flour, and a skin of wine, and presented him at the temple of the LORD in Shiloh. After the boy's father had sacrificed the young bull, Hannah, his mother, approached Eli and said: "Pardon, my lord! As you live, my lord, I am the woman who stood near you here, praying to the LORD. I prayed for this child, and the LORD granted my request. Now I, in turn, give him to the LORD; as long as he lives, he shall be dedicated to the LORD." Hannah left Samuel there.

PSALM RESPONSE
Psalm 84:5a

Blessed are they who dwell in your house, O Lord.

SECOND READING
1 John 3:1–2, 21–24

Beloved: See what love the Father has bestowed on us that we may be called the children of God. And so we are. The reason the world does not know us is that it did not know him. Beloved, we are God's children now; what we shall be has not yet been revealed. We do know that when it is revealed we shall be like him, for we shall see him as he is.

Beloved, if our hearts do not condemn us, we have confidence in God and receive from him whatever we ask, because we keep his commandments and do what pleases him. And his commandment is this: we should believe in the name of his Son, Jesus Christ, and love one another just as he commanded us. Those who keep his commandments remain in him, and he in them, and the way we know that he remains in us is from the Spirit he gave us.

GOSPEL
Luke 2:41–52

Each year Jesus' parents went to Jerusalem for the feast of Passover, and when he was twelve years old, they went up according to festival custom. After they had completed its days, as they were returning, the boy Jesus remained behind in Jerusalem, but his parents did not know it. Thinking that he was in the caravan, they journeyed for a day and looked for him among their relatives and acquaintances, but not finding him, they returned to Jerusalem to look for him.

After three days they found him in the temple, sitting in the midst of the teachers, listening to them and asking them questions, and all who heard him were astounded at his understanding and his answers.

When his parents saw him, they were astonished, and his mother said to him, "Son, why have you done this to us? Your father and I have been looking for you with great anxiety." And he said to them, "Why were you looking for me? Did you not know that I must be in my Father's house?" But they did not understand what he said to them.

He went down with them and came to Nazareth, and was obedient to them; and his mother kept all these things in her heart. And Jesus advanced in wisdom and age and favor before God and man.

Understanding the Word

Today's Gospel about the finding of the boy Jesus in the Temple offers important teachings about Jesus and also about the Holy Family of Jesus, Mary, and Joseph. The principal teaching is the special relationship between Christ and his heavenly Father. "I *must* be in my Father's house" (Luke 2:49). The verb in the Greek text is the same one that Luke uses to refer to necessary aspects of salvation history. Thus the relationship of Jesus to the Father and his mission are stressed as keys to salvation history.

The Gospel is helpful for all Christian families as it teaches the piety of the Holy Family. They regularly went to the three pilgrimage feasts: the Passover of today's Gospel, Booths, and Pentecost. Even though women and children under thirteen were not required to attend, Mary and Jesus do accompany Joseph. When the Holy Family returned to Nazareth, the Greek text says that he was continually obedient to his parents (2:51). The Savior continued his observance of Jewish law throughout his public life. For instance, he "went according to his custom into the synagogue on the sabbath day" (4:16).

Mary and Joseph have a difficult time understanding why Jesus remained in the Temple. Their problem reflects the basic difficulty all the followers of Christ had in trying to understand him. No one at that time, for instance, had ever heard of the Trinity, three Persons in one God. Though Mary had been told many things about her Son, today's Gospel shows that hers would be a gradual learning process. The sword of judgment that Simeon had promised forced Mary to make judgments about her Son. She responded with faith and became the prime believer, the first and greatest disciple. "[H]is mother kept all these things in her heart" (2:51).

Jerusalem and the Temple are important not only in today's Gospel, but throughout the Gospel of Luke. The infancy narrative begins and ends in the Temple of Jerusalem. At the end of the Gospel his disciples "were continually in the temple praising God" (24:53). Jesus himself makes a final trip to Jerusalem (9:51 — 19:27) and the early church goes from "Jerusalem, throughout Judea and Samaria, and to the ends of the earth" (Acts 1:8).

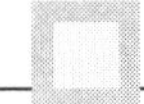

Reflecting on the Word

It was mid-December and the red-and-green combustion of Christmas was everywhere. So when I heard my name called out in the mall, I turned to look back. "It's me, Paul. Remember me?" I did, easily so, though the last time I had seen him was long before when he was in grade school. He'd grown up now, taller, married, and a father, too, he quickly and proudly proclaimed. Then Paul did what every new father has ever done since the invention of the camera. He pulled out his wallet and began flipping through the pictures of his daughter.

"I've been thinking about you," he said to me. "I'd like to have her baptized and was wondering if you would be able to." Paul grinned. He was pleased with himself, I could tell, for wanting to do what a good parent does.

The mall swished about us in a frenzy of Christmas, yet there stood Paul in a very different Christmas field of dreams, somewhere between the memories of his own childhood and the early stirrings of his daughter's new life and what that life might produce in her. Like Mary and Joseph and all who came to the Temple, so Paul and every other parent as well come to the Church, believing not only that their child's life can be filled with holiness and peace, but also believing that something in that child can be the very revelation of a God who is in our midst.

I doubt if most parents think about it in those terms. I'm sure they don't. But they do look upon their own love made flesh and find themselves believing that maybe this child could be more than they themselves ever were.

CONSIDER/ DISCUSS:

- What events have sparked for you the belief that life can and will be more than what it is?
- Among the people whom you know as family, what longings burn eternal?

Family is family because we struggle to nurture in one another what so often no one else will. We try to clothe one another with mercy and kindness and meekness and patience. We choose to be willing to bear with one another, forgive grievances, and put on the sort of love that holds us all together. Could any of us be family without that?

Spend a few minutes in quiet prayer. Ask God to show you one (or more) ways that you may be called to respond to this week's scriptures—

- in your relationship with God
- with family and friends
- at work, school, or church
- in the broader community

January 1, 2007

THE BLESSED VIRGIN MARY, THE MOTHER OF GOD

Today's Focus: Soul Noise

The turn of the year stirs reminiscing and dreaming, attentiveness as well to births and deaths, comings and goings, successes and failures. And if we stay for a bit with such ruminations, we're more than likely to grow aware of what is stirring deep within us as well.

FIRST READING *Numbers 6: 22–27*

The LORD said to Moses: "Speak to Aaron and his sons and tell them: This is how you shall bless the Israelites. Say to them:

The LORD bless you and keep you!
The LORD let his face shine upon you, and be gracious to you!
The LORD look upon you kindly and give you peace!

So shall they invoke my name upon the Israelites, and I will bless them."

PSALM RESPONSE *Psalm 67:2a*

May God bless us in his mercy.

SECOND READING *Galatians 4:4–7*

Brothers and sisters: When the fullness of time had come, God sent his Son, born of a woman, born under the law, to ransom those under the law, so that we might receive adoption as sons. As proof that you are sons, God sent the Spirit of his Son into our hearts, crying out, "Abba, Father!" So you are no longer a slave but a son, and if a son then also an heir, through God.

GOSPEL *Luke 2:16–21*

The shepherds went in haste to Bethlehem and found Mary and Joseph, and the infant lying in the manger. When they saw this, they made known the message that had been told them about this child. All who heard it were amazed by what had been told them by the shepherds. And Mary kept all these things, reflecting on them in her heart. Then the shepherds returned, glorifying and praising God for all they had heard and seen, just as it had been told to them.

When eight days were completed for his circumcision, he was named Jesus, the name given him by the angel before he was conceived in the womb.

Understanding the Word

The readings begin today with the priestly prayer from the book of Numbers. The prayer ends with this blessing, "The LORD look upon you kindly and give you peace" (Numbers 6:26). "Peace" in the biblical tradition means much more than the absence of hostility. It is a very positive concept, implying fullness, completion, perfection. It promises the fullness of God's messianic blessings. A strong Old Testament theme sees the mother of the Messiah as one of those special blessings.

In the book of Genesis, immediately after the sin of Adam and Eve, God promises future salvation. "I will put enmity between you and the woman, / and between your offspring and hers; / he will strike at your head, / while you strike at his heel" (Genesis 3:15). Since this is a promise of salvation, the complete fulfillment of the promise is seen in Jesus, the son of Mary.

The book of Isaiah has a key text about Mary, which is quoted by Matthew in his infancy narrative (Matthew 1:23). "[T]he virgin shall be with child, and bear a son, and shall name him Immanuel" (Isaiah 7:14). "The church has always followed St. Matthew in seeing the transcendent fulfillment of this verse in Christ and his Virgin Mother" (*New American Bible*, footnote, Isaiah 7:14).

The prophet Micah is perhaps best known for his identifying Bethlehem as the place of the Messiah's birth (Micah 5:1). Micah portrays the Messiah as a king, "ruler in Israel," for he will be the ideal David. He goes on to say about the Israelites, "Therefore the Lord will give them up, until the time / when she who is to give birth has borne" (5:2). This is another reference to the mother of the Messiah.

With this Old Testament preparation, it is not surprising to see the key role that Mary plays in the New Testament. In today's second reading, for instance, Saint Paul notes that "God sent his Son, born of a woman, born under the law" (Galatians 4:4). Today's Gospel and the infancy narratives in general make clear that Jesus was born of the Virgin Mary. Her role continues throughout Jesus' public life, and she is with the church at the time of its birth on Pentecost (Acts 1:14).

Reflecting on the Word

In her poem "The Noise of the Soul" Mary Rose O'Reilley tries to describe what goes on in us when we're restless, when we're not paying attention to stirrings deep within us. One way or another, she suggests, those noises make themselves heard. She writes of our souls,

They start to run their invisible nails over the blackboard,
get you to notice them,
get you to feed them,
get you to play catch.

from *Living the Questions: Essays Inspired by the Life and Work of Parker J. Palmer* by Sam Intrator, p. 53.

Saint Luke, another poet of sorts, tells the story of Mary and all what was happening to her son, and how she kept all these things in her heart—perhaps her way of giving attention to the noises in her soul. It's how she came over time to understand the events going on in her life and what their meaning might be. Our heart is the very same place where we, too, make sense of things and do some sorting of our own.

St. Paul, yet another kind of poet, pointed out to the believers in Galatia how we cry out "Abba, Father!" (Galatians 4:6). He said it was God sent into our hearts, drawing us to what is good and holy and pure. All the stirrings and the restlessness, then, those noises that demand our attention, come from God.

Still, there is more going on in our hearts than the urgings of God. Here our own urgings also find a home. We no longer speak much of the seven capital sins, but they're still around: pride, anger, envy, greed, gluttony, sloth, lust. They, too, make noise in our souls, and it's good to be aware of them as well lest they drown out the divine noise.

CONSIDER/ DISCUSS:

- How do you give attention to the noises in your soul? How do you listen in your life?
- How do you know which noises come from God and which come from your own ego?

Responding to the Word

The noises in our soul, the voices crying out in our heart, they may very well be a tug-of-war of sorts between God and us, each wanting to be heard. Perhaps it is this constant chatter and wisdom that ultimately shape our lives.

Spend a few minutes in quiet prayer. Ask God to show you one (or more) ways that you may be called to respond to this week's scriptures—

- in your relationship with God
- with family and friends
- at work, school, or church
- in the broader community

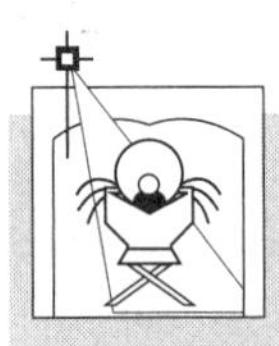

January 7, 2007

THE EPIPHANY OF THE LORD

Today's Focus: The Wisdom of the Magi

Every Christmas we hear warnings about how to prepare for the post-holiday letdown and avoid January's blue blahs. Somewhere along the way you would think we'd catch on that the payback from our own strivings for joy and good times is somewhat limited, and that worlds of our own making tend to be global houses of cards.

FIRST READING
Isaiah 60:1–6

Rise up in splendor, Jerusalem! Your light has come,
the glory of the Lord shines upon you.
See, darkness covers the earth,
and thick clouds cover the peoples;
but upon you the LORD shines,
and over you appears his glory.
Nations shall walk by your light,
and kings by your shining radiance.
Raise your eyes and look about;
they all gather and come to you:
your sons come from afar,
and your daughters in the arms of their nurses.

Then you shall be radiant at what you see,
your heart shall throb and overflow,
for the riches of the sea shall be emptied out before you,
the wealth of nations shall be brought to you.
Caravans of camels shall fill you,
dromedaries from Midian and Ephah;
all from Sheba shall come
bearing gold and frankincense,
and proclaiming the praises of the LORD.

PSALM RESPONSE
Psalm 72:11

Lord, every nation on earth will adore you.

SECOND READING
Ephesians 3: 2–3a, 5–6

Brothers and sisters: You have heard of the stewardship of God's grace that was given to me for your benefit, namely, that the mystery was made known to me by revelation. It was not made known to people in other generations as it has now been revealed to his holy apostles and prophets by the Spirit: that the Gentiles are coheirs, members of the same body, and copartners in the promise in Christ Jesus through the gospel.

GOSPEL
Matthew 2: 1–12

When Jesus was born in Bethlehem of Judea, in the days of King Herod, behold, magi from the east arrived in Jerusalem, saying, "Where is the newborn king of the Jews? We saw his star at its rising and have come to do him homage." When King Herod heard this, he was greatly troubled, and all Jerusalem with him. Assembling all the chief priests and the scribes of the people, he inquired of them where the Christ was to be born. They said to him, "In Bethlehem of Judea, for thus it has been written through the prophet:

And you, Bethlehem, land of Judah,
are by no means least among the rulers of Judah;
since from you shall come a ruler,
who is to shepherd my people Israel."

Then Herod called the magi secretly and ascertained from them the time of the star's appearance. He sent them to Bethlehem and said, "Go and search diligently for the child. When you have found him, bring me word, that I too may go and do him homage."

After their audience with the king they set out. And behold, the star that they had seen at its rising preceded them, until it came and stopped over the place where the child was. They were overjoyed at seeing the star, and on entering the house they saw the child with Mary his mother. They prostrated themselves and did him homage. Then they opened their treasures and offered him gifts of gold, frankincense, and myrrh.

And having been warned in a dream not to return to Herod, they departed for their country by another way.

Understanding the Word

As the name Epiphany indicates, there is a remarkable manifestation of Jesus on the occasion of the visit of the magi (Matthew 2:1–12) He is called "king of the Jews" by the magi. Herod then uses "Christ" interchangeably with "king of the Jews." It reflects the concept of a royal Messiah, popular since God promised David an everlasting kingdom (see 2 Samuel 7:13). "King of the Jews" will appear on the cross on Good Friday (Matthew 27:37), but will be as hypocritical then as Herod's indication that he wants to pay homage to the Christ Child.

The expression "pay homage" also teaches that Jesus is regarded as a person of great dignity, of great authority. It is repeated three times in this account of the magi (2:2, 8, 11). The magi show their respect also through gifts of gold, frankincense, and myrrh. The fact that the magi are Gentiles prepares us for Christ's great commission: "Go, therefore, and make disciples of all nations" (Matthew 28:19).

Bethlehem is identified by the Jewish chief priests and scribes as the place of the Messiah's birth. The quotation is a combination of Micah 5:1 and 2 Samuel 5:2. The star that is so prominent in this incident may well reflect the colorful story of Balaam in the book of Numbers (22 — 24). Balaam is hired by Balak, king of Moab, to curse the Israelites; but God forces him to bless them instead. In the fourth of these blessings, Balaam promises, "A star shall advance from Jacob" (24:17).

Herod the Great was "king of the Jews" from 37 to 4 B.C. (Jesus probably was born between 9 and 5 B.C.) Herod was always willing to shed blood to keep his title. He even killed two of his own sons who were a threat. As the Gospel indicates (Matthew 2:16), he was determined to remove Jesus whom the magi called "the newborn king of the Jews" (Matthew 2:2).

To end on a positive note, in commenting on the words "they saw the child with Mary his mother" (2:11), the *New Jerome Biblical Commentary* says, "The magi offer a model of sound mariology as worshippers of Christ in a Marian context" (p. 636).

Reflecting on the Word

Henry David Thoreau made the observation that "it is not enough to be busy. So are the ants. The question is, What are we busy about?" So some of the wisdom we eventually come to in life is what to be busy about and what not to be busy about. All of which seems to suggest that perhaps what we are caught up in during much of December is not what we should be about at all, not in December or in any month of the year.

Perhaps "the right things" to be busy about are those life pieces that bring joy and love and peace to others regardless (and this seems to be the important part) of whether or not they bring joy and love and peace to us. "The right things" are others and not us. Perhaps, then, it's only when we make ourselves the object of Christmas that depression and downers set in because, of course, that sort of joy and love and peace eventually run down whether the Energizer™ bunny is our sidekick or not.

The three wise men had to have wrestled with that same quandary. What does one do once one has arrived at the end of the searching? Does one give a regal nod along with a royal gesture of gratitude and then casually go back home, as the story suggests? Months of mapless wandering only to undo the journey just after arriving? It seems so futile, to surrender what they had just come to have at hand. Yet that is what they found themselves doing. Love found must also be love set free; only then does it stay with the seeker. So also with wisdom and joy and peace and every other such divine gift.

CONSIDER/ DISCUSS:

- What precious gift have you been called to leave behind, undoubtedly at great pain and sadness? Have you yet found it again?
- Have you yet been called to leave one way of believing in exchange for a new path? What has been its fruit?

Responding to the Word

Love (whether at Christmas time or at any other time of the year) is not really love if it's a search for what we get out of it. That is the wisdom of Jesus for all peoples, believers and nonbelievers alike. What makes it salvific is to know it even before one arrives.

Spend a few minutes in quiet prayer. Ask God to show you one (or more) ways that you may be called to respond to this week's scriptures—

- in your relationship with God
- with family and friends
- at work, school, or church
- in the broader community

Notes

The Gospel of Luke is the beginning of a two-volume work. The Acts of the Apostles is the second volume. In order to have the four Gospels together, the Acts of the Apostles was separated from Luke's Gospel by the Gospel of John. Luke is the author of both volumes. Though they are only two books, in quantity they constitute almost one-fourth of the New Testament.

Luke is a non-Jewish Semite, a convert who travels occasionally with St. Paul. His writings indicate that he is very well educated. His audience appears to be a community of mostly Gentile Christians. He wrote between 80 and 90 A.D.

A unique feature of Luke's Gospel is an extended literary prologue, telling the reader the purpose of the writer, his sources, and his own personal contribution. He writes to give "certainty of the teachings that you have received" (1:4). He has done careful research, searching out eyewitnesses and ministers of the word. He explains his own contribution, "I too have decided, after investigating everything accurately anew, to write it down in an orderly sequence" (1:3).

As the Gospel is proclaimed throughout this liturgical year, Luke's principal teachings will become clear. First and foremost, Luke wants the reader to understand that Jesus came into the world to save every human being. In his genealogy of our Lord he goes back to Adam to stress this universal aspect of the Savior's work. Jesus shows special zeal in reaching out to sinners. "For the Son of Man has come to seek and to save what was lost" (19:10). Jesus saw the danger of wealth and the need for renunciation. "Take care to guard against all greed, for though one may be rich, one's life does not consist of possessions" (12:15).

Jesus also has special love for the poor and vulnerable. The Beatitudes are a strong statement that the poor are close to the heart of God. Among the vulnerable at that time were women. Luke stresses Jesus' constant reaching out to women. The Gospel gives special attention not only to Mary, but to many others, including Elizabeth, Simon's mother-in-law, the widow of Nain, the sinful woman who is pardoned, the Galilean women who follow Jesus, Mary and Martha, the daughter of Jairus, the crippled woman cured on the Sabbath, the persistent widow, the poor widow contributing her two coins, the women mourning Jesus on his way to Calvary, and Mary Magdalene.

Prayer is an important teaching of Luke's Gospel. Christ gives the example, often spending the night in prayerful union with his Father. The qualities of prayer are also noted: confidence, humility, and especially perseverance.

Finally, the Holy Spirit is prominent in the Third Gospel as guiding the life of Jesus and his disciples. "Jesus returned to Galilee in the power of the Spirit" (4:14). This role of the Spirit will be even more evident in the Acts of the Apostles, which is often referred to as the "Gospel of the Spirit."

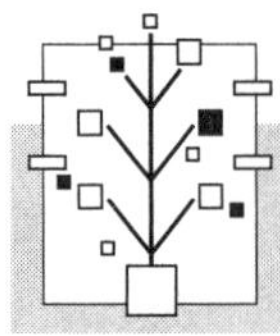

January 14, 2007

SECOND SUNDAY IN ORDINARY TIME

Today's Focus: A Toast to New Wine

The thing about new wine is just that—it's new. Because it's new and hasn't yet been tasted, no one knows if it's any good. The only way to know, of course, is by tasting it. So when life runs out of wine, taste the new wine, if for no other reason than that it may be better than the old.

FIRST READING
Isaiah 62:1–5

For Zion's sake I will not be silent,
 for Jerusalem's sake I will not be quiet,
until her vindication shines forth like the dawn
 and her victory like a burning torch.

Nations shall behold your vindication,
 and all the kings your glory;
you shall be called by a new name
 pronounced by the mouth of the LORD.
You shall be a glorious crown in the hand of the LORD,
 a royal diadem held by your God.
No more shall people call you "Forsaken,"
 or your land "Desolate,"
but you shall be called "My Delight,"
 and your land "Espoused."
For the LORD delights in you
 and makes your land his spouse.
As a young man marries a virgin,
 your Builder shall marry you;
and as a bridegroom rejoices in his bride
 so shall your God rejoice in you.

PSALM RESPONSE
Psalm 96:3

Proclaim his marvelous deeds to all the nations.

SECOND READING
1 Corinthians 12:4–11

Brothers and sisters: There are different kinds of spiritual gifts but the same Spirit; there are different forms of service but the same Lord; there are different workings but the same God who produces all of them in everyone. To each individual the manifestation of the Spirit is given for some benefit. To one is given through the Spirit the expression of wisdom; to another, the expression of knowledge according to the same Spirit; to another, faith by the same Spirit; to another, gifts of healing by the one Spirit; to another, mighty deeds; to another, prophecy; to another, discernment of spirits; to another, varieties of tongues; to another, interpretation of tongues. But one and the same Spirit produces all of these, distributing them individually to each person as he wishes.

GOSPEL
John 2:1–11

There was a wedding at Cana in Galilee, and the mother of Jesus was there. Jesus and his disciples were also invited to the wedding. When the wine ran short, the mother of Jesus said to him, "They have no wine." And Jesus said to her, "Woman, how does your concern affect me? My hour has not yet come." His mother said to the servers, "Do whatever he tells you." Now there were six stone water jars there for Jewish ceremonial washings, each holding twenty to thirty gallons. Jesus told them, "Fill the jars with water." So they filled them to the brim. Then he told them, "Draw some out now and take it to the headwaiter." So they took it. And when the headwaiter tasted the water that had become wine, without knowing where it came from—although the servers who had drawn the water knew—, the headwaiter called the bridegroom and said to him, "Everyone serves good wine first, and then when people have drunk freely, an inferior one; but you have kept the good wine until now." Jesus did this as the beginning of his signs at Cana in Galilee and so revealed his glory, and his disciples began to believe in him.

Understanding the Word

Seven significant miracles of Jesus in the Gospel of John are referred to as signs. The miracle at the wedding feast of Cana is the first of these. The signs are intended to point the reader to a deeper understanding of Jesus and his ministry. The change by Jesus of an immense amount of water into choice wine symbolizes the end of the Period of Israel and the beginning of the Period of Jesus. The Old Testament often uses an abundance of wine as a symbol of the Messianic era. "And then, on that day, / the mountains shall drip new wine" (Joel 4:18). Also, a wedding feast was seen as a symbol of the Messianic banquet.

Scripture scholars have difficulty with several parts of John 2:4. Mary is called "woman" by Jesus, who then goes on to say, "[H]ow does your concern affect me? My hour has not yet come." The use of "woman" is not disrespectful, but symbolic. Genesis 3:15 speaks of a woman and her offspring defeating Satan. Christians see Mary as the woman involved. When Christ engages in the final defeat of Satan on the cross, Mary is present and is again called "woman" by her Son. This symbolism is also seen in Revelation, "A great sign appeared in the sky, a woman clothed with the sun, with the moon under her feet, and on her head a crown of twelve stars" (12:1). Here, too, the child of the woman defeats Satan.

Jesus always insisted that his hour will be the time of his death, resurrection, and ascension. Until then his ministry is under the control of his Father. Mary will find her true role at the cross. She will become the new Eve, the mother of all who live the life of Jesus (see Genesis 3:20).

This first sign has wonderful results: it manifests the glory of Jesus and leads his disciples to faith in him (2:11). The glory of Yahweh in the Old Testament and of Jesus in the New represents a manifestation of their presence. Jesus' messianic miracle makes it possible for his followers to reach firm faith in their Lord.

Reflecting on the Word

"Do whatever he tells you," is what today's Gospel pointedly suggests. Perhaps too pointedly, because it just may turn out that none of what he tells us seems appealing. Be that as it may, life does serve up new wine.

Yet as always the question remains, how does anyone know what we're being told to do? How does one read the signs of personal times? A good marker, it would seem, is to pay attention to one's gifts. It may not be the only marker, but certainly one not to be ignored. St. Paul writes to the Corinthians that our strengths and talents come from the Spirit, and that each is given for some benefit. Other translations say they are given for the common good, which seems to be a better way of putting it, because it broadens our view and prevents us from understanding any gift in terms of personal benefit or preference. It may be that the old wine we just drained did quench our personal thirst, but that the new wine is for the common good.

So when the old wine runs out and we're offered new wine, it's worth considering whether we're being called to some new role in life. It may be that life is ratcheting up our degree of participation, calling us to make some new contribution we have not even considered. And we may be surprised. It may enrich the taste of life.

On this day, then, raise a toast to God's new creation. To new wine. The British say Cheers! The Germans, *Prosit*! Poles, *Na Zdrowie*! In Spain, *Salud*! And Lithuanians, *Sveikas*! Believers, well, they say Alleluia!

CONSIDER/ DISCUSS:

- In your life, when has the new wine tasted better than the old?
- What new gifts and contributions showed themselves later on in your life, after the more obvious had been well established or run their course?

Responding to the Word

It does seem that somewhere along the path of life, the wine runs out for each of us. We get bored with jobs, or relationships, or maybe just the same four old walls. Or life gets bored with us, or exhausted by our demands and expectations. We can lament the loss of old wine, or we can open a new bottle, and carry on God's work perhaps in a new way.

Spend a few minutes in quiet prayer. Ask God to show you one (or more) ways that you may be called to respond to this week's scriptures—

- in your relationship with God
- with family and friends
- at work, school, or church
- in the broader community

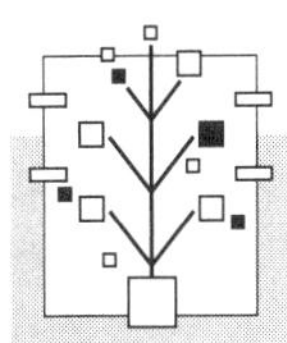

January 21, 2007

THIRD SUNDAY IN ORDINARY TIME

Today's Focus: The Flip Side of God's Word

Most realities of any worth are two-sided. Family nurtures and challenges. Love sustains and demands sacrifice. On any day one should work as well as play. A healthy person will be able both to laugh and cry. Much of life is a two-sided coin.

FIRST READING
Nehemiah 8: 2–4a, 5–6, 8–10

Ezra the priest brought the law before the assembly, which consisted of men, women, and those children old enough to understand. Standing at one end of the open place that was before the Water Gate, he read out of the book from daybreak till midday, in the presence of the men, the women, and those children old enough to understand; and all the people listened attentively to the book of the law. Ezra the scribe stood on a wooden platform that had been made for the occasion. He opened the scroll so that all the people might see it—for he was standing higher up than any of the people—; and, as he opened it, all the people rose. Ezra blessed the LORD, the great God, and all the people, their hands raised high, answered, "Amen, amen!" Then they bowed down and prostrated themselves before the LORD, their faces to the ground. Ezra read plainly from the book of the law of God, interpreting it so that all could understand what was read. Then Nehemiah, that is, His Excellency, and Ezra the priest-scribe and the Levites who were instructing the people said to all the people: "Today is holy to the LORD your God. Do not be sad, and do not weep"—for all the people were weeping as they heard the words of the law. He said further: "Go, eat rich foods and drink sweet drinks, and allot portions to those who had nothing prepared; for today is holy to our LORD. Do not be saddened this day, for rejoicing in the LORD must be your strength!"

PSALM RESPONSE
John 6:63c

Your words, Lord, are Spirit and life.

In the shorter form of the reading, the passages in brackets are omitted.

SECOND READING
1 Corinthians 12:12–30

Brothers and sisters: As a body is one though it has many parts, and all the parts of the body, though many, are one body, so also Christ. For in one Spirit we were all baptized into one body, whether Jews or Greeks, slaves or free persons, and we were all given to drink of one Spirit.

Now the body is not a single part, but many. [If a foot should say, "Because I am not a hand I do not belong to the body," it does not for this reason belong any less to the body. Or if an ear should say, "Because I am not an eye I do not belong to the body," it does not for this reason belong any less to the body. If the whole body were an eye, where would the hearing be? If the whole body were hearing, where would the sense of smell be? But as it is, God placed the parts, each one of them, in the body as he intended. If they were all one part, where would the body be? But as it is, there are many parts, yet one body. The eye cannot say to the hand, "I do not need you," nor again the head to the feet, "I do not need you." Indeed, the parts of the body that seem to be weaker are all the more necessary, and those parts of the body that we consider less honorable we surround with greater honor, and our less presentable parts are treated with greater propriety, whereas our more presentable parts do not need this. But God has so constructed the body as to give greater honor to a part that is without it, so that there may be no division in the body, but that the parts may have the same concern for one another. If one part suffers, all the parts suffer with it; if one part is honored, all the parts share its joy.]

Now you are Christ's body, and individually parts of it. [Some people God has designated in the church to be, first, apostles; second, prophets; third, teachers; then, mighty deeds; then gifts of healing, assistance, administration, and varieties of tongues. Are all apostles? Are all prophets? Are all teachers? Do all work mighty deeds? Do all have gifts of healing? Do all speak in tongues? Do all interpret?]

GOSPEL
Luke 1:1–4; 4:14–21

Since many have undertaken to compile a narrative of the events that have been fulfilled among us, just as those who were eyewitnesses from the beginning and ministers of the word have handed them down to us, I too have decided, after investigating everything accurately anew, to write it down in an orderly sequence for you, most excellent Theophilus, so that you may realize the certainty of the teachings you have received.

Jesus returned to Galilee in the power of the Spirit, and news of him spread throughout the whole region. He taught in their synagogues and was praised by all.

He came to Nazareth, where he had grown up, and went according to his custom into the synagogue on the sabbath day. He stood up to read and was handed a scroll of the prophet Isaiah. He unrolled the scroll and found the passage where it was written:

The Spirit of the Lord is upon me,
because he has anointed me
to bring glad tidings to the poor.
He has sent me to proclaim liberty to captives
and recovery of sight to the blind,
to let the oppressed go free,
and to proclaim a year acceptable to the Lord.

Rolling up the scroll, he handed it back to the attendant and sat down, and the eyes of all in the synagogue looked intently at him. He said to them, "Today this Scripture passage is fulfilled in your hearing."

Understanding the Word

The public life and ministry of Jesus in the Gospel of Luke began with a visit to Nazareth, "where he had grown up" (Luke 4:16). The reader is told that the Holy Spirit guides the life of Jesus. The Spirit brings him to Galilee. Jesus will say, "The Spirit of the Lord is upon me, because he has anointed me" (4:18). Jesus is quoting Isaiah 61:1–2, where the anointing is prophetic anointing. Later in chapter 4 (vs. 24) Jesus identifies himself as a prophet, a key part of his ministry. A prophet essentially tells people what God has sent the prophet to communicate. Christ is the final revelation of the Father.

Jesus appears at the synagogue in Nazareth. Apparently the Jewish people began to establish synagogues at the time of the Babylonian Exile in the sixth century before Christ. The synagogue was and still is a vital part of Jewish life. It serves as a focus for liturgy, for education, for meetings. As a faithful Jew, Jesus goes regularly to the synagogue. In today's Gospel Jesus is portrayed as one who teaches continually. This is important because it is this teaching that gives the reader the "certainty" that Luke had promised in the Prologue (1:1–4).

In addition to presenting Jesus as an anointed prophet, the text of Isaiah highlights an important part of Jesus' ministry, namely his care for the poor, for the marginalized, the downtrodden, the vulnerable. "Blessed are you who are poor, / for the kingdom of God is yours" (see Luke 6:20). "[W]hen you hold a banquet, invite the poor, the crippled, the lame, the blind; blessed indeed will you be because of their inability to repay you" (Luke 14:13–14). Luke is so concerned about this aspect of Jesus' teaching that his work deserves the title "Gospel of Social Justice."

Jesus marks the fulfillment of the Period of Israel. The Old Testament longing for the Messianic blessings is realized by these words of Jesus, "Today this Scripture passage is fulfilled in your hearing" (4:21). Now the Period of Jesus begins, which in the Acts of the Apostles will lead to the Period of the Church.

Reflecting on the Word

These day I live in a former parish convent with a handful of other priests. All of us have become terribly aware of one another's idiosyncrasies. In the end there is little else to do but tolerate these peculiarities.

One of us is a seventy-year-old priest who simply finds it most difficult to throw anything away. A few years back he befriended a "Charlie Brown" weeping fig tree. In the summer he puts it outside, and while it doesn't thrive, it does fairly well at surviving. During the winter months the fig tree finds a home next to his lounge chair. I'm not sure why he cares so much for the scrawny fig tree, except that by this time I suspect it brings him a certain amount of comfort just having it by his side. All of us need to be comforted.

While the Word of God is a two-edged sword, it seems we've been quite conditioned to its surgical edge, the hewn edge of judgment and confrontation, the prophetic edge. In part, I suppose, it's because both the Church and its preachers recognize we are all sinners, and so they want us to be saved and holy.

Still, we need to be comforted as well. Maybe that is why Nehemiah and Ezra tell the people not to weep or be sad upon hearing God's word. Instead they say, "Go, eat rich foods and drink sweet drinks" (Nehemiah 8:10) and rejoice in the Lord. And Jesus, too, comes to bring glad tidings, proclaiming liberty and freeing the oppressed. We need the Word to comfort us and not only challenge us.

CONSIDER/ DISCUSS:

- Pick three passages from sacred scripture that you find comforting. Why do you find them so? Do they provide comfort to the same areas of your life or different areas?
- The people of this week's scriptures heard the word in the context of a community of believers. Do you find the word more powerful when heard in community or in your own personal prayer?

Responding to the Word

Week upon week we stand in the shadow of God's word. It can be light for holy living. It can be wisdom for recognizing God's presence. It can be truth for understanding. It can hold us accountable to our commitments. It can be a source of joy and peace.

Spend a few minutes in quiet prayer. Ask God to show you one (or more) ways that you may be called to respond to this week's scriptures—

- in your relationship with God
- with family and friends
- at work, school, or church
- in the broader community

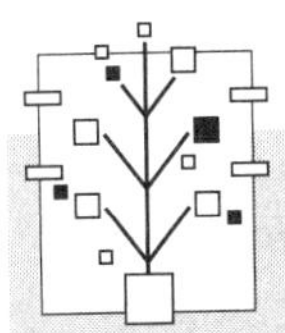

January 28, 2007

FOURTH SUNDAY IN ORDINARY TIME

Today's Focus: A Time for Passion

At some point in life most of us make a commitment, either to someone or something. That's the first time, but usually we are called to remake that commitment again and again. It's seldom as exciting as the first time, and often more demanding. Still we stand upon the commitments we make.

FIRST READING
Jeremiah 1:4–5, 17–19

The word of the LORD came to me, saying:
Before I formed you in the womb I knew you,
before you were born I dedicated you,
a prophet to the nations I appointed you.

But do you gird your loins;
stand up and tell them
all that I command you.
Be not crushed on their account,
as though I would leave you crushed before them;
for it is I this day
who have made you a fortified city,
a pillar of iron, a wall of brass,
against the whole land:
against Judah's kings and princes,
against its priests and people.
They will fight against you but not prevail over you,
for I am with you to deliver you, says the LORD.

PSALM RESPONSE
Psalm 71:15ab

I will sing of your salvation.

In the shorter form of the reading, the passages in brackets are omitted.

SECOND READING
1 Corinthians 12:31 — 13:13

Brothers and sisters: [Strive eagerly for the greatest spiritual gifts. But I shall show you a still more excellent way.

If I speak in human and angelic tongues, but do not have love, I am a resounding gong or a clashing cymbal. And if I have the gift of prophecy, and comprehend all mysteries and all knowledge; if I have all faith so as to move mountains, but do not have love, I am nothing. If I give away everything I own, and if I hand my body over so that I may boast, but do not have love, I gain nothing.]

Love is patient, love is kind. It is not jealous, it is not pompous, it is not inflated, it is not rude, it does not seek its own interests, it is not quick-tempered, it does not brood over injury, it does not rejoice over wrongdoing but rejoices with the truth. It bears all things, believes all things, hopes all things, endures all things.

Love never fails. If there are prophecies, they will be brought to nothing; if tongues, they will cease; if knowledge, it will be brought to nothing. For we know partially and we prophesy partially, but when the perfect comes, the partial will pass away. When I was a child, I used to talk as a child, think as a child, reason as a child; when I became a man, I put aside childish things. At present we see indistinctly, as in a mirror, but then face to face. At present I know partially; then I shall know fully, as I am fully known. So faith, hope, love remain, these three; but the greatest of these is love.

GOSPEL
Luke 4:21–30

Jesus began speaking in the synagogue, saying: "Today this Scripture passage is fulfilled in your hearing." And all spoke highly of him and were amazed at the gracious words that came from his mouth. They also asked, "Isn't this the son of Joseph?"

He said to them, "Surely you will quote me this proverb, 'Physician, cure yourself,' and say, 'Do here in your native place the things that we heard were done in Capernaum.' " And he said, "Amen, I say to you, no prophet is accepted in his own native place. Indeed, I tell you, there were many widows in Israel in the days of Elijah when the sky was closed for three and a half years and a severe famine spread over the entire land. It was to none of these that Elijah was sent, but only to a widow in Zarephath in the land of Sidon. Again, there were many lepers in Israel during the time of Elisha the prophet; yet not one of them was cleansed, but only Naaman the Syrian."

When the people in the synagogue heard this, they were all filled with fury. They rose up, drove him out of the town, and led him to the brow of the hill on which their town had been built, to hurl him down headlong. But Jesus passed through the midst of them and went away.

Understanding the Word

Luke puts the visit of Jesus to Nazareth, his hometown, at the very beginning of the public ministry. His purpose is to have the reader realize that the initial acceptance of Jesus and then the sudden reversal to angry rejection foreshadows his entire public life. After a period of acceptance he will be victimized by the leaders, rejected, and finally crucified.

The initial favorable reaction to Jesus' gracious words is followed by concern about his background. "Isn't this the son of Joseph?" (Luke 4:22). In the parallel passage in the Gospel of Mark the people refer to Jesus as a carpenter. Their problem is, how can a carpenter, the son of a carpenter, interpret scripture and tell them, "Today this Scripture passage is fulfilled in your hearing" (4:21)?

The response of the Savior is to point out that he is a prophet. He makes the strong assertion, "Amen, I say to you, no prophet is accepted in his own native place" (4:24). Only Jesus uses that "Amen." He uses it frequently in all four Gospels as he teaches with conviction and with a prophetic mission. Opposition is building up among his neighbors because he has not worked miracles in Nazareth as he did in Capernaum. He teaches that he will reach out to the poor and vulnerable. He cites the example of Elijah (1 Kings 17:7–16) and Elisha (2 Kings 5:1–14), who worked miracles for Gentiles because they were persons of faith. The Gospel of Mark adds, "He was amazed at their lack of faith" (Mark 6:6).

Finally, Jesus went on his way, a way that will lead to the cross and the Resurrection. The synoptic Gospels (Matthew, Mark, and Luke) narrate the public life of Jesus as though it all happened in one year. As Jesus goes on his way there is always the goal of Jerusalem. For example, at a critical juncture in the life of Jesus, Luke highlights this purpose in his journey, "When the days for his being taken up were fulfilled, he resolutely determined to journey to Jerusalem" (Luke 9:51).

Reflecting on the Word

I sometimes wonder if Jesus ever second-guessed himself, questioning his decisions or wishing he'd kept his mouth shut even if he was right. Or did he simply decide and proceed forward without even a glance in hindsight to what might have been, like a seedling committed to the sun? Is that what happened in the synagogue—that he came to see what needed to be said and so he said it, plainly and without hesitation and with passion?

Passions drive us and commit us to the count of ten. They don't second-guess. And if they are worthwhile, if they come from God as did those in the life of Jesus, then we stand in quiet and sometimes silent courage upon committed lives, as if driven to goodness by some preordained call.

It happens. In Nelson Mandela, imprisoned as if in transparent amber by the unrelenting truth of his convictions. In Rosa Parks, calmly refusing to go not only to the back of the bus but also to the back of life. In a lone and anonymous student remembered forever because he stood in defiance of the military in Tiananmen Square. In the prophet Jeremiah, impelled to be faithful to a word whose very power reduced his desire to ashes. To say nothing of teenagers daring to practice uncommon mores among their peers, and heads of households working in jobs without satisfaction in order to nurture their family, and elderly people reluctantly raising yet a second family of their children's children. Passionate commitments happen. They don't always feel like passion, maybe not even most of the time, but they do happen.

CONSIDER/ DISCUSS:

- To what in your life are you committed over the long term? Can you, would you label that your passion?
- What gifts of life have chosen you?

Responding to the Word

The apostle Paul challenged the Corinthian community to remember their gifts and their once-passionate commitment to them. "So faith, hope, love remain, these three; but the greatest of these is love" (1 Corinthians 13:13). Commitment does happen.

Spend a few minutes in quiet prayer. Ask God to show you one (or more) ways that you may be called to respond to this week's scriptures—

- in your relationship with God
- with family and friends
- at work, school, or church
- in the broader community

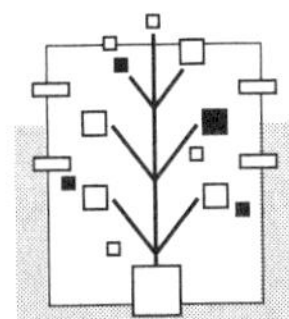

February 4, 2007

FIFTH SUNDAY IN ORDINARY TIME

Today's Focus: Once Upon a Time

Once upon a time . . . and ever since we've lived with the hope that today might just be such a time. Once upon a time the good guys and the bad guys did battle, and the good guys won. Once upon a time Prince Charming kissed a sleeping beauty, and she awoke to love him happily ever after. Once upon a time the sun rose and a new day happened like never before.

FIRST READING
Isaiah 6:1–2a, 3–8

In the year King Uzziah died, I saw the Lord seated on a high and lofty throne, with the train of his garment filling the temple. Seraphim were stationed above.

They cried one to the other, "Holy, holy, holy is the LORD of hosts! All the earth is filled with his glory!" At the sound of that cry, the frame of the door shook and the house was filled with smoke.

Then I said, "Woe is me, I am doomed! For I am a man of unclean lips, living among a people of unclean lips; yet my eyes have seen the King, the LORD of hosts!" Then one of the seraphim flew to me, holding an ember that he had taken with tongs from the altar.

He touched my mouth with it, and said, "See, now that this has touched your lips, your wickedness is removed, your sin purged."

Then I heard the voice of the Lord saying, "Whom shall I send? Who will go for us?" "Here I am," I said; "send me!"

PSALM RESPONSE
Psalm 138:1c

In the sight of the angels I will sing your praises, Lord.

In the shorter form of the reading, the passages in brackets are omitted.

SECOND READING
1 Corinthians 15: 1–11

[I am reminding you,] brothers and sisters,[of the gospel I preached to you, which you indeed received and in which you also stand. Through it you are also being saved, if you hold fast to the word I preached to you, unless you believed in vain. For] I handed on to you as of first importance what I also received: that Christ died for our sins in accordance with the Scriptures; that he was buried; that he was raised on the third day in accordance with the Scriptures; that he appeared to Cephas, then to the Twelve. After that, he appeared to more than five hundred brothers at once, most of whom are still living, though some have fallen asleep. After that he appeared to James, then to all the apostles. Last of all, as to one born abnormally, he appeared to me. [For I am the least of the apostles, not fit to be called an apostle, because I persecuted the church of God. But by the grace of God I am what I am, and his grace to me has not been ineffective. Indeed, I have toiled harder than all of them; not I, however, but the grace of God that is with me.] Therefore, whether it be I or they, so we preach and so you believed.

GOSPEL
Luke 5:1–11

While the crowd was pressing in on Jesus and listening to the word of God, he was standing by the Lake of Gennesaret. He saw two boats there alongside the lake; the fishermen had disembarked and were washing their nets. Getting into one of the boats, the one belonging to Simon, he asked him to put out a short distance from the shore. Then he sat down and taught the crowds from the boat. After he had finished speaking, he said to Simon, "Put out into deep water and lower your nets for a catch." Simon said in reply, "Master, we have worked hard all night and have caught nothing, but at your command I will lower the nets." When they had done this, they caught a great number of fish and their nets were tearing. They signaled to their partners in the other boat to come to help them. They came and filled both boats so that the boats were in danger of sinking. When Simon Peter saw this, he fell at the knees of Jesus and said, "Depart from me, Lord, for I am a sinful man." For astonishment at the catch of fish they had made seized him and all those with him, and likewise James and John, the sons of Zebedee, who were partners of Simon. Jesus said to Simon, "Do not be afraid; from now on you will be catching men." When they brought their boats to the shore, they left everything and followed him.

Understanding the Word

In today's Gospel Luke highlights the role of Simon, who had witnessed Jesus' acts of power in an exorcism and a number of miraculous cures (see Luke 4:33–41). Now he benefits from a miracle in his own field of expertise. Jesus helps him and his companions make a huge catch of fish when his knowledge of fishing tells him there should be no results. But he has faith in his Lord and says simply, "[A]t your command I will lower the nets" (5:5). His trust is rewarded with a huge catch of fish. Two boats were filled to the point "that the boats were in danger of sinking" (5:7).

In light of this miracle Simon does not feel worthy to be with Jesus because he realizes that he is a sinful person. Isaiah had the same reaction when he experienced a vision of God. As he said in today's first reading, "Woe is me, I am doomed! For I am a man of unclean lips" (Isaiah 6:5). The fear of doom reflects an Old Testament belief that seeing God or a remarkable divine intervention could lead to one's death. So Jesus says to Simon, "Do not be afraid." Simon then receives this promise from Christ: "[F]rom now on you will be catching men" (5:10).

Simon and his fishing companions "left everything and followed him" (5:11). To leave everything is in harmony with Jesus' insistence on detachment from material possessions. The Greek word for "follow" is an important word in all the Gospels. It indicates a disciple's commitment to Jesus and his ministry. From this point on Simon will be an outstanding missionary and the spokesperson for all the disciples.

Today's Gospel continues to stress the role of Jesus as teacher. He "taught the crowds from the boat" (5:3). Luke also speaks of the "word of God" (5:1) for the first time. He will use this expression frequently both in his Gospel and in the Acts of the Apostles for the preaching of Jesus. However, the very phrase "word of God" makes one realize that God is the ultimate source of Jesus' preaching.

Reflecting on the Word

You and I live in dreams of once-upon-a-time, and so, too, once in every while such a someone or something invites us into new life. Then we turn away from old and worn paths to walk new dreams. We move from the city to the country, or from fields and meadows to high-rise condos. Or we exchange our work for other climes. Or we fall in love and leave everything and everyone behind. Or sometimes, too, something stirs us to a journey of uncertain following, to change our way and follow a new path, even when it seems little more than a promise. It's what happened to Isaiah, touched by God so that his lips spoke new words. It's what happened to Simon and his fellows, and to Paul and all those to whom he preached. For them all, the promised once-upon-a-time came to be. Then they changed the way they lived.

Sometimes once-upon-a-times do take place. Like when the grasping for more gets tiring or boring or maybe just seems useless, and we begin to think life could be better if we were simply content with what is. Or when we grow weary of playing the game of one-upmanship and so decide to play the game of life like a game of checkers, the way we do with children. Then we let them win and never feel we lost, and somehow life seems so much more whole.

CONSIDER/ DISCUSS:

- When have you tried a new way of dealing with life? Why? How did it turn out?
- What would you like to try doing differently in life? What is keeping you from trying it?

Responding to the Word

Life is marked with turning points when we choose to walk in a different direction. It isn't always because life was not good. Sometimes it's simply because we've realized we had to be true to ourselves. Then we take on new roles, become different persons.

Spend a few minutes in quiet prayer. Ask God to show you one (or more) ways that you may be called to respond to this week's scriptures—

- in your relationship with God
- with family and friends
- at work, school, or church
- in the broader community

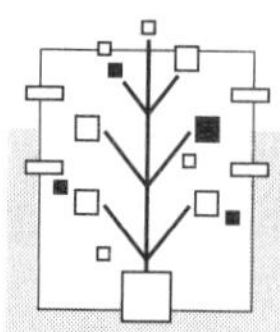

February 11, 2007

SIXTH SUNDAY IN ORDINARY TIME

Today's Focus: Roots Matter

Life never stands still. We are always being made or remade, and for the most part it reflects the choices we make in life. Which values we choose to live by and how we choose to relate to one another, they all move us in one direction or another.

FIRST READING
Jeremiah 17:5–8

Thus says the LORD:
Cursed is the one who trusts in human beings,
who seeks his strength in flesh,
whose heart turns away from the LORD.
He is like a barren bush in the desert
that enjoys no change of season,
but stands in a lava waste,
a salt and empty earth.
Blessed is the one who trusts in the LORD,
whose hope is the LORD.
He is like a tree planted beside the waters
that stretches out its roots to the stream:
it fears not the heat when it comes;
its leaves stay green;
in the year of drought it shows no distress,
but still bears fruit.

PSALM RESPONSE
Psalm 1:40:5a

Blessed are they who hope in the Lord.

SECOND READING
1 Corinthians 15: 12, 16–20

Brothers and sisters: If Christ is preached as raised from the dead, how can some among you say there is no resurrection of the dead? If the dead are not raised, neither has Christ been raised, and if Christ has not been raised, your faith is vain; you are still in your sins. Then those who have fallen asleep in Christ have perished. If for this life only we have hoped in Christ, we are the most pitiable people of all.

But now Christ has been raised from the dead, the firstfruits of those who have fallen asleep.

GOSPEL *Luke 6:17, 20–26*

Jesus came down with the Twelve and stood on a stretch of level ground with a great crowd of his disciples and a large number of the people from all Judea and Jerusalem and the coastal region of Tyre and Sidon.

And raising his eyes toward his disciples he said:
"Blessed are you who are poor,
for the kingdom of God is yours.
Blessed are you who are now hungry,
for you will be satisfied.
Blessed are you who are now weeping,
for you will laugh.
Blessed are you when people hate you,
and when they exclude and insult you,
and denounce your name as evil
on account of the Son of Man.

Rejoice and leap for joy on that day! Behold, your reward will be great in heaven. For their ancestors treated the prophets in the same way.

But woe to you who are rich,
for you have received your consolation.
Woe to you who are filled now,
for you will be hungry.
Woe to you who laugh now,
for you will grieve and weep.
Woe to you when all speak well of you,
for their ancestors treated the false prophets in this way."

Understanding the Word

The prophet Jeremiah provides a perfect introduction for today's Gospel. He outlines contrasting religious attitudes. "Cursed is the one who trusts in human beings, / . . . Blessed is the one who trusts in the LORD, / whose hope is in the LORD" (Jeremiah 17:5, 8).

Jesus began his preaching with a major sermon, giving his values and his expectations for his disciples. The words are addressed to the disciples, but Luke's Gospel with its stress on universal salvation notes the presence of a great crowd, made up of Jews and Gentiles (Luke 6:18). Luke 6:20–49 is Luke's version of Matthew's Sermon on the Mount (5 — 7). Both authors begin this discourse of Jesus with beatitudes.

The Beatitudes of Luke's Gospel reflect the social and economic conditions of that time. People at that very moment are poor, hungry, weeping, and victims of hate. But Jesus says that they are blessed because God will reverse their lot. The poor shall be part of the kingdom of God; the hungry will be satisfied; those who are weeping will laugh. In this context laughter reflects a joyful awareness of God's favor. "Those who sow in tears / will reap with cries of joy" (Psalm 126:5). The ones who are hated because of the name "Christian" will share joyfully in the redeeming work of the Son of Man.

In exact opposition to the Beatitudes are the four woes. Woe to the rich; they have already received their consolation, material possessions. Those who are filled with an abundance of food will go hungry. Grief and tears will be the lot of those who are laughing now. Laughter here has a different meaning from that in the Beatitudes. It refers to self-centered satisfaction with present worldly good fortune. Those receiving popular acclaim will find that praise deceptive. The false prophets of the Old Testament were also esteemed highly; but that was because they curried favor by telling the rulers and people what they wanted to hear, instead of what God wanted said.

Jesus wants every Christian to seek the kingdom of God by pursuing the values of the Beatitudes rather than earthly values and material possessions.

Reflecting on the Word

Where we put down our roots matters. Greatly. We don't do it often, put down roots, that is. It takes time and energy, and to pull up roots and move on is no easy thing. So we settle in and make serious commitments infrequently, maybe only a few times in our lives.

A passage often attributed to the German poet Goethe notes how a commitment sets into motion an entire series of events. "Until one is committed, there is hesitancy, the chance to draw back, always ineffectiveness. Concerning all acts of initiative (and creation) there is one elementary truth, the ignorance of which kills countless ideas and splendid plans: that the moment one definitely commits oneself, then Providence moves too. All sorts of things occur to help one that would never otherwise have occurred. A whole stream of events issues from the decision, raising in one's favor all manner of unforeseen incidents and meetings and material assistance which no man could have dreamed would have come his way.

Whatever you can do,
Or dream you can, begin it.
Boldness has genius,
Power and magic in it."

The poet and prophet Jeremiah made the same point in different words. He spoke of it in terms of trust, which is one way that we commit ourselves. Trust in human flesh, he says, and it's like putting down roots in a lava waste. Trust in the Lord and it's like putting down roots beside an ever-flowing stream of fresh water. Then one bears fruit even during a drought.

Where one puts down one's roots matters. Whom we draw life from makes a difference.

CONSIDER/ DISCUSS:

- Make a list of your long-term commitments. How many are there? Are they what you want to be committed to? What do they tell you about yourself?
- How have your commitments affected your life?
- With the benefit of 20/20 hindsight, have changed commitments had a positive or negative impact on the quality of your life?

Responding to the Word

Where we put down our roots matters. Commitments matter, so that in the end they are the means by which we are made into the divine image and likeness—or also unmade, should we become the instruments of some other force.

Spend a few minutes in quiet prayer. Ask God to show you one (or more) ways that you may be called to respond to this week's scriptures—

- in your relationship with God
- with family and friends
- at work, school, or church
- in the broader community

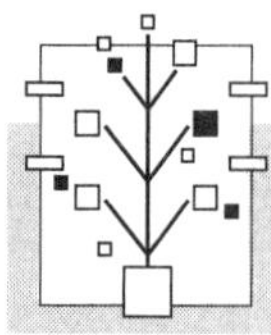

February 18, 2007

SEVENTH SUNDAY IN ORDINARY TIME

Today's Focus: Addiction and Grace

Sooner or later we all get to the point of thinking about the things in life that have slipped past us without much notice on our part. In some instances, we may never even have noticed what we were missing, oblivious to our very selves.

FIRST READING
1 Samuel 26:2, 7–9, 12–13, 22–23

In those days, Saul went down to the desert of Ziph with three thousand picked men of Israel, to search for David in the desert of Ziph. So David and Abishai went among Saul's soldiers by night and found Saul lying asleep within the barricade, with his spear thrust into the ground at his head and Abner and his men sleeping around him.

Abishai whispered to David: "God has delivered your enemy into your grasp this day. Let me nail him to the ground with one thrust of the spear; I will not need a second thrust!" But David said to Abishai, "Do not harm him, for who can lay hands on the LORD's anointed and remain unpunished?" So David took the spear and the water jug from their place at Saul's head, and they got away without anyone's seeing or knowing or awakening. All remained asleep, because the LORD had put them into a deep slumber.

Going across to an opposite slope, David stood on a remote hilltop at a great distance from Abner, son of Ner, and the troops. He said: "Here is the king's spear. Let an attendant come over to get it. The LORD will reward each man for his justice and faithfulness. Today, though the LORD delivered you into my grasp, I would not harm the LORD's anointed."

PSALM RESPONSE
Psalm 103:8a

The Lord is kind and merciful.

SECOND READING
1 Corinthians 15: 45–49

Brothers and sisters: It is written, *The first man, Adam, became a living being,* the last Adam a life-giving spirit. But the spiritual was not first; rather the natural and then the spiritual. The first man was from the earth, earthly; the second man, from heaven. As was the earthly one, so also are the earthly, and as is the heavenly one, so also are the heavenly. Just as we have borne the image of the earthly one, we shall also bear the image of the heavenly one.

GOSPEL
Luke 6:27–38

Jesus said to his disciples: "To you who hear I say, love your enemies, do good to those who hate you, bless those who curse you, pray for those who mistreat you. To the person who strikes you on one cheek, offer the other one as well, and from the person who takes your cloak, do not withhold even your tunic. Give to everyone who asks of you, and from the one who takes what is yours do not demand it back. Do to others as you would have them do to you. For if you love those who love you, what credit is that to you? Even sinners love those who love them. And if you do good to those who do good to you, what credit is that to you? Even sinners do the same. If you lend money to those from whom you expect repayment, what credit is that to you? Even sinners lend to sinners, and get back the same amount.

But rather, love your enemies and do good to them, and lend expecting nothing back; then your reward will be great and you will be children of the Most High, for he himself is kind to the ungrateful and the wicked.

Be merciful, just as your Father is merciful. "Stop judging and you will not be judged. Stop condemning and you will not be condemned. Forgive and you will be forgiven. Give, and gifts will be given to you; a good measure, packed together, shaken down, and overflowing, will be poured into your lap. For the measure with which you measure will in return be measured out to you."

Understanding the Word

Today's Gospel challenges every follower of Christ. Jesus says twice, "Love your enemies"(Luke 6:27, 35). That was not easy for those listening to Jesus to hear. Nor is it easy for Christians down through the centuries. Retaliation is the natural instinct in dealing with an enemy. But Jesus insists not only that we love our enemies, but that we do good to them, bless them, and pray for them (6:27).

Christ allows no exceptions to the rule of loving one's enemies. In today's first reading David spares the life of Saul, his sworn enemy, because he has been anointed as king of Israel. Christians are to love their enemies even when they have no redeeming qualities. God the Father has set the example, "kind to the ungrateful and the wicked" (Luke 6:35). Jesus adds this command, "Be merciful, just as [also] your Father is merciful" (6:36). The Old Testament background for that imperative is found in the book of Leviticus, "Be holy, for I, the LORD, your God, am holy" (Leviticus 19:2). Leviticus goes on to say, "You shall love your neighbor as yourself" (19:18). Jesus brings that Old Testament concept to fulfillment by stressing that one's enemies must always be seen as neighbors and loved.

While it is right for everyone to love those who love them, to do good to those who do good to them, to lend money to those from whom they expect repayment, Jesus points out that those acts of natural kindness have no heavenly reward; "even sinners do the same" (Luke 6:33). He goes on to promise, "Love your enemies and do good to them, and lend expecting nothing back; then your reward will be great and you will be children of the Most High" (6:35).

The Christian must also avoid judging, condemning. Rather, every follower of Jesus must forgive (see 6:37). The promise here is that God will deal with us as we deal with others. If you forgive, you will be forgiven. If you reach out with gifts to the poor and vulnerable, "giving to everyone who asks of you" (6:30), the Father will pour an overflowing abundance of divine gifts into your lap (see 6:38).

Reflecting on the Word

In his book *Addiction and Grace* Gerald May lists one hundred six slices of life to which people find themselves addicted, attractively so, and then another seventy-seven that people addictively avoid—another way of talking about phobias. The obvious attractions find their way onto his list, like alcohol and smoking and gambling. But then he also includes many unexpected behaviors—addictions to the stock market, being right, power, happiness, revenge, nail biting, music, potato chips, and almost a hundred more.

Gerald May confesses that he finds at least fourteen lurking in his own shadows. For all of us they are blind spots of sorts, ways of structuring other worlds when the real one in which we live grows a bit too stressful. What is sad is that too often we're not even aware of it. In short, we become addicted to who we are, both to our sin as well as our grace. We like ourselves well enough not to recognize the need to change.

Interestingly, many of the addictions May notes have become contemporary expressions of the very behaviors against which Jesus warns us. Our addiction to the ups and downs of the stock market can easily get in the way of generous lending or sharing of resources. Cursing our enemies sounds much like revenge. And the need to be right will blind us to the need to forgive.

Thankfully we are not only sinful but also graced. Though each of us has our own addictions, some of them sinful, each of us is also free of other ones. St. Paul had it right: "Just as we have borne the image of the earthly one, we shall also bear the image of the heavenly one" (1 Corinthians 15:49).

CONSIDER/ DISCUSS:

- Which blessing or personal quality of your life would be the last you would surrender? Would you call it an addiction?
- Each day for a week, name for yourself the one personal quality you most need to overcome. Admit to God that you are powerless over it. Then ask God to do what you cannot. After a week, how are you different?

Responding to the Word

How we live too often seems to arise instinctively from somewhere deep within us. What we can decide is where our heart lies, what we will treasure and nurture. And then from the heart of our heart comes forth the real us, and we can acknowledge God's presence there.

Spend a few minutes in quiet prayer. Ask God to show you one (or more) ways that you may be called to respond to this week's scriptures—

- in your relationship with God
- with family and friends
- at work, school, or church
- in the broader community

Notes

Lent is intended to prepare the Christian for a renewed celebration of the death and resurrection of Jesus Christ. Some basic themes in the readings of the Lenten liturgy anticipate those events of Holy Week.

At Christmas Jesus is hailed as Savior by the angels; he has come into the world to save all from their sins. Lent develops this point by stressing the love of God in forgiving sinners. On the Fifth Sunday of Lent Jesus will say to the woman caught in the act of adultery, "Neither do I condemn you. Go, and from now on do not sin any more" (John 8:11). Even more amazing is the parable of the prodigal son on the fourth Sunday of Lent (Luke 15:11–32). Here is a man who has done everything wrong; yet God, in the person of the father, is not only willing to forgive and forget, incredibly he does it with joy. Most comforting on Palm Sunday are the words of Jesus from the cross: "Father, forgive them, they know not what they do" (Luke 23:34). Jesus is very much aware that our sins have made the cross necessary, but he willingly forgives us. Then he forgives and promises salvation to the criminal crucified with him: "Amen, I say to you, today you will be with me in Paradise" (23:43).

The Lenten readings will insist on repentance as the Christian's response to this loving forgiveness of Jesus. On the Third Sunday of Lent Jesus will be very explicit on this point. Talking about Galileans who had been killed by Pilate, Jesus says, "But I tell you, if you do not repent, you will all perish as they did!" (Luke 13:3). Repentance means a true reformation of one's life, the sincere effort always to put God first. Love of God then must be accompanied by love for all neighbors, even enemies, since every human being is a child of God.

Baptism is a central theme in the season of Lent, especially for those preparing to enter the Church. But every Christian should recall the great grace of baptism and also the baptismal commitment. The readings from Year A, which may be used any year, highlight the role of baptism. These readings for the Third, Fourth, and Fifth Sundays of Lent are all from the Gospel of John: the Samaritan woman (4:5–42), the man born blind (9:1–41) and Lazarus (11:1–45). Each has a special connection with baptism. In the account of the Samaritan woman, for example, one phrase is a perfect description of the grace of baptism: "[T]he water I shall give will become in him a spring of water welling up to eternal life" (4:14).

The Church wants to stress two principal themes during the season of Lent: "the recalling of baptism or the preparation for it, and penance" (*Constitution on the Sacred Liturgy*, 109). The readings of Lent achieve that purpose of the Church by recalling God's willingness to share this abundant life with Christ's followers in baptism and also to forgive those who sin, but who repent.

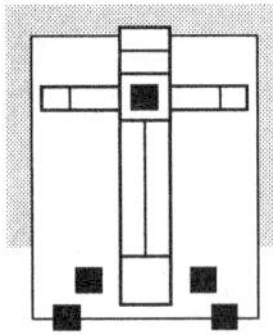

February 25, 2007

FIRST SUNDAY OF LENT

Today's Focus: Dreams of a Past Future

Sometimes nostalgia gets a bad rap for being too much cotton candy, for living on borrowed dreams. But nostalgia can also be that means by which we remember what we once held onto as true, back to a time not yet polluted by our sin, a time when everything was possible.

FIRST READING
Deuteronomy 26: 4–10

Moses spoke to the people, saying: "The priest shall receive the basket from you and shall set it in front of the altar of the LORD, your God. Then you shall declare before the LORD, your God, 'My father was a wandering Aramean who went down to Egypt with a small household and lived there as an alien. But there he became a nation great, strong, and numerous. When the Egyptians maltreated and oppressed us, imposing hard labor upon us, we cried to the LORD, the God of our fathers, and he heard our cry and saw our affliction, our toil, and our oppression. He brought us out of Egypt with his strong hand and outstretched arm, with terrifying power, with signs and wonders; and bringing us into this country, he gave us this land flowing with milk and honey. Therefore, I have now brought you the firstfruits of the products of the soil which you, O LORD, have given me.' And having set them before the Lord, your God, you shall bow down in his presence."

PSALM RESPONSE
Psalm 91:15b

Be with me, Lord, when I am in trouble.

SECOND READING
Romans 10: 8–13

Brothers and sisters: What does Scripture say?

The word is near you,
in your mouth and in your heart

—that is, the word of faith that we preach—, for, if you confess with your mouth that Jesus is Lord and believe in your heart that God raised him from the dead, you will be saved. For one believes with the heart and so is justified, and one confesses with the mouth and so is saved. For the Scripture says,

No one who believes in him will be put to shame.

For there is no distinction between Jew and Greek; the same Lord is Lord of all, enriching all who call upon him. For "everyone who calls on the name of the Lord will be saved."

GOSPEL
Luke 4:1–13

Filled with the Holy Spirit, Jesus returned from the Jordan and was led by the Spirit into the desert for forty days, to be tempted by the devil. He ate nothing during those days, and when they were over he was hungry. The devil said to him, "If you are the Son of God, command this stone to become bread." Jesus answered him, "It is written,

One does not live on bread alone."

Then he took him up and showed him all the kingdoms of the world in a single instant. The devil said to him, "I shall give to you all this power and glory; for it has been handed over to me, and I may give it to whomever I wish. All this will be yours, if you worship me." Jesus said to him in reply, "It is written:

You shall worship the Lord, your God,
and him alone shall you serve."

Then he led him to Jerusalem, made him stand on the parapet of the temple, and said to him, "If you are the Son of God, throw yourself down from here, for it is written:

He will command his angels concerning you, to guard you,
and:
With their hands they will support you,
lest you dash your foot against a stone."

Jesus said to him in reply, "It also says,
You shall not put the Lord, your God, to the test."

When the devil had finished every temptation, he departed from him for a time.

Understanding the Word

The temptations of Jesus in the desert are intended by the devil to take him away from his God-given mission and lead him to embrace the role of wonder-worker, a person with political power. Jesus insists that he is to be a gentle, humble Messiah who will bring salvation to all by following the will of his Father.

The thread that unites the three temptations is the use of scripture by Jesus. He answers each temptation with a quotation from the book of Deuteronomy. The Israelites in the desert during their forty years of wandering were also tempted, but failed to pass the test. Luke emphasizes the role of the Spirit in the success of Jesus. He is "filled with the Holy Spirit" and "was led by the Spirit into the desert" (4:1).

In the third temptation the devil even quotes scripture to assure Jesus of angelic protection (Psalm 91:11, 12). But the psalmist has in mind God's ordinary protection of those whom God loves, not helping a person who is tempting God by rash action. "You shall not put the LORD, your God, to the test" (Deuteronomy 6:16). Luke's Gospel sets the third temptation in Jerusalem because that city is always the place of destiny for Jesus.

In the first and third temptations, the devil uses the phrase, "If you are the Son of God." This is a follow-up to the baptismal scene in which "a voice came from heaven, 'You are my beloved Son; with you I am well pleased' " (Luke 3:22). The devil is putting that title of Jesus to the test. Jesus' responses not only accept the title, but prove that he deserves it as an obedient Son. His rejection of these temptations is an example for all his followers.

After these temptations the devil "departed from him for a time" (4:13). Temptation is a regular part of Jesus' ministry, but the most dramatic encounter will occur at the time of the Passion, which Jesus refers to as "the time for the power of darkness" (22:53). But then, as in today's Gospel, Jesus will be the victor.

Reflecting on the Word

I went back to the old neighborhood a while ago and realized there what everyone who has ever tried to go home discovers: the trees have grown smaller and easier for climbing, the alley where we played hide-and-go-seek has grown narrower, the trip to the corner less daring, and all the old haunts so much less intriguing. But going back also drew forth in me a power I had not imagined or expected. Not only did it reintroduce me to who I am, it renewed the dream of who I could be. Going back to one's roots can do that because it's a going back to where it all began.

Lent can be such a time of returning to our roots. Some would see the season as penitential, a time of reparation for sin; others as a time for growing more prayerful or for reestablishing lives of service or for deepening faith. And it can be all of that. Yet the readings of this Lenten Sunday take us back to how it once was and who was once doing the shaping of life.

There are myriad ways of making the Lenten journey back to our roots. Spend time with the scriptures. Read the lives of the saints. Go on a retreat. Visit a shrine. Keep a journal. Pray the rosary again. Sit with silence. Make the Stations of the Cross. Offer peace to an enemy. Visit the sick or a shut-in. Give enough alms to notice the pinch. Do some spiritual reading. Fast and abstain from meat. They are all part of our tradition and shards of our own pasts. In them we will once more meet ourselves, perhaps as if for the first time, and remember dreams long lost in the clutter of life's demands.

CONSIDER/ DISCUSS:

- We have "outer dreams," dreams about what we can accomplish with our lives. We also have "inner dreams," dreams about what sort of person we can become, dreams for our spirit. Name an "inner dream" you once had for yourself that has since faded. What sort of Lenten penance could bring you back home to the roots of that dream?
- Was there a "best time" to your faith? Would you go back to it?

Responding to the Word

If we seek to make a journey back to our roots and not simply into nostalgia, we need to remember that roots are always found in the dirt and the mud. A journey back to our roots, then, will also place us square in the midst of all of our life's unattractive earthiness.

Spend a few minutes in quiet prayer. Ask God to show you one (or more) ways that you may be called to respond to this week's scriptures—

- in your relationship with God
- with family and friends
- at work, school, or church
- in the broader community

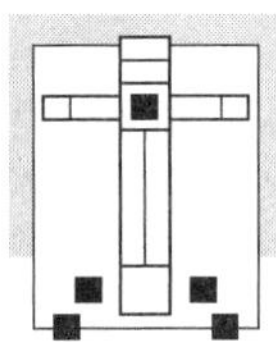

March 4, 2007

SECOND SUNDAY OF LENT

Today's Focus: On Befriending Darkness

Grownups always talk of childhood as if it were carefree and wonderful and without any of the labors that make being an adult stressful and weighted. But being a child, too, has its own work to be done, its own darknesses to negotiate.

FIRST READING
Genesis 15: 5–12, 17–18

The Lord God took Abram outside and said, "Look up at the sky and count the stars, if you can. Just so," he added, "shall your descendants be." Abram put his faith in the LORD, who credited it to him as an act of righteousness.

He then said to him, "I am the LORD who brought you from Ur of the Chaldeans to give you this land as a possession." "O Lord GOD," he asked, "how am I to know that I shall possess it?" He answered him, "Bring me a three-year-old heifer, a three-year-old she-goat, a three-year-old ram, a turtledove, and a young pigeon." Abram brought him all these, split them in two, and placed each half opposite the other; but the birds he did not cut up. Birds of prey swooped down on the carcasses, but Abram stayed with them. As the sun was about to set, a trance fell upon Abram, and a deep, terrifying darkness enveloped him.

When the sun had set and it was dark, there appeared a smoking fire pot and a flaming torch, which passed between those pieces. It was on that occasion that the LORD made a covenant with Abram, saying: "To your descendants I give this land, from the Wadi of Egypt to the Great River, the Euphrates."

PSALM RESPONSE
Psalm 27:1a

The Lord is my light and my salvation.

In the shorter form of the reading, the passage in brackets is omitted.

SECOND READING
Philippians 3: 17 — 4:1 or 3:20 — 4:1

[Join with others in being imitators of me, brothers and sisters, and observe those who thus conduct themselves according to the model you have in us. For many, as I have often told you and now tell you even in tears, conduct themselves as enemies of the cross of Christ. Their end is destruction. Their God is their stomach; their glory is in their "shame." Their minds are occupied with earthly things. But] our citizenship is in heaven, and from it we also await a savior, the Lord Jesus Christ. He will change our lowly body to conform with his glorified body by the power that enables him also to bring all things into subjection to himself.

Therefore, my brothers and sisters, whom I love and long for, my joy and crown, in this way stand firm in the Lord.

GOSPEL
Luke 9:28b–36

Jesus took Peter, John, and James and went up the mountain to pray. While he was praying his face changed in appearance and his clothing became dazzling white. And behold, two men were conversing with him, Moses and Elijah, who appeared in glory and spoke of his exodus that he was going to accomplish in Jerusalem. Peter and his companions had been overcome by sleep, but becoming fully awake, they saw his glory and the two men standing with him. As they were about to part from him, Peter said to Jesus, "Master, it is good that we are here; let us make three tents, one for you, one for Moses, and one for Elijah." But he did not know what he was saying. While he was still speaking, a cloud came and cast a shadow over them, and they became frightened when they entered the cloud. Then from the cloud came a voice that said, "This is my chosen Son; listen to him." After the voice had spoken, Jesus was found alone. They fell silent and did not at that time tell anyone what they had seen.

Understanding the Word

After telling the disciples that he will suffer and be killed, Jesus adds "and on the third day be raised" (Luke 9:22). The Transfiguration gives a preview of the glory of that resurrection.

Jesus is transfigured before Peter, James, and John. "[H]is face changed in appearance and his clothing became dazzling white" (9:29). Moses and Elijah appear with him representing the Old Testament. Suddenly they are overshadowed by a cloud, the sign of God's presence. From the cloud the heavenly voice says, "This is my chosen Son; listen to him" (9:35). Jesus is then left alone—he alone now will be the spokesperson for his Father. All must listen to Jesus.

The Transfiguration story also appears in Matthew and Mark, but Luke offers some interesting additions. First of all, he notes that Jesus "went up the mountain to pray" (9:28). In the Gospel of Luke a mountain is seen as a place of prayer. Luke notes that Jesus often spends the entire evening on a mountain in prayer with the Father, especially before important decisions, such as the choice of the Twelve (6:12–16).

Another contribution of Luke is the indication of "glory" with Moses and Elijah (9:31) and then with Jesus (9:32). "Glory" in the Biblical tradition reflects the wonder of the presence of God. After the Father orders that people should listen to his Son, Jesus is alone. The Old Testament has yielded to the universal mission of the Savior. The "glory" of God, the presence of the Father, will always be with the Son.

Perhaps the most important addition by Luke is the indication of what Jesus, Moses, and Elijah were discussing. They "spoke of his exodus that he was going to accomplish in Jerusalem" (9:31). Already in 9:51 Luke says of Jesus, "[H]e resolutely determined to journey to Jerusalem." For Luke the exodus, the departure of Jesus, will include not only the death and Resurrection, but also the Ascension (24:50–53). The Transfiguration will support the faith of the disciples as they, too, will suffer and be killed. They will see the Resurrection as the ultimate goal.

Reflecting on the Word

One of my childhood tasks at the end of each day was to befriend the fearsome denizens of the dark. By the time I was eight I had evolved a simple ritual for myself so that I might ensure safe and undisturbed dreams. One by one in established rotation I would check the three caverns of darkness where the foes of peaceful nighttime could hide—beneath my bed, behind the door to the attic stairway that ascended from my bedroom, and finally in the closet behind the winter coats where the forces of evil could hide and be less easily detected. Only after these three possible hiding places had been secured could I then give my head to the place of dreams.

The trio of Peter and James and John, as well as Abram long before them, found their experience of darkness to be more than a bit unsettling. The Gospel says Peter and his friends were frightened, and the book of Genesis says Abram was terrified. Nevertheless, the events became turning points for a new way of understanding what their lives were to be about.

For my own childhood the bedroom darkness was where I worked out who and what I was. There I said my prayers, but also wondered whether they mattered at all to God or to anyone. There, too, I worked out my relationship with my parents, on occasion running away from home but also slinking on back, both mostly in my imagination. In that tamed darkness there were times, too, I suppose, when I cried myself to sleep, though mostly I remember slipping from the day's busyness with peace and a sense of being loved. In that nightly darkness I met my angers and my loves, my dreams and my sins, the people with whom I lived, and mostly myself.

CONSIDER/ DISCUSS:

- Name your darknesses. Name your current fears. List your possible responses. Choose one.
- What are the promises of God that you count on today?

Responding to the Word

Not being able to see very clearly what's in store for us does not mean that we should back away from such darkness. Being frightened, even terrified, by a future lost in fog does not suggest we're meant for some other path. To the contrary, it is in the midst of that clouded unknown that we meet the future to which our God is calling us.

Spend a few minutes in quiet prayer. Ask God to show you one (or more) ways that you may be called to respond to this week's scriptures—

- in your relationship with God
- with family and friends
- at work, school, or church
- in the broader community

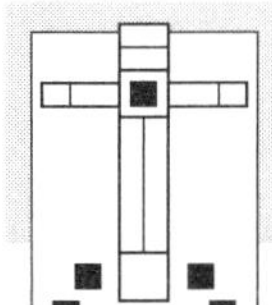

March 11, 2007

THIRD SUNDAY OF LENT, YEAR C

Today's Focus: The Quiet Side of Patience

When it comes to holiness, however we might define it, we're all more or less cast from the same mold. Whether old or young, wise or simple, priests or parishioners, like good wine we all take time to age into something worthwhile.

For pastoral reasons, the readings given for Year A may be used in place of these readings. *See page 77.*

FIRST READING
Exodus 3:1–8a, 13–15

Moses was tending the flock of his father-in-law Jethro, the priest of Midian. Leading the flock across the desert, he came to Horeb, the mountain of God. There an angel of the LORD appeared to Moses in fire flaming out of a bush. As he looked on, he was surprised to see that the bush, though on fire, was not consumed. So Moses decided, "I must go over to look at this remarkable sight, and see why the bush is not burned."

When the LORD saw him coming over to look at it more closely, God called out to him from the bush, "Moses! Moses!" He answered, "Here I am." God said, "Come no nearer! Remove the sandals from your feet, for the place where you stand is holy ground. I am the God of your fathers," he continued, "the God of Abraham, the God of Isaac, the God of Jacob." Moses hid his face, for he was afraid to look at God. But the LORD said, "I have witnessed the affliction of my people in Egypt and have heard their cry of complaint against their slave drivers, so I know well what they are suffering. Therefore I have come down to rescue them from the hands of the Egyptians and lead them out of that land into a good and spacious land, a land flowing with milk and honey."

Moses said to God, "But when I go to the Israelites and say to them, 'The God of your fathers has sent me to you,' if they ask me, 'What is his name?' what am I to tell them?" God replied, "I am who am." Then he added, "This is what you shall tell the Israelites: I AM sent me to you."

God spoke further to Moses, "Thus shall you say to the Israelites: The LORD, the God of your fathers, the God of Abraham, the God of Isaac, the God of Jacob, has sent me to you.

"This is my name forever; thus am I to be remembered through all generations."

PSALM RESPONSE
Psalm 103:8a

The Lord is kind and merciful.

SECOND READING
1 Corinthians 10: 1–6, 10–12

I do not want you to be unaware, brothers and sisters, that our ancestors were all under the cloud and all passed through the sea, and all of them were baptized into Moses in the cloud and in the sea. All ate the same spiritual food, and all drank the same spiritual drink, for they drank from a spiritual rock that followed them, and the rock was the Christ. Yet God was not pleased with most of them, for they were struck down in the desert.

These things happened as examples for us, so that we might not desire evil things, as they did. Do not grumble as some of them did, and suffered death by the destroyer. These things happened to them as an example, and they have been written down as a warning to us, upon whom the end of the ages has come. Therefore, whoever thinks he is standing secure should take care not to fall.

GOSPEL
Luke 13:1–9

Some people told Jesus about the Galileans whose blood Pilate had mingled with the blood of their sacrifices. Jesus said to them in reply, "Do you think that because these Galileans suffered in this way they were greater sinners than all other Galileans? By no means! But I tell you, if you do not repent, you will all perish as they did! Or those eighteen people who were killed when the tower at Siloam fell on them—do you think they were more guilty than everyone else who lived in Jerusalem? By no means! But I tell you, if you do not repent, you will all perish as they did!"

And he told them this parable: "There once was a person who had a fig tree planted in his orchard, and when he came in search of fruit on it but found none, he said to the gardener, 'For three years now I have come in search of fruit on this fig tree but have found none. So cut it down. Why should it exhaust the soil?' He said to him in reply, 'Sir, leave it for this year also, and I shall cultivate the ground around it and fertilize it; it may bear fruit in the future. If not you can cut it down.'"

Understanding the Word

In today's first reading God's name is revealed to Moses. Yahweh is the proper personal name of God in the Hebrew scriptures. Someone's name in Old Testament times was very important because it revealed that person's reality. So, too, with the name of God. But God is purposely somewhat mysterious in revealing the name Yahweh. Yahweh comes from the basic Hebrew verb "to be." In the original Hebrew text there were no vowels. It was simply YHWH. Some interpret this as a reference to God's absolute existence. Others, by adding different vowels, understand it as God the creator, the one who causes to be.

Out of great reverence for the divine name the Israelites said *adonai* (my lord) in place of Yahweh. In a Hebrew reading class I took, an Orthodox Jewish student would not even say *adonai*. He wanted that reserved for prayer. When Yahweh would appear in the text, he would say in Hebrew "the name." Jehovah is the result of putting the vowels of *adonai* with the consonants of Yahweh. It is not really a Hebrew word.

Whatever the etymological understanding of Yahweh, everyone agrees that it refers to an active, loving relationship between Yahweh and the chosen people. "I am" exists for them, as seen in creation, in the covenant, in the Exodus. What God expects of the Israelites in return is to "[b]e holy, for I, the LORD, your God, am holy" (Leviticus 19:2).

In the Gospel today Jesus warns his followers to be holy for there is always the possibility of sudden death. Even if God spares the sinner, as the fig tree is spared, it is only for a limited time. Ultimately all will be called to judgment. What is required, therefore, is repentance. The Greek word involved here, *metanoia*, demands a true reformation of life based on the values of Yahweh and of the Son. Not surprisingly, repentance is a basic theme of Lent. The Christian is to prepare for the events of Holy Week by a sincere effort to repent for past sins and to seek greater holiness in the future.

Reflecting on the Word

I live in an old Milwaukee house with five college students. In many ways they are little different from many other college students. They're sorting out what they want to do with their lives and loves. They like good times, though they can also be quite serious. They study sometimes, and watch TV a lot, and eat their apportioned share of frozen pizzas. So it does appear that they and their peers have been cut from the same bolt of cloth—except that these are also thinking about becoming priests.

What amazes me about all those students who have moved in and out of this house over the years is how they mature and grow reflective, how they garner morsels of wisdom. They do change. Something happens to them well beyond my understanding. Perhaps that's how it is with us all, young and old alike. All of which echoes the parable in this Sunday's Gospel, that we need to be patient with the ways any of us come to holiness, if for no other reason than the fact that God is patient with us.

So it might be good for parents to be patient with their adult children who do not yet live out faith as they had hoped. And believers may need to be patient with the institutional Church; it, too, has not yet finished the journey of growing into holiness. And society needs to be patient with those in its prisons; they are places that should not be so much about punishment as about finding ways of nurturing someone into better living over the long term. And ultimately it is good to be patient with ourselves as well; after all, holiness is not our own doing, but God's. It just takes time, mostly a good portion of it.

CONSIDER/ DISCUSS:

- How has God been patient with you?
- As you notice the people and circumstances that are scattered about your life, what need for maturity and growth is currently calling forth patience in you?

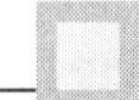

Responding to the Word

It may be that as we all grow older and pile up years, one by one we add more and more experiences like that of Moses and his now famous bush. Or perhaps it may be that as we simply become accustomed to the holy, just because it is so ordinary, it happens in ways we never even notice.

Spend a few minutes in quiet prayer. Ask God to show you one (or more) ways that you may be called to respond to this week's scriptures—

- in your relationship with God
- with family and friends
- at work, school, or church
- in the broader community

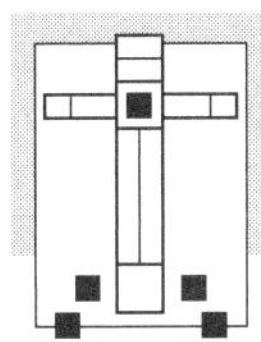

March 11, 2007

THIRD SUNDAY OF LENT, YEAR A

Today's Focus: A Restless Thirst

There is an edge of dissatisfaction to our living, or perhaps a thirst that is never quite quenched. St. Augustine, who prayed, "Restless is our heart until it rests in God," knew that longing well and the struggle that accompanied it.

FIRST READING
Exodus 17: 3–7

In those days, in their thirst for water, the people grumbled against Moses, saying, "Why did you ever make us leave Egypt? Was it just to have us die here of thirst with our children and our livestock?" So Moses cried out to the LORD, "What shall I do with this people? A little more and they will stone me!" The LORD answered Moses, "Go over there in front of the people, along with some of the elders of Israel, holding in your hand, as you go, the staff with which you struck the river. I will be standing there in front of you on the rock in Horeb. Strike the rock, and the water will flow from it for the people to drink." This Moses did, in the presence of the elders of Israel. The place was called Massah and Meribah, because the Israelites quarreled there and tested the LORD, saying, "Is the LORD in our midst or not?"

PSALM RESPONSE
Psalm 95:8

If today you hear his voice, harden not your hearts.

SECOND READING
Romans 5: 1–2, 5–8

Brothers and sisters: Since we have been justified by faith, we have peace with God through our Lord Jesus Christ, through whom we have gained access by faith to this grace in which we stand, and we boast in hope of the glory of God.

And hope does not disappoint, because the love of God has been poured out into our hearts through the Holy Spirit who has been given to us. For Christ, while we were still helpless, died at the appointed time for the ungodly. Indeed, only with difficulty does one die for a just person, though perhaps for a good person one might even find courage to die. But God proves his love for us in that while we were still sinners Christ died for us.

In the shorter version of the reading, the three passages in brackets are omitted.

GOSPEL
John 4:5–42 or 4:5–15, 19b–26, 39a, 40–42

Jesus came to a town of Samaria called Sychar, near the plot of land that Jacob had given to his son Joseph. Jacob's well was there. Jesus, tired from his journey, sat down there at the well. It was about noon.

A woman of Samaria came to draw water. Jesus said to her, "Give me a drink." His disciples had gone into the town to buy food. The Samaritan woman said to him, "How can you, a Jew, ask me, a Samaritan woman, for a drink?"—For Jews use nothing in common with Samaritans.—Jesus answered and said to her, "If you knew the gift of God and who is saying to you, 'Give me a drink,' you would have asked him and he would have given you living water." The woman said to him, "Sir, you do not even have a bucket and the cistern is deep; where then can you get this living water? Are you greater than our father Jacob, who gave us this cistern and drank from it himself with his children and his flocks?" Jesus answered and said to her, "Everyone who drinks this water will be thirsty again; but whoever drinks the water I shall give will never thirst; the water I shall give will become in him a spring of water welling up to eternal life." The woman said to him, "Sir, give me this water, so that I may not be thirsty or have to keep coming here to draw water."

[Jesus said to her, "Go call your husband and come back." The woman answered and said to him, "I do not have a husband." Jesus answered her, "You are right in saying, 'I do not have a husband.' For you have had five husbands, and the one you have now is not your husband. What you have said is true." The woman said to him, "Sir,] I can see that you are a prophet. Our ancestors worshiped on this mountain; but you people say that the place to worship is in Jerusalem." Jesus said to her, "Believe me, woman, the hour is coming when you will worship the Father neither on this mountain nor in Jerusalem. You people worship what you do not understand; we worship what we understand, because salvation is from the Jews. But the hour is coming, and is now here, when true worshipers will worship the Father in Spirit and truth; and indeed the Father seeks such people to worship him. God is Spirit, and those who worship him must worship in Spirit and truth."

The woman said to him, "I know that the Messiah is coming, the one called the Christ; when he comes, he will tell us everything." Jesus said to her, "I am he, the one speaking with you."

[At that moment his disciples returned, and were amazed that he was talking with a woman, but still no one said, "What are you looking for?" or "Why are you talking with her?" The woman left her water jar and went into the town and said to the people, "Come see a man who told me everything I have done. Could he possibly be the Christ?" They went out of the town and came to him. Meanwhile, the disciples urged him, "Rabbi, eat." But he said to them, "I have food to eat of which you do not know." So the disciples said to one another, "Could someone have brought him something to eat?" Jesus said to them, "My food is to do the will of the one who sent me and to finish his work. Do you not say, 'In four months the harvest will be here'? I tell you, look up and see the fields ripe for the harvest. The reaper is already receiving payment and gathering crops for eternal life, so that the sower and reaper can rejoice together. For here the saying is verified that 'One sows and another reaps.' I sent you to reap what you have not worked for; others have done the work, and you are sharing the fruits of their work."]

Many of the Samaritans of that town began to believe in him [because of the word of the woman who testified, "He told me everything I have done."] When the Samaritans came to him, they invited him to stay with them; and he stayed there two days. Many more began to believe in him because of his word, and they said to the woman, "We no longer believe because of your word; for we have heard for ourselves, and we know that this is truly the savior of the world."

Understanding the Word

The scripture readings today stress in a comforting way the unconditional, unique love of God for every human being. The account in Exodus narrates how God gives life-sustaining water from a rock to the people despite their quarreling and testing. The account of the Samaritan woman shows Jesus giving us life-giving water, "a spring of water welling up to eternal life" (John 4:14). This is a wonderful description of baptism and its effects.

Paul's letter to the Romans makes the point emphatically that God's love for us is a free gift, not deserved, but needed. The proof of this is the fact that the death of Christ on the cross took place when we were helpless, ungodly, even sinners (Romans 5:6, 8). Because of that death the Christian can be justified by faith (5:1). Later Paul will stress that baptism must accompany the faith. "We were indeed buried with him through baptism into death, so that, just as Christ was raised from the dead by the glory of the Father, we too might live in newness of life" (6:4).

Paul enumerates the effects of justification for the follower of Jesus in today's reading. First of all, there is "peace with God through our Lord Jesus Christ" (5:1). Peace in the biblical background denotes the fullness, the completeness of one's relationship with God and the blessings that flow from that relationship. "Through our Lord Jesus Christ" makes clear that Jesus is the mediator of the New Covenant. The Christian enjoys grace, God's abiding favor (5:2). Importantly there is also confident hope for eternal salvation because "the love of God has been poured out into our hearts through the Holy Spirit who has been given to us" (5:5). "Then afterward I will pour out / my spirit upon all mankind" (Joel 3:1). For those preparing for baptism and all who are recalling their baptismal commitment, these words are most encouraging. Because of the death of Jesus, God the Father will give us the gift of the Holy Spirit. All three persons of the Trinity are very involved at the moment of baptism and throughout the Christian life.

Reflecting on the Word

Patrick is a freshman in college. He tends to be introspective and somewhat on the quiet side by nature. While in high school he was introduced to creative writing and still finds it to be something that stirs his soul, though lately he's begun to discover poetry. But what really taps into his spirit, says Patrick, is drumming. He's a percussionist and in high school played in the orchestra but also as part of a rock band. When Patrick talks about that, he does so with energy and a glint in his eyes. After a while, when he comes to trust you, he'll tell you that at times his drumming is a spiritual experience, as close to sensing God's presence as he ever comes.

Patrick wonders if his drumming could be prayer. I think it could. More recently he's come with questions about praying, and amid all the questions he talks about wanting to grow closer to God, and what to do with such a thirst. Patrick is only nineteen, and before long he'll learn that nothing ever quite satisfies that thirst, at least not for long. At that point he'll be faced with choosing—on the one hand an endless quest with continual disappointments, on the other a growing realization that what he's sensing in his thirst is the soul's desire for God, a thirst that's never quenched this side of death. It's a thirst he'll have to live with, like the rest of us. Still, in the meantime Patrick and we live as restless seekers for the fountain of life.

CONSIDER/ DISCUSS:

- When in life are you "most thirsty" for more? When are you "least thirsty"? What conclusions might you draw?
- When have you unexpectedly found water flowing in the desert, that is, deep meaning to life when there seemed to be no reason for its presence?

Responding to the Word

One of the gifts of belonging to a community of believers is that we make the journey together—like the Samaritans of the town who came to listen to Jesus. When we seek to quench our thirst, at times we do so alone and at other times together like the townsfolk.

Spend a few minutes in quiet prayer. Ask God to show you one (or more) ways that you may be called to respond to this week's scriptures—

- in your relationship with God
- with family and friends
- at work, school, or church
- in the broader community

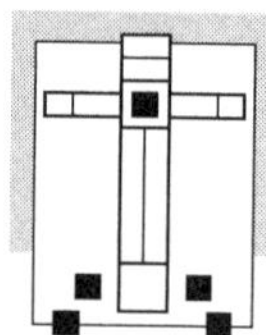

March 18, 2007

FOURTH SUNDAY OF LENT, YEAR C

Today's Focus: The Bite of Forgiveness

It's been said that forgiving is the most difficult thing we do. I suspect it's true. Too often we find ourselves living with fractured lives and fractured loves, sometimes because we don't know how to do the mending, and sometimes because we don't wish to do the mending. In either case, we suffer.

For pastoral reasons, the readings given for Year A may be used in place of these readings. See page 86.

FIRST READING
Joshua 5:9a, 10–12

The LORD said to Joshua, "Today I have removed the reproach of Egypt from you."

While the Israelites were encamped at Gilgal on the plains of Jericho, they celebrated the Passover on the evening of the fourteenth of the month. On the day after the Passover, they ate of the produce of the land in the form of unleavened cakes and parched grain. On that same day after the Passover, on which they ate of the produce of the land, the manna ceased. No longer was there manna for the Israelites, who that year ate of the yield of the land of Canaan.

PSALM RESPONSE
Psalm 34:9a

Taste and see the goodness of the Lord.

SECOND READING
2 Corinthians 5: 17–21

Brothers and sisters: Whoever is in Christ is a new creation: the old things have passed away; behold, new things have come. And all this is from God, who has reconciled us to himself through Christ and given us the ministry of reconciliation, namely, God was reconciling the world to himself in Christ, not counting their trespasses against them and entrusting to us the message of reconciliation. So we are ambassadors for Christ, as if God were appealing through us. We implore you on behalf of Christ, be reconciled to God. For our sake he made him to be sin who did not know sin, so that we might become the righteousness of God in him.

GOSPEL *Luke 15:1–3, 11–32*

Tax collectors and sinners were all drawing near to listen to Jesus, but the Pharisees and scribes began to complain, saying, "This man welcomes sinners and eats with them." So to them Jesus addressed this parable: "A man had two sons, and the younger son said to his father, 'Father give me the share of your estate that should come to me.' So the father divided the property between them. After a few days, the younger son collected all his belongings and set off to a distant country where he squandered his inheritance on a life of dissipation. When he had freely spent everything, a severe famine struck that country, and he found himself in dire need. So he hired himself out to one of the local citizens who sent him to his farm to tend the swine. And he longed to eat his fill of the pods on which the swine fed, but nobody gave him any. Coming to his senses he thought, 'How many of my father's hired workers have more than enough food to eat, but here am I, dying from hunger. I shall get up and go to my father and I shall say to him, "Father, I have sinned against heaven and against you. I no longer deserve to be called your son; treat me as you would treat one of your hired workers."' So he got up and went back to his father. While he was still a long way off, his father caught sight of him, and was filled with compassion. He ran to his son, embraced him and kissed him. His son said to him, 'Father, I have sinned against heaven and against you; I no longer deserve to be called your son.' But his father ordered his servants, 'Quickly bring the finest robe and put it on him; put a ring on his finger and sandals on his feet. Take the fattened calf and slaughter it. Then let us celebrate with a feast, because this son of mine was dead, and has come to life again; he was lost, and has been found.' Then the celebration began. Now the older son had been out in the field and, on his way back, as he neared the house, he heard the sound of music and dancing. He called one of the servants and asked what this might mean. The servant said to him, 'Your brother has returned and your father has slaughtered the fattened calf because he has him back safe and sound.' He became angry, and when he refused to enter the house, his father came out and pleaded with him. He said to his father in reply, 'Look, all these years I served you and not once did I disobey your orders; yet you never gave me even a young goat to feast on with my friends. But when your son returns who swallowed up your property with prostitutes, for him you slaughter the fattened calf.' He said to him, 'My son, you are here with me always; everything I have is yours. But now we must celebrate and rejoice, because your brother was dead and has come to life again; he was lost and has been found.'"

Understanding the Word

Chapter 15 of Luke's Gospel is an amazing tribute to the love of God, who is willing to forgive our sins, to forget them, and to do all that with joy! The audience represents two very different groups. The tax collectors and sinners are the outcasts, the marginalized of that time. They are eager to hear Jesus. The self-righteous Pharisees and scribes are complaining because Jesus is reaching out to sinners.

The three parables deal with a lost sheep, a lost coin, and a lost son. But the true focus of all three parables is the loving God who rejoices to welcome lovingly the lost sinner. The major difference in the parable of the prodigal son is that he has free will. He uses his freedom to abandon his father and squander his possessions. Finally he reaches the lowest stage of degradation—a Jewish man tending pigs and contesting with them for their food.

He then uses his free will to return to his father. He knows that he has sinned against God and his father and is repentant. He wants only a job as a hired worker. But the father sees him at a distance and not only forgives him, but welcomes him with a joyous celebration. Clearly the teaching here is that God as the father sees sinners at a distance and pursues them with graces. But the sinner must follow the example of the prodigal son and return with love and repentance to God.

The father shows his compassionate love also for the elder son in the second part of the parable; but this son is bitter, self-righteous, unforgiving of his brother. He represents the Pharisees and scribes who refuse to join with Jesus in welcoming and joyfully forgiving the "tax collectors and sinners" (Luke 15:1).

This incredible forgiveness of God was made possible by the death and resurrection of the Savior. Our second reading today has a remarkable statement of St. Paul, "For our sake [God] made him to be sin who did not know sin, so that we might become the righteousness of God in him" (2 Corinthians 5:21).

Reflecting on the Word

The world was at war in 1944, at war with itself. Then there were not simply two sides, as if evil could have been so easily diagnosed; but rather a jumble of alliances were cast upon the political landscape so that everything seemed to grow and recede and constantly shift like an overlay of evening shadows, blurring the boundaries of all that we thought we knew.

In the midst of the war Russia and Germany engaged in a game of chess played by Stalin and Hitler, each seeking to checkmate the other. In his autobiography the poet Yevgeny Yevtushenko tells of being brought from Siberia to Moscow by his mother, where he watched as twenty thousand German prisoners-of-war were marched across Red Square. Thousands of Russian peasant onlookers, all of whom must have all lost someone they loved to the German war machine, watched the shattered army. The hatred was palpable. Then something changed, says Yevtushenko.

"Then I saw an elderly woman in broken-down boots push herself forward and touch a policeman's shoulder, saying, 'Let me through.' There must have been something about her which made him step aside. She went up to the column, took from inside her coat something wrapped in a colored handkerchief and unfolded it. It was a crust of black bread. She pushed it awkwardly into the pocket of a soldier, so exhausted that he was tottering on his feet. And now from every side women were running toward the soldiers, pushing into their hands bread, cigarettes, whatever they had. The soldiers were no longer enemies. They were people."

How does anyone ever imagine such forgiveness before time chooses to call it forth? We don't. Sometimes, maybe always, forgiveness stretches us beyond ourselves, beyond balancing scales or restoring justice to life. Maybe that is why we sometimes find it so difficult, just because we cannot imagine what it looks like, at least until someone comes along and shows us, the way the Russian women did, and before them, the way Jesus did.

CONSIDER/ DISCUSS:

- If you do only one thing this Lent, consider doing something lavishly generous to someone who may seek your forgiveness.
- For one week, do something generous for a different person each day. It'll change their world, and yours, too.

Responding to the Word

Whenever real forgiveness happens, we tell its story. Because Jesus knows the difficulty in imagining what such forgiveness looks like, he tells a story as well. It's his way of letting us know how the old things have passed away and new things have come, and how all of this is from God.

Spend a few minutes in quiet prayer. Ask God to show you one (or more) ways that you may be called to respond to this week's scriptures—

- in your relationship with God
- with family and friends
- at work, school, or church
- in the broader community

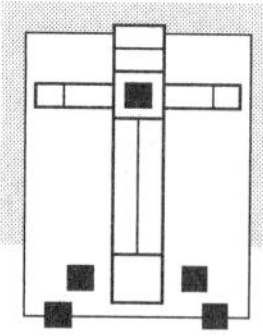

March 18, 2007

FOURTH SUNDAY OF LENT, YEAR A

Today's Focus: To See or Not to See

Children and adults look at life differently. So do parents and those who are not, single people and the married, the healthy and those who are dying. In the end, the more we experience of life, the more the way we see life changes.

FIRST READING
1 Samuel 16: 1b, 6–7, 10–13a

The LORD said to Samuel: "Fill your horn with oil, and be on your way. I am sending you to Jesse of Bethlehem, for I have chosen my king from among his sons."

As Jesse and his sons came to the sacrifice, Samuel looked at Eliab and thought, "Surely the Lord's anointed is here before him." But the LORD said to Samuel: "Do not judge from his appearance or from his lofty stature, because I have rejected him. Not as man sees does God see, because man sees the appearance but the LORD looks into the heart." In the same way Jesse presented seven sons before Samuel, but Samuel said to Jesse, "The LORD has not chosen any one of these." Then Samuel asked Jesse, "Are these all the sons you have?" Jesse replied, "There is still the youngest, who is tending the sheep." Samuel said to Jesse, "Send for him; we will not begin the sacrificial banquet until he arrives here." Jesse sent and had the young man brought to them. He was ruddy, a youth handsome to behold and making a splendid appearance. The LORD said, "There—anoint him, for this is the one!" Then Samuel, with the horn of oil in hand, anointed David in the presence of his brothers; and from that day on, the spirit of the LORD rushed upon David.

PSALM RESPONSE
Psalm 23:1

The Lord is my shepherd; there is nothing I shall want.

SECOND READING
Ephesians 5: 8–14

Brothers and sisters: You were once darkness, but now you are light in the Lord. Live as children of light, for light produces every kind of goodness and righteousness and truth. Try to learn what is pleasing to the Lord. Take no part in the fruitless works of darkness; rather expose them, for it is shameful even to mention the things done by them in secret; but everything exposed by the light becomes visible, for everything that becomes visible is light. Therefore, it says:

> "Awake, O sleeper,
> and arise from the dead,
> and Christ will give you light."

In the shorter version of the reading, the four passages in brackets are omitted.

GOSPEL *John 9:1–41 or 9:1, 6–9, 13–17, 34–38*

As Jesus passed by he saw a man blind from birth. [His disciples asked him, "Rabbi, who sinned, this man or his parents, that he was born blind?" Jesus answered,

"Neither he nor his parents sinned;
it is so that the works of God might be made visible through him.

We have to do the works of the one who sent me while it is day. Night is coming when no one can work. While I am in the world, I am the light of the world." When he had said this,] he spat on the ground and made clay with the saliva, and smeared the clay on his eyes, and said to him, "Go wash in the Pool of Siloam"—which means Sent—. So he went and washed, and came back able to see.

His neighbors and those who had seen him earlier as a beggar said, "Isn't this the one who used to sit and beg?" Some said, "It is, " but others said, "No, he just looks like him." He said, "I am." [So they said to him, "How were your eyes opened?" He replied, "The man called Jesus made clay and anointed my eyes and told me, 'Go to Siloam and wash.' So I went there and washed and was able to see." And they said to him, "Where is he?" He said, "I don't know."]

They brought the one who was once blind to the Pharisees. Now Jesus had made clay and opened his eyes on a sabbath. So then the Pharisees also asked him how he was able to see. He said to them, "He put clay on my eyes, and I washed, and now I can see." So some of the Pharisees said, "This man is not from God, because he does not keep the sabbath." But others said, "How can a sinful man do such signs?" And there was a division among them. So they said to the blind man again, "What do you have to say about him, since he opened your eyes?" He said, "He is a prophet."

[Now the Jews did not believe that he had been blind and gained his sight until they summoned the parents of the one who had gained his sight. They asked them, "Is this your son, who you say was born blind? How does he now see?" His parents answered and said, "We know that this is our son and that he was born blind. We do not know how he sees now, nor do we know who opened his eyes. Ask him, he is of age; he can speak for himself." His parents said this because they were afraid of the Jews, for the Jews had already agreed that if anyone acknowledged him as the Christ, he would be expelled from the synagogue. For this reason his parents said, "He is of age; question him."

So a second time they called the man who had been blind and said to him, "Give God the praise! We know that this man is a sinner." He replied, "If he is a sinner, I do not know. One thing I do know is that I was blind and now I see." So they said to him, "What did he do to you? How did he open your eyes?" He answered them, "I told you already and you did not listen. Why do you want to hear it again? Do you want to become his disciples, too?" They ridiculed him and said, "You are that man's disciple; we are disciples of Moses! We know that God spoke to Moses, but we do not know where this one is from." The man answered and said to them, "This is what is so amazing, that you do not know where he is from, yet he opened my eyes. We know that God does not listen to sinners, but if one is devout and does his will, he listens to him. It is unheard of that anyone ever opened the eyes of a person born blind. If this man were not from God, he would not be able to do anything."] They answered and said to him, "You were born totally in sin, and are you trying to teach us?" Then they threw him out.

When Jesus heard that they had thrown him out, he found him and said, "Do you believe in the Son of Man?" He answered and said, "Who is he, sir, that I may believe in him?" Jesus said to him, "You have seen him, the one speaking with you is he." He said, "I do believe, Lord," and he worshiped him. [Then Jesus said, "I came into this world for judgment, so that those who do not see might see, and those who do see might become blind."

Some of the Pharisees who were with him heard this and said to him, "Surely we are not also blind, are we?" Jesus said to them,

"If you were blind, you would have no sin;
but now you are saying, 'We see,' so your sin remains."]

Understanding the Word

The anointing of David by the prophet Samuel marks an important step in salvation history. Anointing in the biblical tradition indicated that the person had been selected by God and was to have a special role in God's plans. As a result of the anointing, "from that day on, the spirit of the LORD rushed upon David"(1 Samuel 16:13). The phrase "from that day on" indicates that this was a permanent gift. God promises to be with the anointed one because he is sacred. David, though at war with Saul, refused to kill him when he had the opportunity. "But the LORD forbid that I touch his anointed!" (1 Samuel 26:11). Saul had been anointed and later rejected by God, but David understood that Saul was still God's anointed.

Anointing is an important part of the sacraments of baptism and confirmation. Recall that "anointed one" is translated into Greek as "Christ" and into Hebrew as "Messiah," suggesting the importance of the Christian's anointing. Saint Paul has these encouraging words for the followers of Jesus: "But the one who gives us security with you in Christ and who has anointed us is God; he has also put his seal upon us and given the Spirit in our hearts as a first installment" (2 Corinthians 1:21–22).

The second reading also has strong baptismal significance, as does the entire Letter to the Ephesians. In today's Gospel reading, Jesus proclaims, "While I am in the world, I am the light of the world" (John 9:5). Ephesians develops this theme of light. Darkness is used to describe the life of persons before conversion to Christ. Light represents their new situation when they have faith and receive baptism. Verse 14 is seen as an early Christian baptismal hymn. Jesus also says, "You are the light of the world" (Matthew 5:14). The followers of Jesus are to "learn what is pleasing to the Lord" (Ephesians 5:10). They receive "goodness and righteousness and truth" (5:9) from the light of Christ. Those virtues must be reflected in their way of life as they try to influence their contemporaries by a good moral life.

Reflecting on the Word

There are scores of checklists with which to compare some aspect of our lives to some predetermined norm. "Ten Signs of a Successful Marriage." "How to Tell If Your Newborn Infant Is a Creative Genius." "The Fifty Marks of a Successful Parish." It seems there is one for just about any facet of life that we care to measure. There are some, as well, that measure prayerfulness, though it does seem a bit presumptuous to think that the power and effectiveness of the Holy Spirit could be quantified. Still, spiritual writers do make mention of the fruits of a life of prayerfulness.

One such fruit is hope. It is not about wishing, as when one hopes to win the lottery. Rather, the virtue of hope is about believing, about a different way of seeing. Hope looks at the future and believes that it will be as God has said simply because God has said. Hope is about promises, those that one lives by without hesitation. It is the conviction that God is indeed making all things new.

It takes time to come to see in a new way. The Gospel's man born blind first said Jesus was a man who made clay and anointed his eyes. Later he said, "He is a prophet" (John 9:17). Still later he identified himself as a disciple of Jesus. And finally he called him Lord. His story is also our story, one of coming to see over time who this Jesus is and how God is making all things new.

CONSIDER/ DISCUSS:

- Is your faith in who Jesus is different today from what it was ten years ago? Twenty or twenty-five years ago? How is it different?
- Where do you see God remaking life and making it new?
- What do you expect from your prayer?

Responding to the Word

It's been said that we don't become full believers before the age of thirty-five. There is some truth in that. It takes time to see with the eyes of faith, to have lived enough of life to see in a new way.

Spend a few minutes in quiet prayer. Ask God to show you one (or more) ways that you may be called to respond to this week's scriptures—

- in your relationship with God
- with family and friends
- at work, school, or church
- in the broader community

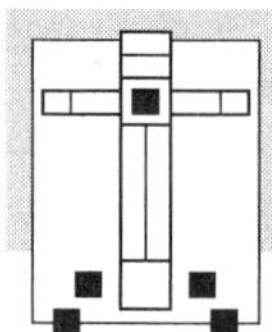

March 25, 2007

FIFTH SUNDAY OF LENT, YEAR C

Today's Focus: On Becoming Human

There is so much about each of us that yet needs to be worked out. We are all still becoming—intellectually, emotionally, spiritually—all of us still evolving into the sorts of people God envisions us to be. Even physically we humans continue to be in process.

For pastoral reasons, the readings given for Year A may be used in place of these readings. See page 94.

FIRST READING
Isaiah 43:16–21

Thus says the LORD,
  who opens a way in the sea
  and a path in the mighty waters,
who leads out chariots and horsemen,
  a powerful army,
till they lie prostrate together, never to rise,
  snuffed out and quenched like a wick.
Remember not the events of the past,
  the things of long ago consider not;
see, I am doing something new!
  Now it springs forth, do you not perceive it?
In the desert I make a way,
  in the wasteland, rivers.
Wild beasts honor me,
  jackals and ostriches,
for I put water in the desert
  and rivers in the wasteland
  for my chosen people to drink,
the people whom I formed for myself,
  that they might announce my praise.

PSALM RESPONSE
Psalm 126:3

The Lord has done great things for us; we are filled with joy.

SECOND READING
Philippians 3: 8–14

Brothers and sisters: I consider everything as a loss because of the supreme good of knowing Christ Jesus my Lord. For his sake I have accepted the loss of all things and I consider them so much rubbish, that I may gain Christ and be found in him, not having any righteousness of my own based on the law but that which comes through faith in Christ, the righteousness from God, depending on faith to know him and the power of his resurrection and the sharing of his sufferings by being conformed to his death, if somehow I may attain the resurrection from the dead.

It is not that I have already taken hold of it or have already attained perfect maturity, but I continue my pursuit in hope that I may possess it, since I have indeed been taken possession of by Christ Jesus. Brothers and sisters, I for my part do not consider myself to have taken possession. Just one thing: forgetting what lies behind but straining forward to what lies ahead, I continue my pursuit toward the goal, the prize of God's upward calling, in Christ Jesus.

GOSPEL
John 8:1–11

Jesus went to the Mount of Olives. But early in the morning he arrived again in the temple area, and all the people started coming to him, and he sat down and taught them. Then the scribes and the Pharisees brought a woman who had been caught in adultery and made her stand in the middle. They said to him, "Teacher, this woman was caught in the very act of committing adultery. Now in the law, Moses commanded us to stone such women. So what do you say?" They said this to test him, so that they could have some charge to bring against him. Jesus bent down and began to write on the ground with his finger. But when they continued asking him, he straightened up and said to them, "Let the one among you who is without sin be the first to throw a stone at her." Again he bent down and wrote on the ground. And in response, they went away one by one, beginning with the elders. So he was left alone with the woman before him. Then Jesus straightened up and said to her, "Woman, where are they? Has no one condemned you?" She replied, "No one, sir." Then Jesus said, "Neither do I condemn you. Go, and from now on do not sin any more."

Understanding the Word

It is not surprising that today's reading from the Gospel of John appears in the Lukan Year C. There is general agreement that this account of the woman caught in adultery does not belong in the Fourth Gospel. Many scholars believe that it is, in fact, the work of Luke. In style and vocabulary, in themes such as the mercy of Jesus and his concern for women, it is much more Lukan than Johannine. It does not appear in the best Greek manuscripts of John. It does appear in some later manuscripts of both John and Luke. It is found in some manuscripts after Luke 21:38, where it fits perfectly. The Catholic Church has, however, defined the account to be inspired and canonical despite these problems with its transmission.

The principal point of this account is the mercy of Jesus. The scribes and Pharisees attempt to trap him, using the woman for their purposes. They ask Jesus if she should be executed for her sin. If he says no, he is going against the law of Moses. If he says yes, he is going against the law of the Romans, who had taken from the Jewish people the right to execute anyone. But more importantly, it would go against the teaching and practice of Jesus concerning mercy. Jesus first writes on the ground, and the nature of that writing has led to much speculation on the part of students of the Bible. Father Raymond E. Brown writes, "There remains the much simpler possibility that Jesus was simply tracing lines on the ground while he was thinking, or wished to show imperturbability, or to contain his feelings of disgust for the violent zeal shown by the accusers" (*Anchor Bible*, "The Gospel According to John," vol. 29, p. 334).

The account ends with a dialogue between Jesus and the woman. Jesus has saved her from execution. Now he offers her the possibility of a spiritual life, "Go, and from now on do not sin any more" (John 8:11). Jesus clearly does not condone the sin of the woman; but even more clearly he reaches out to her with mercy and forgiveness—important themes in the Gospel of Luke.

Reflecting on the Word

The color blue seems to be the most recent hue of the color spectrum to which human beings have become visually sensitive. It is the most frequent color missing in color blindness. Our creative sense of sound is still becoming as well. Musical harmony is an occurrence not coming to full blossom in the West until the fifteenth and sixteenth centuries. Even the gift of smell is a sense that continues to be finely tuned. We have not yet found one word to describe the smell of innocence given off by a newborn baby's hair.

More recently authors write of growing beyond the five senses and becoming multi-sensory human beings, of experiencing more than the physical. Our five senses together do help us perceive our physical reality, but slowly, generation by generation, we are developing an awareness of the fact that there is more to life than simply the physical. We listen to our intuition; we pay attention to our "sixth sense"; we discover a spiritual side to our personalities. Many have mystical experiences, occurrences about which they hesitate to talk yet ones that are so real that those moments give direction to the rest of their lives.

So when we hear the story of Jesus forgiving the woman caught in adultery and forgiving so unconditionally, of course we squirm. Most of us have not yet evolved to the point of being able to forgive very well, to forgive without any need to equalize the suffering. Maybe that's why we still like the idea of capital punishment and a kind of justice that balances scales pain for pain. Maybe it's because we are still in the process of becoming human with such a long way yet to go.

CONSIDER/ DISCUSS:

- On the spectrum between justice and mercy, toward which end do you lean when it comes to capital punishment and the purpose of our penal system?
- Have you ever experienced great mercy from someone? Spend some time remembering the moment.

Responding to the Word

Jesus showed us most clearly what our God is creating us to be: compassionate and just, generous and merciful, loving in a wasteland of indifference. Profound forgiveness must be new on the human scene simply because for most of us we are so deeply touched whenever we come upon it.

Spend a few minutes in quiet prayer. Ask God to show you one (or more) ways that you may be called to respond to this week's scriptures—

- in your relationship with God
- with family and friends
- at work, school, or church
- in the broader community

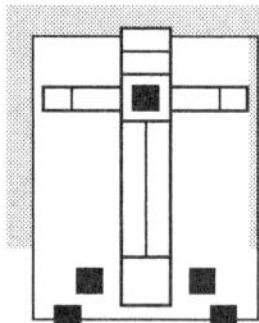

March 25, 2007

FIFTH SUNDAY OF LENT, YEAR A

Today's Focus: Death, Life, and All That Is in Between

We live in a world fearful of death, in part because it surrounds us, in part because we have no control over it. Yet as with most fears, the best way to deal with death is not to go around it but to go through it.

FIRST READING
Ezekiel 37: 12–14

Thus says the LORD GOD: O my people, I will open your graves and have you rise from them, and bring you back to the land of Israel. Then you shall know that I am the LORD, when I open your graves and have you rise from them, O my people! I will put my spirit in you that you may live, and I will settle you upon your land; thus you shall know that I am the LORD. I have promised, and I will do it, says the LORD.

PSALM RESPONSE
Psalm 130:7

With the Lord there is mercy and fullness of redemption.

SECOND READING
Romans 8:8–11

Brothers and sisters: Those who are in the flesh cannot please God. But you are not in the flesh; on the contrary, you are in the spirit, if only the Spirit of God dwells in you. Whoever does not have the Spirit of Christ does not belong to him. But if Christ is in you, although the body is dead because of sin, the spirit is alive because of righteousness. If the Spirit of the one who raised Jesus from the dead dwells in you, the one who raised Christ from the dead will give life to your mortal bodies also, through his Spirit dwelling in you.

In the shorter version of the reading, the five passages in brackets are omitted.

GOSPEL
John 11:1–45 or 11:3–7, 17, 20–27, 33b–45

[Now a man was ill, Lazarus from Bethany, the village of Mary and her sister Martha. Mary was the one who had anointed the Lord with perfumed oil and dried his feet with her hair; it was her brother Lazarus who was ill. So] the sisters sent word to him saying, "Master, the one you love is ill." When Jesus heard this he said,

"This illness is not to end in death,
but is for the glory of God,
that the Son of God may be glorified through it."

Now Jesus loved Martha and her sister and Lazarus. So when he heard that he was ill, he remained for two days in the place where he was. Then after this he said to his disciples, "Let us go back to Judea." [The disciples said to him, "Rabbi, the Jews were just trying to stone you, and you want to go back there?" Jesus answered,

"Are there not twelve hours in a day?
If one walks during the day, he does not stumble,
because he sees the light of this world.
But if one walks at night, he stumbles,
because the light is not in him."

He said this, and then told them, "Our friend Lazarus is asleep, but I am going to awaken him." So the disciples said to him, "Master, if he is asleep, he will be saved." But Jesus was talking about his death, while they thought that he meant ordinary sleep. So then Jesus said to them clearly, "Lazarus has died. And I am glad for you that I was not there, that you may believe. Let us go to him." So Thomas, called Didymus, said to his fellow disciples, "Let us also go to die with him."]

When Jesus arrived, he found that Lazarus had already been in the tomb for four days. [Now Bethany was near Jerusalem, only about two miles away. And many of the Jews had come to Martha and Mary to comfort them about their brother.] When Martha heard that Jesus was coming, she went to meet him; but Mary sat at home. Martha said to Jesus, "Lord, if you had been here, my brother would not have died. But even now I know that whatever you ask of God, God will give you." Jesus said to her, "Your brother will rise." Martha said to him, "I know he will rise, in the resurrection on the last day." Jesus told her,

"I am the resurrection and the life;
whoever believes in me, even if he dies, will live,
and everyone who lives and believes in me will never die.

Do you believe this?" She said to him, "Yes, Lord. I have come to believe that you are the Christ, the Son of God, the one who is coming into the world."

[When she had said this, she went and called her sister Mary secretly, saying, "The teacher is here and is asking for you." As soon as she heard this, she rose quickly and went to him. For Jesus had not yet come into the village, but was still where Martha had met him. So when the Jews who were with her in the house comforting her saw Mary get up quickly and go out, they followed her, presuming that she was going to the tomb to weep there. When Mary came to where Jesus was and saw him, she fell at his feet and said to him, "Lord, if you had been here, my brother would not have died." When] Jesus [saw her weeping and the Jews who had come with her weeping, he] became perturbed and deeply troubled, and said, "Where have you laid him?" They said to him, "Sir, come and see." And Jesus wept. So the Jews said, "See how he loved him." But some of them said, "Could not the one who opened the eyes of the blind man have done something so that this man would not have died?"

So Jesus, perturbed again, came to the tomb. It was a cave, and a stone lay across it. Jesus said, "Take away the stone." Martha, the dead man's sister, said to him, "Lord, by now there will be a stench; he has been dead for four days." Jesus said to her, "Did I not tell you that if you believe you will see the glory of God?" So they took away the stone. And Jesus raised his eyes and said,

"Father, I thank you for hearing me.
I know that you always hear me;
but because of the crowd here I have said this,
that they may believe that you sent me."

And when he had said this, he cried out in a loud voice, "Lazarus, come out!" The dead man came out, tied hand and foot with burial bands, and his face was wrapped in a cloth. So Jesus said to them, "Untie him and let him go."

Now many of the Jews who had come to Mary and seen what he had done began to believe in him.

Understanding the Word

The Holy Spirit plays a key role in the sacraments of baptism and confirmation. In the Old Testament the spirit of God was characterized by the Hebrew word *ruah*, which could mean wind, breath, or spirit. At the beginning of creation, for example, in the book of Genesis the wind/breath/spirit of God "swept over the waters" (Genesis 1:2). In today's first reading from Ezekiel the spirit is God's dynamic, creative presence for the Chosen People. The spirit of God is infused into the people of Israel to give them a deeper knowledge of God and to raise them from the terrible experience of the Babylonian exile to a new life in the Promised Land.

In the New Testament Jesus appeared as the final revelation of the Father. He made known the Trinity: Father, Son, and Holy Spirit. This was difficult for the Jewish Christians to assimilate. For two thousand years there was great stress on one God. To teach now that there is still one God but three persons required time to understand. Saint Paul in today's second reading highlights the role of the Spirit. "If the Spirit of the one who raised Jesus from the dead dwells in you, the one who raised Christ from the dead will give life to your mortal bodies also, through his Spirit that dwells in you" (Romans 8:11). Father Joseph A. Fitzmyer comments, "In all of this one must recall the role of both faith and baptism. Christ and his Spirit dwell in Christians because of faith that justifies" (*Anchor Bible*, "Romans," vol. 33, p. 491).

Today's Gospel from John has great baptismal symbolism. One particular example is found in the words of Jesus, "I am the resurrection and the life; / whoever believes in me, even if he dies, will live, / and everyone who lives and believes in me will never die" (John 11:25–26). These words reflect a strong teaching of the Fourth Gospel, namely realized eschatology. That concept means that when one is baptized, the presence of Christ is already realized in that person. Christ's words stress that the spiritual life of the Christian, which begins at baptism, will never die.

Reflecting on the Word

The shelf of coffee mugs in our house is a menagerie of wisdom quotes, vacation remembrances, and business promotions. There is even a political cup with pictures of George and Laura Bush that someone slipped in unannounced, though the cup continually disappears and reappears depending upon the political leanings of the one who spied it last.

Among all those cups sits one that offers a listing of well-known persons who have struggled with mental illness in their lives. The names include Mozart and Benjamin Franklin and Mark Twain and Rosemary Clooney and Mike Wallace and Bette Midler and Robert Young and Winston Churchill and Irving Berlin and Sting and Abraham Lincoln and Patty Duke and Dick Clark and many others.

The prophet Ezekiel once proclaimed to the people of his day, "Thus says the LORD GOD: O my people, I will open your graves and have you rise from them" (Ezekiel 37:12). So sometimes I wonder if there is a connection between the genius of these cup-folk and their struggle, if perhaps their creativity flowed from their pain like life from a grave. The theologian Karl Rahner once said that one of the tasks of life is to learn how to die well. If so, then having learned that skill, we will also come to learn that life itself is called forth, Lazarus-fashion, out of those same dark and deathly tombs. There is an integrity to the journey, a wholeness on the part of God's Spirit that will not be undone.

CONSIDER/ DISCUSS:

- What is the deadliest aspect of living in the tombs? How have you dealt with those times?
- What or who has called you forth and freed you from the wrappings of death?

Responding to the Word

Disciples of Jesus believe not that life ends in death but that death ends in life. It is always God's Spirit that calls us forth into life even when all that exists within us insists that there is no hope.

Spend a few minutes in quiet prayer. Ask God to show you one (or more) ways that you may be called to respond to this week's scriptures—

- in your relationship with God
- with family and friends
- at work, school, or church
- in the broader community

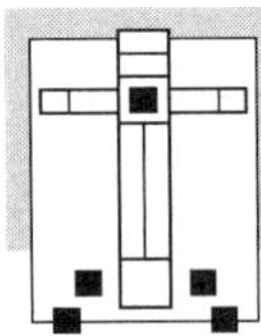

April 1, 2007

PALM SUNDAY OF THE LORD'S PASSION

Today's Focus: Cloaks, Not Palms

Sometimes our encounters with life seem to unmask us before the world. We find ourselves revealed for who we truly are. Such moments can be graced and move us to conversion, or they can be too filled with fear of being known for our darkness.

FIRST READING
Isaiah 50:4–7

The Lord GOD has given me
a well-trained tongue,
that I might know how to speak to the weary
a word that will rouse them.
Morning after morning
he opens my ear that I may hear;
and I have not rebelled,
have not turned back.
I gave my back to those who beat me,
my cheeks to those who plucked my beard;
my face I did not shield
from buffets and spitting.
The Lord God is my help,
therefore I am not disgraced;
I have set my face like flint,
knowing that I shall not be put to shame.

PSALM RESPONSE
Psalm 22:2a

My God, my God, why have you abandoned me?

SECOND READING
Philippians 2:6–11

Christ Jesus, though he was in the form of God,
did not regard equality with God
something to be grasped.
Rather, he emptied himself,
taking the form of a slave,
coming in human likeness;
and found human in appearance,
he humbled himself,
becoming obedient to the point of death,
even death on a cross.
Because of this, God greatly exalted him
and bestowed on him the name
which is above every name,
that at the name of Jesus
every knee should bend,
of those in heaven and on earth and under the earth,
and every tongue confess that
Jesus Christ is Lord,
to the glory of God the Father.

In the shorter form of the Passion, the passages in brackets are omitted.

GOSPEL *Luke 22: 14 — 23:56 or 23:1–49*

[When the hour came, Jesus took his place at table with the apostles. He said to them, "I have eagerly desired to eat this Passover with you before I suffer, for, I tell you, I shall not eat it again until there is fulfillment in the kingdom of God." Then he took a cup, gave thanks, and said, "Take this and share it among yourselves; for I tell you that from this time on I shall not drink of the fruit of the vine until the kingdom of God comes." Then he took the bread, said the blessing, broke it, and gave it to them, saying, "This is my body, which will be given for you; do this in memory of me." And likewise the cup after they had eaten, saying, "This cup is the new covenant in my blood, which will be shed for you.

"And yet behold, the hand of the one who is to betray me is with me on the table; for the Son of Man indeed goes as it has been determined; but woe to that man by whom he is betrayed." And they began to debate among themselves who among them would do such a deed.

Then an argument broke out among them about which of them should be regarded as the greatest. He said to them, "The kings of the Gentiles lord it over them and those in authority over them are addressed as 'Benefactors'; but among you it shall not be so. Rather, let the greatest among you be as the youngest, and the leader as the servant. For who is greater: the one seated at table or the one who serves? Is it not the one seated at table? I am among you as the one who serves. It is you who have stood by me in my trials; and I confer a kingdom on you, just as my Father has conferred one on me, that you may eat and drink at my table in my kingdom; and you will sit on thrones judging the twelve tribes of Israel.

"Simon, Simon, behold Satan has demanded to sift all of you like wheat, but I have prayed that your own faith may not fail; and once you have turned back, you must strengthen your brothers." He said to him, "Lord, I am prepared to go to prison and to die with you." But he replied, "I tell you, Peter, before the cock crows this day, you will deny three times that you know me."

He said to them, "When I sent you forth without a money bag or a sack or sandals, were you in need of anything?" "No, nothing," they replied. He said to them, "But now one who has a money bag should take it, and likewise a sack, and one who does not have a sword should sell his cloak and buy one. For I tell you that this Scripture must be fulfilled in me, namely,

He was counted among the wicked;

and indeed what is written about me is coming to fulfillment." Then they said, "Lord, look, there are two swords here." But he replied, "It is enough!"

Then going out, he went, as was his custom, to the Mount of Olives, and the disciples followed him. When he arrived at the place he said to them, "Pray that you may not undergo the test." After withdrawing about a stone's throw from them and kneeling, he prayed, saying, "Father, if you are willing, take this cup away from me; still, not my will but yours be done." And to strengthen him an angel from heaven appeared to him. He was in such agony and he prayed so fervently that his sweat became like drops of blood falling on the ground. When he rose from prayer and returned to his disciples, he found them sleeping from grief. He said to them, "Why are you sleeping? Get up and pray that you may not undergo the test."

While he was still speaking, a crowd approached and in front was one of the Twelve, a man named Judas. He went up to Jesus to kiss him. Jesus said to him, "Judas, are you betraying the Son of Man with a kiss?" His disciples realized what was about to happen, and they asked, "Lord, shall we strike with a sword?" And one of them struck the high priest's servant and cut off his right ear. But Jesus said in reply, "Stop, no more of this!" Then he touched the servant's ear and healed him. And Jesus said to the chief priests and temple guards and elders who had come for him, "Have you come out as against a robber, with swords and clubs? Day after day I was with you in the temple area, and you did not seize me; but this is your hour, the time for the power of darkness."

After arresting him they led him away and took him into the house of the high priest; Peter was following at a distance. They lit a fire in the middle of the courtyard and sat around it, and Peter sat down with them. When a maid saw him seated in the light, she looked intently at him and said, "This man too was with him." But he denied it saying, "Woman, I do not know him." A short while later someone else saw him and said, "You too are one of them"; but Peter answered, "My friend, I am not." About an hour later, still another insisted, "Assuredly, this man too was with him, for he also is a Galilean." But Peter said, "My friend, I do not know what you are talking about." Just as he was saying this, the cock crowed, and the Lord turned and looked at Peter; and Peter remembered the word of the Lord, how he had said to him, "Before the cock crows today, you will deny me three times." He went out and began to weep bitterly. The men who held Jesus in custody were ridiculing and beating him. They blindfolded him and questioned him, saying, "Prophesy! Who is it that struck you?" And they reviled him in saying many other things against him.

When day came the council of elders of the people met, both chief priests and scribes, and they brought him before their Sanhedrin. They said, "If you are the Christ, tell us," but he replied to them, "If I tell you, you will not believe, and if I question, you will not respond. But from this time on the Son of Man will be seated at the right hand of the power of God." They all asked, "Are you then the Son of God?" He replied to them, "You say that I am." Then they said, "What further need have we for testimony? We have heard it from his own mouth."]

Then the whole assembly of them arose and brought him before Pilate. They brought charges against him, saying, "We found this man misleading our people; he opposes the payment of taxes to Caesar and maintains that he is the Christ, a king." Pilate asked him, "Are you the king of the Jews?" He said to him in reply, "You say so." Pilate then addressed the chief priests and the crowds, "I find this man not guilty." But they were adamant and said, "He is inciting the people with his teaching throughout all Judea, from Galilee where he began even to here."

On hearing this Pilate asked if the man was a Galilean; and upon learning that he was under Herod's jurisdiction, he sent him to Herod who was in Jerusalem at that time. Herod was very glad to see Jesus; he had been wanting to see him for a long time, for he had heard about him and had been hoping to see him perform some sign. He questioned him at length, but he gave him no answer. The chief priests and scribes, meanwhile, stood by accusing him harshly. Herod and his soldiers treated him contemptuously and mocked him, and after clothing him in resplendent garb, he sent him back to Pilate. Herod and Pilate became friends that very day, even though they had been enemies formerly. Pilate then summoned the chief priests, the rulers, and the people and said to them, "You brought this man to me and accused him of inciting the people to revolt. I have conducted my investigation in your presence and have not found this man guilty of the charges you have brought against him, nor did Herod, for he sent him back to us. So no capital crime has been committed by him. Therefore I shall have him flogged and then release him."

But all together they shouted out, "Away with this man! Release Barabbas to us."—Now Barabbas had been imprisoned for a rebellion that had taken place in the city and for murder.—Again Pilate addressed them, still wishing to release Jesus, but they continued their shouting, "Crucify him! Crucify him!" Pilate addressed them a third time, "What evil has this man done? I found him guilty of no capital crime. Therefore I shall have him flogged and then release him." With loud shouts, however, they persisted in calling for his crucifixion, and their voices prevailed. The verdict of Pilate was that their demand should be granted. So he released the man who had been imprisoned for rebellion and murder, for whom they asked, and he handed Jesus over to them to deal with as they wished.

As they led him away they took hold of a certain Simon, a Cyrenian, who was coming in from the country; and after laying the cross on him, they made him carry it behind Jesus. A large crowd of people followed Jesus, including many women who mourned and lamented him. Jesus turned to them and said, "Daughters of Jerusalem, do not weep for me; weep instead for yourselves and for your children, for indeed, the days are coming when people will say, 'Blessed are the barren, the wombs that never bore and the breasts that never nursed.' At that time people will say to the mountains, 'Fall upon us!' and to the hills, 'Cover us!' for if these things are done when the wood is green what will happen when it is dry?" Now two others, both criminals, were led away with him to be executed.

When they came to the place called the Skull, they crucified him and the criminals there, one on his right, the other on his left. Then Jesus said, "Father, forgive them, they know not what they do." They divided his garments by casting lots. The people stood by and watched; the rulers, meanwhile, sneered at him and said, "He saved others, let him save himself if he is the chosen one, the Christ of God." Even the soldiers jeered at him. As they approached to offer him wine they called out, "If you are King of the Jews, save yourself." Above him there was an inscription that read, "This is the King of the Jews."

Now one of the criminals hanging there reviled Jesus, saying, "Are you not the Christ? Save yourself and us." The other, however, rebuking him, said in reply, "Have you no fear of God, for you are subject to the same condemnation? And indeed, we have been condemned justly, for the sentence we received corresponds to our crimes, but this man has done nothing criminal." Then he said, "Jesus, remember me when you come into your kingdom." He replied to him, "Amen, I say to you, today you will be with me in Paradise."

It was now about noon and darkness came over the whole land until three in the afternoon because of an eclipse of the sun. Then the veil of the temple was torn down the middle. Jesus cried out in a loud voice, "Father, into your hands I commend my spirit"; and when he had said this he breathed his last.

The centurion who witnessed what had happened glorified God and said, "This man was innocent beyond doubt." When all the people who had gathered for this spectacle saw what had happened, they returned home beating their breasts; but all his acquaintances stood at a distance, including the women who had followed him from Galilee and saw these events.

[Now there was a virtuous and righteous man named Joseph who, though he was a member of the council, had not consented to their plan of action. He came from the Jewish town of Arimathea and was awaiting the kingdom of God. He went to Pilate and asked for the body of Jesus. After he had taken the body down, he wrapped it in a linen cloth and laid him in a rock-hewn tomb in which no one had yet been buried. It was the day of preparation, and the sabbath was about to begin. The women who had come from Galilee with him followed behind, and when they had seen the tomb and the way in which his body was laid in it, they returned and prepared spices and perfumed oils. Then they rested on the sabbath according to the commandment.]

Understanding the Word

The followers of Jesus Christ are blessed to have four accounts of the passion of Jesus. While the principal points are the same, each evangelist brings some special insights into his work. Luke's Passion account (chapters 22 and 23) incorporates some of the outstanding themes of the Gospel that to a great extent are proper to Luke.

The Third Gospel has been called the Gospel of Great Pardons. The Passion account manifests that interest of Luke. After Peter denies Jesus, the Savior looks at him kindly with merciful forgiveness. Peter then "went out and began to weep bitterly" (Luke 22:62). His first word from the cross is a prayer to his Father to forgive his executioners. This is comforting, since Christians realize that we, because of our sins, are the true executioners. Also, there is the moving exchange between Jesus and the repentant criminal. The mercy of Christ responds to the penitent with the promise, "Amen, I say to you, today you will be with me in Paradise" (23:43). Jesus ends his life prayerfully and serenely, "Father, into your hands I commend my spirit" (23:46).

Examples of the compassion of Christ include his prayer for his disciples. Luke alone notes that the kindness of Jesus led him to heal the ear of the servant (22:51). He expresses great concern for the "daughters of Jerusalem" who are mourning and lamenting him (23:27–28).

Luke's Gospel has also been identified as a Gospel of Prayer. It is not surprising that prayer plays a large part in the Passion account. Jesus prays for his disciples and especially for Peter. He observes a prayerful celebration of Passover with the institution of the Eucharist. In the garden he encourages his disciples to pray and petitions the Father to be freed from crucifixion, but adds, "not my will but yours be done" (22:42).

The Third Gospel has also been named the Gospel of Women. In the Passion account we hear of the daughters of Jerusalem, of women standing at a distance from the cross, and of women helping to prepare Jesus' body for burial (23:28, 49, 55).

Reflecting on the Word

Prayer can be risky business. I don't mean saying prayers; usually that can be fairly safe. No, I mean the sort of prayer that is reflective, like daydreaming in the presence of one's God, or maybe just wondering about where God's nudges might be moving us and whether we're cooperating or resisting. That's the sort of prayer I mean when I say it can be risky business. It's the kind of prayer that begins in peaceful silence and can end like a peanut butter sandwich—gooey and hard to swallow.

Surprisingly, this year the Church's Palm Sunday story is not at all about palms. In other years there are branches cut from trees and strewn on the roadway, but when Saint Luke tells the story there are only cloaks on the roadway, no palms. This year it's not the trees that are stripped and stand naked so that the Holy-One-made-flesh may be praised. No, it's the people who are stripped—stripped of their cloaks, of that which hides them, of that which conceals the most vulnerable and weakest aspects of who they are as well as the most precious.

When God rides into our lives we do find that God unmasks us, uncloaks us; and when that happens we either respond in praise because we see ourselves for who we are in relationship to our God, or we react out of fear that our true selves might be too checkered to risk being known. Sometimes that fear can even take on the face of violence. As it happens, this week's story tells of both—of people who responded with wonder and awe and of people who responded with deadly violence.

CONSIDER/ DISCUSS:

- When have you found yourself without a cloak to hide beneath? How did you deal with it?
- What sorts of moments reveal the truest you? What has come of them? Were they avenues into more holy living?

Responding to the Word

Prayer can be risky business simply because it's one of the niches in our lives where we can find ourselves without a cloak to hide beneath. It can be one of those times when God rides into our lives and we begin to see our real selves. Whether it takes place willingly or unwillingly, there can be something good about being decloaked.

Spend a few minutes in quiet prayer. Ask God to show you one (or more) ways that you may be called to respond to this week's scriptures—

- in your relationship with God
- with family and friends
- at work, school, or church
- in the broader community

Notes

Introduction to Easter

The resurrection of Jesus Christ is certainly the most important happening in salvation history. In the liturgy of the Easter season there are true riches for the Christian. The Gospels from John give many key teachings of Jesus; the first readings tell much about the history of the early church; the second readings, mostly from the book of Revelation, are informative about the completion of salvation history.

Easter Sunday's Gospel tells of the resurrection of Jesus as seen through the eyes of Mary of Magdala, Peter, and the other disciple whom Jesus loved. There is a Gospel highlighting the appearances of Christ to his disciples. Christ will renew his promise that he knows his sheep. The new commandment, "As I have loved you, so you also should love one another" (John 13:34), is a true challenge to all Jesus' followers. The Holy Spirit is promised as an advocate to be sent by the Father. Christ will pray for the unity of Christianity and will add, "Peace be with you. As the Father has sent me, so I send you" (20:21).

The first readings from the Acts of the Apostles show that the early church understood this commission received from the Lord. Having worked for unity, the early church began to proclaim Jesus to the Jewish people and leaders, even though it met with serious opposition, including the martyrdom of St. Stephen. Paul and associates began the conversion of the Gentiles. At the Council of Jerusalem the church decided formally that converts to Christianity were not first obliged to accept Judaism.

The second readings in this season are mostly from Revelation, a wonderful but difficult book. It is written in apocalyptic language, which is somewhat foreign to anyone coming from a Greek, Latin, or English background. For example, it uses visions, conceptual symbolism, and communications from angels. Apocalyptic works were written between 200 BC and AD 200, intended for people under pressure. The original readers of Revelation were experiencing internal problems in the Christian community and serious persecution by Domitian, the Roman emperor (AD 81–96).

The basic message of the author of Revelation is to continue to have faith in God despite adversity. The readings this season highlight Jesus' special unity with the church. In two interesting phrases, the Christians are told, "I, John, had a vision of a great multitude, which no one could count, from every nation, race, people, and tongue. . . . [T]hey have washed their robes and made them white in the blood of the Lamb" (Revelation 7:9, 14). The followers of Jesus are assured that "the Lamb who is in the center of the throne will shepherd them" (7:17).

The book of Revelation gives Christians hope by showing the final outcome of salvation history. God will triumph over all the forces of evil. Those who have remained faithful will be with God both body and soul. The Lamb and Yahweh will be both the temple and the light in the New Jerusalem (21:22–23). In view of this reality at the *parousia* (the Second Coming of Christ) it is not surprising that the early Christians would pray "Come, Lord Jesus!" (22:20).

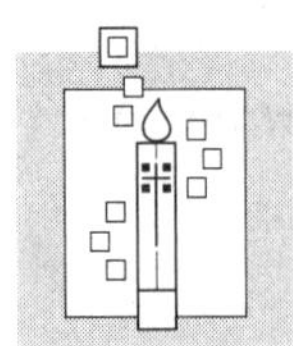

April 8, 2007

EASTER SUNDAY
THE RESURRECTION OF THE LORD

Today's Focus: Lord of All Rings

Stories come in all sorts of shapes and forms, in novels and film and television, in poetry and ballads and love songs. So often the stories we are most drawn to tell tales of great courage, of entering into the abode of death where life is not lost but found—or perhaps, as with Jesus, both lost and found.

FIRST READING
Acts 10:34a, 37–43

Peter proceeded to speak and said: "You know what has happened all over Judea, beginning in Galilee after the baptism that John preached, how God anointed Jesus of Nazareth with the Holy Spirit and power. He went about doing good and healing all those oppressed by the devil, for God was with him. We are witnesses of all that he did both in the country of the Jews and in Jerusalem. They put him to death by hanging him on a tree. This man God raised on the third day and granted that he be visible, not to all the people, but to us, the witnesses chosen by God in advance, who ate and drank with him after he rose from the dead. He commissioned us to preach to the people and testify that he is the one appointed by God as judge of the living and the dead. To him all the prophets bear witness, that everyone who believes in him will receive forgiveness of sins through his name.

PSALM RESPONSE
Psalm 118:24

This is the day the Lord has made; let us rejoice and be glad.

SECOND READING
Colossians 3: 1–4

Brothers and sisters: If then you were raised with Christ, seek what is above, where Christ is seated at the right hand of God. Think of what is above, not of what is on earth. For you have died, and your life is hidden with Christ in God. When Christ your life appears, then you too will appear with him in glory.

– or –

1 Corinthians 5: 6b–8

Brothers and sisters: Do you not know that a little yeast leavens all the dough? Clear out the old yeast, so that you may become a fresh batch of dough, inasmuch as you are unleavened. For our paschal lamb, Christ, has been sacrificed. Therefore, let us celebrate the feast, not with the old yeast, the yeast of malice and wickedness, but with the unleavened bread of sincerity and truth.

GOSPEL
John 20:1–9

On the first day of the week, Mary of Magdala came to the tomb early in the morning, while it was still dark, and saw the stone removed from the tomb. So she ran and went to Simon Peter and to the other disciple whom Jesus loved, and told them, "They have taken the Lord from the tomb, and we don't know where they put him." So Peter and the other disciple went out and came to the tomb. They both ran, but the other disciple ran faster than Peter and arrived at the tomb first; he bent down and saw the burial cloths there, but did not go in. When Simon Peter arrived after him, he went into the tomb and saw the burial cloths there, and the cloth that had covered his head, not with the burial cloths but rolled up in a separate place. Then the other disciple also went in, the one who had arrived at the tomb first, and he saw and believed. For they did not yet understand the Scripture that he had to rise from the dead.

Understanding the Word

It is impossible for a Christian to overemphasize the importance of the resurrection of Jesus Christ. Today's readings for Easter Sunday highlight some important aspects of that great event in salvation history. In the first reading, from the Acts of the Apostles, Saint Peter instructs his audience, "This man God raised on the third day" (Acts 10:40). The apostle also stresses the importance of witnesses chosen by God, especially the Twelve, who were to continue the preaching ministry of Jesus (10:41–42). In one of the choices for the second reading Saint Paul reminds his readers of their baptism and its effects. "If then you were raised with Christ, seek what is above, where Christ is seated at the right hand of God" (Colossians 3:1).

The Gospel brings together the critical combination of the resurrection of Christ and faith on the part of his followers. This text tells how the beloved disciple "saw and believed" (John 20:8). His faith in the resurrected Jesus provides a model for Christians down through the centuries. Before John has seen the risen Savior, he believes. We are asked to believe also without actually seeing Christ in his glorified body.

John 20:9 points out that "they did not yet understand the Scripture that he had to rise from the dead." The appearances of Jesus and the coming of the Holy Spirit will give the needed understanding. Psalm 16:10 is an interesting text from the Old Testament, quoted by Saint Peter in his Pentecost sermon: "[Y]ou will not abandon my soul to the nether world, / nor will you suffer your holy one to see corruption" (Acts 2:27).

The readings this Sunday together with so many other scripture texts indicate the importance of the Resurrection. The *Catechism of the Catholic Church* has an excellent summary of the meaning of this most significant event. "The Resurrection of Jesus is the crowning truth of our faith in Christ, a faith believed and lived as the central truth by the first Christian community; handed on as fundamental by Tradition; established by the documents of the New Testament; and preached as an essential part of the Paschal mystery along with the cross" (Paragraph 638).

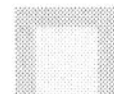

Reflecting on the Word

Andrew is a college senior I met as part of a focus group exploring the quality and nature of the college experience. In the course of the conversation Andrew grew excited and animated about the trilogy film *The Lord of the Rings*. His enthusiasm sparked, he told of how he had seen the first film twenty-three times, the second fourteen times, and the third and most recent six times. Clearly for him *The Lord of the Rings* is a template for understanding life, one that approaches one hundred fifty hours of viewing time.

It may well be our doubt that draws us to such tales simply because the power of good over evil and of life over death seems too preposterous. And so we need to hear the story told again and again so that we might believe that at least it is possible, if not certain. Nevertheless, it all begins with being amazed, as it did for Peter in this Easter's Gospel. Once he hears the story from the three women, Peter can't seem to stay away. He gets up and runs to the tomb, sees the same emptiness the women saw, and goes home amazed. I suspect it is also why Andrew keeps returning to *The Lord of the Rings*, and why I find myself utterly dumbfounded whenever I listen to those who are dying tell me their journey toward death without any fear or anxiety, and why we tell the story of Easter every year, and maybe why we all love springtime so much. It's all so amazing, and perhaps without any of it none of us would ever come to believe.

CONSIDER/ DISCUSS:

- In what amazement is your faith rooted?
- Make a list of the things you find amazing. Pray with it.

Responding to the Word

The stories of Easter are stories of great truth. They are stories in which life and death do battle with each other until the oppressor is vanquished and the victor is exalted and doubt bows in homage. It is why they are so amazing, and why we keep telling them over and over. They become the key to understanding life.

Spend a few minutes in quiet prayer. Ask God to show you one (or more) ways that you may be called to respond to this week's scriptures—

- in your relationship with God
- with family and friends
- at work, school, or church
- in the broader community

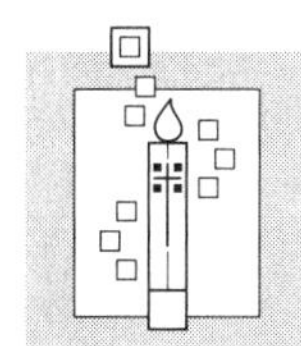

April 15, 2007

SECOND SUNDAY OF EASTER

Today's Focus: Faith Wounds

For some folks the only things they know for sure in life are the hurts and the pains. Not just the nicks and scratches, but the wounds that one carries for the rest of one's life, or at least the memories of those wounds. And sometimes the memories of those wounds can be as painful as the wounds themselves.

FIRST READING
Acts 5:12–16

Many signs and wonders were done among the people at the hands of the apostles. They were all together in Solomon's portico. None of the others dared to join them, but the people esteemed them. Yet more than ever, believers in the Lord, great numbers of men and women, were added to them. Thus they even carried the sick out into the streets and laid them on cots and mats so that when Peter came by, at least his shadow might fall on one or another of them. A large number of people from the towns in the vicinity of Jerusalem also gathered, bringing the sick and those disturbed by unclean spirits, and they were all cured.

PSALM RESPONSE
Psalm 118:1

Give thanks to the Lord for he is good, his love is everlasting.

SECOND READING
Revelation 1: 9–11a, 12–13, 17–19

I, John, your brother, who share with you the distress, the kingdom, and the endurance we have in Jesus, found myself on the island called Patmos because I proclaimed God's word and gave testimony to Jesus. I was caught up in spirit on the Lord's day and heard behind me a voice as loud as a trumpet, which said, "Write on a scroll what you see." Then I turned to see whose voice it was that spoke to me, and when I turned, I saw seven gold lampstands and in the midst of the lampstands one like a son of man, wearing an ankle-length robe, with a gold sash around his chest.

When I caught sight of him, I fell down at his feet as though dead. He touched me with his right hand and said, "Do not be afraid. I am the first and the last, the one who lives. Once I was dead, but now I am alive forever and ever. I hold the keys to death and the netherworld. Write down, therefore, what you have seen, and what is happening, and what will happen afterwards."

GOSPEL *John 20:19–31*

On the evening of that first day of the week, when the doors were locked, where the disciples were, for fear of the Jews, Jesus came and stood in their midst and said to them, "Peace be with you." When he had said this, he showed them his hands and his side. The disciples rejoiced when they saw the Lord. Jesus said to them again, "Peace be with you. As the Father has sent me, so I send you." And when he had said this, he breathed on them and said to them, "Receive the Holy Spirit. Whose sins you forgive are forgiven them, and whose sins you retain are retained."

Thomas, called Didymus, one of the Twelve, was not with them when Jesus came. So the other disciples said to him, "We have seen the Lord." But he said to them, "Unless I see the mark of the nails in his hands and put my finger into the nailmarks and put my hand into his side, I will not believe."

Now a week later his disciples were again inside and Thomas was with them. Jesus came, although the doors were locked, and stood in their midst and said, "Peace be with you." Then he said to Thomas, "Put your finger here and see my hands, and bring your hand and put it into my side, and do not be unbelieving, but believe." Thomas answered and said to him, "My Lord and my God!" Jesus said to him, "Have you come to believe because you have seen me? Blessed are those who have not seen and have believed."

Now Jesus did many other signs in the presence of his disciples that are not written in this book. But these are written that you may come to believe that Jesus is the Christ, the Son of God, and that through this belief you may have life in his name.

Understanding the Word

Both the fact and the importance of the resurrection of Jesus are found in today's second reading from the book of Revelation. Characteristics of this last book of the New Testament are evident in this passage, which recounts a vision received by John on the island of Patmos. Visions are an important aspect of the apocalyptic writing in Revelation.

Symbolism is another key aspect of this type of literature. The trumpet of verse 10 is used in the Old Testament in connection with an appearance of Yahweh (Exodus 19:16) and in the New Testament to announce the second coming of Christ and the resurrection of the dead (1 Thessalonians 4:16). Other symbols are the ankle-length robe, which indicates the priesthood of Jesus (Wisdom 18:24), and the gold sash around Christ's chest, a reference to his role as king (1 Maccabees 11:56).

The author gives an excellent portrayal of Jesus. John speaks of Christ as "one like a son of man" (Revelation 1:13). "Son of man" can simply mean a human being. However, John expects the reader to recall this important passage in the book of Daniel: "One like a son of man coming / on the clouds of heaven; / When he reached the Ancient One / and was presented before him, / He received dominion, glory, and kingship" (Daniel 7:13–14). Of great significance in this passage from Revelation are the words, "I am the first and the last, the one who lives. Once I was dead, but now I am alive forever and ever" (Revelation 1:17–18). Jesus receives titles in these verses normally applied to Yahweh. There is also the clear reference to the resurrection of the Savior.

A significant encouragement for the followers of Jesus is the verse that speaks of "the distress, the kingdom, and the endurance we have in Jesus" (Revelation 1:9). John is telling the Christians that they need continuing endurance in the face of Roman persecution and in life's daily struggles to be truly Christ-like. The result of this continuing patient endurance is the reward of the kingdom, which is life "in Jesus."

Reflecting on the Word

Most of us find ourselves remembering a mixture of both good times and bad times. We are able to call up the blessings, those times when we lie back on the grass, hands behind our head, gazing at clouds and dreaming of how they shape themselves into silhouettes of what we've known and where we've been, a scrapbook of images dear to us. We hang on to such times.

But other memories come along as well, clouds drearier if not also stormier. Adolescence, maybe—it can still taste like a copper penny. Or the growing-up relationship we once had with a parent: some still limp from it, a bruised or broken spirit that never healed the way it should have. Or the feeling that comes from never having made the team—not the basketball team or love's team or even life's team. It's as if we got on the wrong bus when everyone left for the game, and ever after we gaze through the window at all the other buses filled with could've-been friends who never wave back.

Mercifully life moves on. And if we're blessed, it moves on into goodnesses of other sorts. Yet not without the scars, those ways our flesh has of remembering. In some ways they become the buoys that point out the deep-water channel in the river of life, markers for safe sailing as well as for rocky beds that rip us open.

So we remember the wounds, which is what Thomas did. They marked the pain for him, but they also marked the real Jesus. He knew that if the wounds into which he would put his hands were real, so would Jesus be, and so also the demise of death. For Thomas it was the wounds that proved resurrection and so moved him into faith.

CONSIDER/ DISCUSS:

- Have there been wounded portions of life that have led to faith for you?
- What is your opinion? Can someone come to faith if they have never suffered and experienced a life in which there have been no wounds?

Responding to the Word

We all struggle with believing. We all doubt; it is the essence of faith. The difference is in where we look for renewed strength and reaffirmed faith. For some the thermometer or measuring stick is the calm of life. For others it is in our wounded helplessness that we come to faith simply because it is also then that we recognize that the new life that comes is not our doing.

Spend a few minutes in quiet prayer. Ask God to show you one (or more) ways that you may be called to respond to this week's scriptures—

- in your relationship with God
- with family and friends
- at work, school, or church
- in the broader community

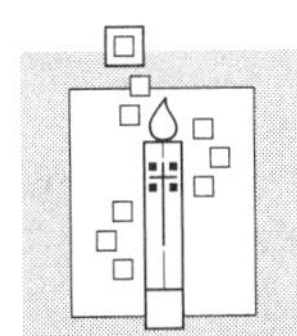

April 22, 2007

THIRD SUNDAY OF EASTER

Today's Focus: Out of Empty Seas

Life can be fickle. Sometimes the words we use are that the river has run dry, and sometimes that the bottle is empty, and sometimes that there aren't any more fish in the sea. Whatever words we put to it, however, don't much matter, only that whatever it was that seemed always to come up roses has turned into a devastated patch of personal crabgrass.

FIRST READING
Acts 5:27–32, 40b–41

When the captain and the court officers had brought the apostles in and made them stand before the Sanhedrin, the high priest questioned them, "We gave you strict orders, did we not, to stop teaching in that name? Yet you have filled Jerusalem with your teaching and want to bring this man's blood upon us." But Peter and the apostles said in reply, "We must obey God rather than men. The God of our ancestors raised Jesus, though you had him killed by hanging him on a tree. God exalted him at his right hand as leader and savior to grant Israel repentance and forgiveness of sins. We are witnesses of these things, as is the Holy Spirit whom God has given to those who obey him."

The Sanhedrin ordered the apostles to stop speaking in the name of Jesus, and dismissed them. So they left the presence of the Sanhedrin, rejoicing that they had been found worthy to suffer dishonor for the sake of the name.

PSALM RESPONSE
Psalm 30:2a

I will praise you, Lord, for you have rescued me.

SECOND READING
Revelation 5: 11–14

I, John, looked and heard the voices of many angels who surrounded the throne and the living creatures and the elders. They were countless in number, and they cried out in a loud voice:

"Worthy is the Lamb that was slain
to receive power and riches, wisdom and strength,
honor and glory and blessing."

Then I heard every creature in heaven and on earth and under the earth and in the sea, everything in the universe, cry out:

"To the one who sits on the throne and to the Lamb
be blessing and honor, glory and might,
forever and ever."

The four living creatures answered, "Amen," and the elders fell down and worshiped.

In the shorter form of the reading, the passage in brackets is omitted.

GOSPEL *John 21:1–19 or 21:1–14*

At that time, Jesus revealed himself again to his disciples at the Sea of Tiberias. He revealed himself in this way. Together were Simon Peter, Thomas called Didymus, Nathanael from Cana in Galilee, Zebedee's sons, and two others of his disciples. Simon Peter said to them, "I am going fishing." They said to him, "We also will come with you." So they went out and got into the boat, but that night they caught nothing. When it was already dawn, Jesus was standing on the shore; but the disciples did not realize that it was Jesus. Jesus said to them, "Children, have you caught anything to eat?" They answered him, "No." So he said to them, "Cast the net over the right side of the boat and you will find something." So they cast it, and were not able to pull it in because of the number of fish. So the disciple whom Jesus loved said to Peter, "It is the Lord." When Simon Peter heard that it was the Lord, he tucked in his garment, for he was lightly clad, and jumped into the sea. The other disciples came in the boat, for they were not far from shore, only about a hundred yards, dragging the net with the fish. When they climbed out on shore, they saw a charcoal fire with fish on it and bread. Jesus said to them, "Bring some of the fish you just caught." So Simon Peter went over and dragged the net ashore full of one hundred fifty-three large fish. Even though there were so many, the net was not torn. Jesus said to them, "Come, have breakfast." And none of the disciples dared to ask him, "Who are you?" because they realized it was the Lord. Jesus came over and took the bread and gave it to them, and in like manner the fish. This was now the third time Jesus was revealed to his disciples after being raised from the dead.

[When they had finished breakfast, Jesus said to Simon Peter, "Simon, son of John, do you love me more than these?" Simon Peter answered him, "Yes, Lord, you know that I love you." Jesus said to him, "Feed my lambs." He then said to Simon Peter a second time, "Simon, son of John, do you love me?" Simon Peter answered him, "Yes, Lord, you know that I love you." Jesus said to him, "Tend my sheep." Jesus said to him the third time, "Simon, son of John, do you love me?" Peter was distressed that Jesus had said to him a third time, "Do you love me?" and he said to him, "Lord, you know everything; you know that I love you." Jesus said to him, "Feed my sheep. Amen, amen, I say to you, when you were younger, you used to dress yourself and go where you wanted; but when you grow old, you will stretch out your hands, and someone else will dress you and lead you where you do not want to go." He said this signifying by what kind of death he would glorify God. And when he had said this, he said to him, "Follow me."]

Understanding the Word

Today's Gospel teaches much about Jesus and about the early church and its mission. An important preliminary question concerns the relationship of this chapter to the rest of the Gospel. Chapter 20, the preceding chapter, has a clear and effective ending (20:30–31). The readers are told that the basic purpose of the Gospel is to support faith in Jesus as Messiah and Son of God, a faith that leads to life in Christ. Chapter 21 starts anew with Resurrection appearances of Christ in Galilee whereas the appearances in the preceding chapter were in Jerusalem. There are also differences in vocabulary and style between the two chapters. As a result, most scholars consider John 21 an epilogue to the Gospel. It is an early, inspired addition, preserving important material about Jesus and the church. This final chapter of the Gospel is found in all biblical manuscripts of the Fourth Gospel.

There are significant teachings in today's Gospel. The amazing catch of one hundred fifty-three fish symbolizes the universal mission of the church. St. Jerome notes that zoologists of his time believed that there were just one hundred fifty-three types of fish.

The role given to Peter here is also noteworthy. To the triple question concerning his love for Christ, Peter responds with strong, positive affirmations. Being reminded of his triple denial of Jesus no doubt upset Peter. The major point of the incident, however, is his present willingness to be a faithful follower of Jesus. After this expression of his conversion Jesus puts Peter in charge of his flock: "Feed my lambs . . . Tend my sheep . . . Feed my sheep" (John 21:15, 16, 17). This commission brings with it the authority of Christ, but also the mission to continue the example of the Good Shepherd's devotion to his flock. "A good shepherd lays down his life for the sheep" (John 10:11).

The evangelist presents Jesus' prediction of the future martyrdom of Peter: "[W]hen you grow old, you will stretch out your hands, and someone else will dress you and lead you where you do not want to go" (21:18). When the author is writing this (about AD 100), Peter had already died a martyr's death in Rome (about AD 65).

Reflecting on the Word

Somewhere along the line most of us come to realize that life can't be all abundance, all the way we'd like it to be. We know that there'll be nights of fishing when all that our nets have snagged is more darkness, and while that disappoints us, it doesn't necessarily keep us from hope and the belief that tides do turn. So when somebody says, "Try one more time," well, sometimes we think, "Maybe this time. You never know."

If there are moments of Godliness in our lives, it is such moments when abundance overflows from barren labors, simply because it in is such moments that we realize that it wasn't our doing, couldn't have been anybody's doing, except the One who has the power to contradict every pattern of life and predictability. It's also when we realize that God or life or chance or however we choose to name it is taking us where we never intended to go or even dreamt of going, as Jesus reminded Peter. For the believer it's all a bit of resurrection out of death, like abundance from an empty sea.

I don't suppose any of us ever goes looking for such emptiness just so we can experience resurrection. In fact we tend to run from it, from sickness or loss of love or the confusion of midlife or adolescent unpopularity or whatever it is that fills in those blanks in our lives. From all such frightening ghouls we tend to turn and frantically dash into life's next scene. Sooner or later, however, the monster once more shows its dread and deadly face, and if we are willing to sit with it for a while, if we can somehow make friends with it or at least muster up a forced smile, that's when new life begins to rise as well.

CONSIDER/ DISCUSS:

- Return to visit a place where you once found abundant life in the midst of emptiness—a place where perhaps you once resolved a dispute or rediscovered meaning or found unexpected courage. Revisit it as one visits a shrine or holy place.
- Or visit a church and light a candle in memory of that event's darkness turned to light.

Responding to the Word

We learn something about ourselves in the midst of our emptiness. That's when confusion over the pieces of life's puzzle can reveal a new picture. All of it is an undreamed-of abundance from a sea we had thought to be fished out—all of it either a beneficent twist of fate or our risen Lord inviting us to breakfast with him on a new shore of our lives.

Spend a few minutes in quiet prayer. Ask God to show you one (or more) ways that you may be called to respond to this week's scriptures—

- in your relationship with God
- with family and friends
- at work, school, or church
- in the broader community

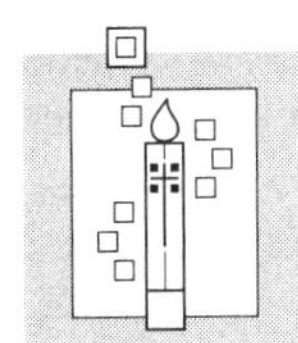

April 29, 2007

FOURTH SUNDAY OF EASTER

Today's Focus: A Walk through the Maze

To be led is to follow. To follow is to allow another to decide the path. To walk the path chosen by another is to be brought to a new place. And we may not even know it until the end of the path.

FIRST READING
Acts 13:14, 43–52

Paul and Barnabas continued on from Perga and reached Antioch in Pisidia. On the sabbath they entered the synagogue and took their seats.

Many Jews and worshipers who were converts to Judaism followed Paul and Barnabas, who spoke to them and urged them to remain faithful to the grace of God.

On the following sabbath almost the whole city gathered to hear the word of the Lord. When the Jews saw the crowds, they were filled with jealousy and with violent abuse contradicted what Paul said. Both Paul and Barnabas spoke out boldly and said, "It was necessary that the word of God be spoken to you first, but since you reject it and condemn yourselves as unworthy of eternal life, we now turn to the Gentiles. For so the Lord has commanded us,

I have made you a light to the Gentiles,
that you may be an instrument of salvation
to the ends of the earth."

The Gentiles were delighted when they heard this and glorified the word of the Lord. All who were destined for eternal life came to believe, and the word of the Lord continued to spread through the whole region. The Jews, however, incited the women of prominence who were worshipers and the leading men of the city, stirred up a persecution against Paul and Barnabas, and expelled them from their territory. So they shook the dust from their feet in protest against them, and went to Iconium. The disciples were filled with joy and the Holy Spirit.

PSALM RESPONSE
Psalm 100:3c

We are his people, the sheep of his flock.

SECOND READING
Revelation 7:9, 14b–17

I, John, had a vision of a great multitude, which no one could count, from every nation, race, people, and tongue. They stood before the throne and before the Lamb, wearing white robes and holding palm branches in their hands.

Then one of the elders said to me, "These are the ones who have survived the time of great distress; they have washed their robes and made them white in the blood of the Lamb.

"For this reason they stand before God's throne
  and worship him day and night in his temple.
The one who sits on the throne will shelter them.
They will not hunger or thirst anymore,
  nor will the sun or any heat strike them.
For the Lamb who is in the center of the throne
  will shepherd them
  and lead them to springs of life-giving water,
  and God will wipe away every tear from their eyes."

GOSPEL
John 10:27–30

Jesus said: "My sheep hear my voice; I know them, and they follow me. I give them eternal life, and they shall never perish. No one can take them out of my hand. My Father, who has given them to me, is greater than all, and no one can take them out of the Father's hand. The Father and I are one."

Understanding the Word

In the Easter season the Church draws from the Acts of the Apostles, rather than the Old Testament, for the first reading on Sunday. These readings show the immediate effects of the death, resurrection, and ascension of Jesus, namely the establishment and spread of his church. Before returning to the Father, Jesus tells the apostles, "[Y]ou will receive power when the holy Spirit comes upon you, and you will be my witnesses in Jerusalem, throughout Judea and Samaria, and to the ends of the earth" (Acts 1:8).

Luke, the author of the Acts of the Apostles, chose the work of Paul to illustrate the fulfillment of that key promise made by Jesus. What happens at Antioch in Asia Minor sets the pattern for most of Paul's ministry. It is God's will that he first present the Word to the Jewish community (Acts 13:46). Paul meets with initial acceptance, but later rejection. He then announces that he will turn to the Gentiles, quoting a text about the Suffering Servant: "I have made you a light to the Gentiles, / that you may be an instrument of salvation / to the ends of the earth" (13:47; see Isaiah 49:6). Paul sees this text as representing the Lord's command to him and enabling him to share in the work of Jesus himself, also a "light . . . to the Gentiles" (Acts 26:23).

Some Gentiles at that time were partial converts to Judaism (Acts 13:43), referred to as "God fearing." They had accepted monotheism and much of Jewish morality, but did not feel compelled to accept other matters, such as circumcision and dietary laws. Beginning with Cornelius (10:2), many of these converts to Judaism were open to accepting Christianity.

Paul and Barnabas are expelled from the city, but have established a community of believers, "filled with joy and the Holy Spirit" (Acts 13:52). Interestingly, Luke makes joy a principal theme at the birth of Jesus and also at the birth of the church in the Acts of the Apostles. The presence of joy and the Holy Spirit created a solid Christian community while "the word of the Lord continued to spread through the whole region" (Acts 13:49).

Reflecting on the Word

Adolescence is not the only time we are brought to a new place in life, but it can certainly be one of the more poignant times, and for some the first time among many yet to be cracked and scrambled upon our plate. How we make it through adolescence can baffle anyone who seeks order and predictability. The years can be a silent call of the wild, or they can drag us out of childhood's bed into a new and far-off morning. Somehow we do find our way through that maze of adolescence and into various sizes of maturity, yet never without dead ends or blind alleys, and always over time—sometimes much time.

There are other mazes as well—midlife, parenthood, divorce, the death of a spouse, retirement—enough of them, it seems, that we are tempted to think of it all as one maze, life-long, groping our way on some endless quest. Hindsight offers some clarity, though at times it seems too late. Nevertheless, we look back and say we made it, even if with bruises and scars. Yet we made it, now wondering how, then with continual plodding because the treadmill would not stop.

For the disciples of Jesus his words then begin to make sense. "I know them, and they follow me. I give them eternal life, and they shall never perish. No one can take them out of my hand" (John 10:27–28).

CONSIDER/ DISCUSS:

- To be brought to a new place, one must be willing to move. How has God gotten you to move when you have resisted?
- What has been your most difficult time in life? What are the new blessings that were brought forth at that time?

Responding to the Word

At some point believers look at their lives through the lens of faith and recognize some greater wisdom, some nurturing presence, intertwined with their own, that has led them to a new place of grace. It is a grace to acknowledge God's presence in this way.

Spend a few minutes in quiet prayer. Ask God to show you one (or more) ways that you may be called to respond to this week's scriptures—

- in your relationship with God
- with family and friends
- at work, school, or church
- in the broader community

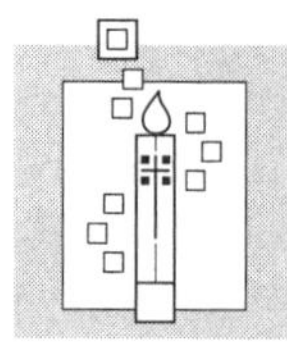

May 6, 2007

FIFTH SUNDAY OF EASTER

Today's Focus: The Ultimate Makeover

There seems to be a longing deep inside each of us, a yearning of sorts that we be made new. Though it grows and ebbs, it never really ever goes away. It seems simply to wait for another time to show its face.

FIRST READING
Acts 14:21–27

After Paul and Barnabas had proclaimed the good news to that city and made a considerable number of disciples, they returned to Lystra and to Iconium and to Antioch. They strengthened the spirits of the disciples and exhorted them to persevere in the faith, saying, "It is necessary for us to undergo many hardships to enter the kingdom of God." They appointed elders for them in each church and, with prayer and fasting, commended them to the Lord in whom they had put their faith. Then they traveled through Pisidia and reached Pamphylia. After proclaiming the word at Perga they went down to Attalia. From there they sailed to Antioch, where they had been commended to the grace of God for the work they had now accomplished. And when they arrived, they called the church together and reported what God had done with them and how he had opened the door of faith to the Gentiles.

PSALM RESPONSE
Psalm 145:1

I will praise your name forever, my king and my God.

SECOND READING
Revelation 21: 1–5a

Then I, John, saw a new heaven and a new earth. The former heaven and the former earth had passed away, and the sea was no more. I also saw the holy city, a new Jerusalem, coming down out of heaven from God, prepared as a bride adorned for her husband. I heard a loud voice from the throne saying, "Behold, God's dwelling is with the human race. He will dwell with them and they will be his people and God himself will always be with them as their God. He will wipe every tear from their eyes, and there shall be no more death or mourning, wailing or pain, for the old order has passed away."

The One who sat on the throne said, "Behold, I make all things new."

GOSPEL
John 13: 31–33a, 34–35

When Judas had left them, Jesus said, "Now is the Son of Man glorified, and God is glorified in him. If God is glorified in him, God will also glorify him in himself, and God will glorify him at once. My children, I will be with you only a little while longer. I give you a new commandment: love one another. As I have loved you, so you also should love one another. This is how all will know that you are my disciples, if you have love for one another."

Understanding the Word

Today's Gospel is very short, but extremely meaningful for the development of Christianity. In the preceding verse the reader is told that Judas "took the morsel and left at once. And it was night" (John 13:30). This begins the process of death, resurrection, and ascension of Jesus. As he dies on the cross in obedience to the will of the Father, Jesus gives glory to God. The glory of the Father is also seen in the love and power involved with the events of the Son's paschal mystery (13:31).

With tender words, "My children," Jesus reminds his disciples that he will be leaving, but also assures them, "I will come back again and take you to myself, so that where I am you also may be" (14:3). In the meantime they are to accept and practice his new commandment: "As I have loved you, so you also should love one another" (13:34). The greatness of Christ's love for his disciples and for everyone will be clear as he lays down his life on Good Friday for the salvation of the entire human race. This love demanded by Jesus' new commandment will be a cornerstone of the New Covenant. In fact, this love will identify the Christian disciple (13:35).

In chapter 15 Jesus makes the amazing statement, "As the Father loves me, so I also love you" (15:9). This incredible love of the Savior for us makes it essential that we in turn love all people. Jesus says very clearly during his public life that we cannot truly follow his example of love if we do not reach out to each and every person. "You have heard that it was said, 'You shall love your neighbor and hate your enemy.' But I say to you, love your enemies, and pray for those who persecute you, that you may be children of your heavenly Father" (Matthew 5:43–45). Jesus is making the point that the Father and he love everyone. The goal of each Christian must be to follow that wonderful example. With this new commandment of love Jesus will give the strength that is required. Father Raymond E. Brown comments, "Thus, as long as Christian love is in the world, the world is still encountering Jesus" (*Anchor Bible*, "The Gospel according to John," vol. 29A, p. 614).

Reflecting on the Word

A while ago the Lysol® brand of cleaning products was promoting a new toilet brush, one that has the liquid cleanser and disinfectant stored inside the handle. Television became its midwife, promoting it as the new generation of toilet bowl cleaners. The ad concluded with a series of housewife testimonials, the final one of which attested, "It has changed my life!" It was but another appeal to our hidden longing that our lives be made new. Or consider the abundance of television makeover programs, even a surgical makeover—the "extreme" makeover. Each of us in some way longs to be made new, sometimes vicariously and sometimes personally.

One of the paradoxes of life is that the more we seek ourselves, the more we lose ourselves; and the more we are willing to lose ourselves, the more we find ourselves. It is, of course, only another way of speaking about love. It seems to be a simple rule of thumb. If your life is in chaos or disarray, if you find yourself unsettled and discombobulated, then forget about your own life and begin to focus on the lives of others. It is how love works, if indeed love does any work at all. It is love that makes us new. It is the ultimate makeover, simply because God is love.

Weapons will never create a new Iraq; only compassion will, and justice, and heartfelt care for the Iraqi people. Punishment and the inhumane conditions of prison life will never remake the soul of one who is incarcerated, only hope for a future and a nurturing of the human spirit. More liturgical regulations and prescriptions will never bring deepening faith life to our eucharistic assemblies; only love for one another will, and the healing we so desperately need.

CONSIDER/ DISCUSS:

- How is the community in which you live being made new, even beyond deliberate human efforts?
- In what ways has love for others been a transforming dimension of your own life? How are you different because of it?

Responding to the Word

All of our efforts to remake life can only be meager strivings. In the end it is God who makes all things new, and we are but sparks of God's creation who seek to live in harmony with the Spirit set free by Jesus who is Lord.

Spend a few minutes in quiet prayer. Ask God to show you one (or more) ways that you may be called to respond to this week's scriptures—

- in your relationship with God
- with family and friends
- at work, school, or church
- in the broader community

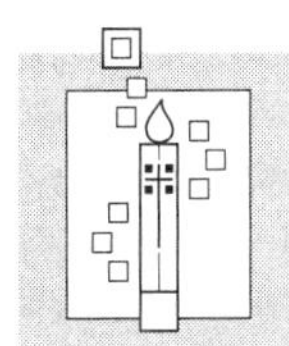

May 13, 2007

SIXTH SUNDAY OF EASTER

Today's Focus: Remembering the Holy

We spend much time daydreaming when we are young. As we grow older daydreams give way to memories. Remembering, then, may be the most sacred thing we do, for our memories are the very story of how God has shaped us out of clay.

FIRST READING
Acts 15:1–2, 22–29

Some who had come down from Judea were instructing the brothers, "Unless you are circumcised according to the Mosaic practice, you cannot be saved." Because there arose no little dissension and debate by Paul and Barnabas with them, it was decided that Paul, Barnabas, and some of the others should go up to Jerusalem to the apostles and elders about this question.

The apostles and elders, in agreement with the whole church, decided to choose representatives and to send them to Antioch with Paul and Barnabas. The ones chosen were Judas, who was called Barsabbas, and Silas, leaders among the brothers. This is the letter delivered by them:

"The apostles and the elders, your brothers, to the brothers in Antioch, Syria, and Cilicia of Gentile origin: greetings. Since we have heard that some of our number who went out without any mandate from us have upset you with their teachings and disturbed your peace of mind, we have with one accord decided to choose representatives and to send them to you along with our beloved Barnabas and Paul, who have dedicated their lives to the name of our Lord Jesus Christ. So we are sending Judas and Silas who will also convey this same message by word of mouth: 'It is the decision of the Holy Spirit and of us not to place on you any burden beyond these necessities, namely, to abstain from meat sacrificed to idols, from blood, from meats of strangled animals, and from unlawful marriage. If you keep free of these, you will be doing what is right. Farewell.' "

PSALM RESPONSE
Psalm 67:4

O God, let all the nations praise you!

SECOND READING
Revelation 21: 10–14, 22–23

The angel took me in spirit to a great, high mountain and showed me the holy city Jerusalem coming down out of heaven from God. It gleamed with the splendor of God. Its radiance was like that of a precious stone, like jasper, clear as crystal. It had a massive, high wall, with twelve gates where twelve angels were stationed and on which names were inscribed, the names of the twelve tribes of the Israelites. There were three gates facing east, three north, three south, and three west. The wall of the city had twelve courses of stones as its foundation, on which were inscribed the twelve names of the twelve apostles of the Lamb.

I saw no temple in the city for its temple is the Lord God almighty and the Lamb. The city had no need of sun or moon to shine on it, for the glory of God gave it light, and its lamp was the Lamb.

GOSPEL
John 14:23–29

Jesus said to his disciples: "Whoever loves me will keep my word, and my Father will love him, and we will come to him and make our dwelling with him. Whoever does not love me does not keep my words; yet the word you hear is not mine but that of the Father who sent me.

"I have told you this while I am with you. The Advocate, the Holy Spirit, whom the Father will send in my name, will teach you everything and remind you of all that I told you. Peace I leave with you; my peace I give to you. Not as the world gives do I give it to you. Do not let your hearts be troubled or afraid. You heard me tell you, 'I am going away and I will come back to you.' If you loved me, you would rejoice that I am going to the Father; for the Father is greater than I. And now I have told you this before it happens, so that when it happens you may believe."

Understanding the Word

The Last Supper discourse in the Gospel of John (14:1 — 17:26) is a farewell discourse. In today's Gospel, for example, Jesus says, "I am going away and I will come back to you" (14:28). Christ consoles his disciples at the thought of his departure with a number of significant promises.

To one who loves him, Jesus promises that the Father and he "will come to him and make our dwelling with him" (14:23). This dwelling begins in this life and reaches its perfection at the time of the *parousia*, the Second Coming of Jesus. Through the prophets Yahweh had made similar promises in the Old Testament. "Sing and rejoice, O daughter Zion! See, I am coming to dwell among you, says the Lord" (Zechariah 2:14). Christ also sounds the note of joy because he is leaving to return to his Father, having completed the work of salvation assigned to him by the Father (John 14:28).

Another important promise is that the Father will send them the Advocate, the Holy Spirit, as their teacher. He will help them understand and put into practice the teachings of Jesus that they had received. This will be the ongoing role of the Holy Spirit for the church and for each Christian.

A third promise for Jesus' followers is peace. The biblical concept of peace involves far more than the absence of hostility. It is a positive term, denoting the fullness, the perfection of God's blessings. In the New Testament it promises all the messianic blessings, especially salvation to those who love Jesus and keep his commandments (John 14:23). This indwelling of Father and Son in the followers of Jesus is one of the fruits of peace.

In today's Gospel Jesus says that "the Father is greater than I" (14:28). Earlier in John's Gospel he said, "The Father and I are one" (10:30). Since the Father sent Jesus to carry out the divine purposes, the Father can be seen as greater than the one sent. The Incarnation and the relationship of Father and Son will be developed in great detail by later theology.

Reflecting on the Word

Do you remember the first rays of freedom dawning for you? Was it walking to school by yourself for the first time? Or having your own money to spend as you would? Or moving away from home? Or was that only yesterday?

Do you remember pain as well? Both feeling pained when you were pruned from the vine that is love; and causing pain when you turned your back to another's face? Do you remember pain? And sin? Or was that, too, only yesterday?

Remembering is good and holy. It is of God's Spirit and where that Spirit works, and why Jesus said, "[N]ow I have told you this before it happens, so that when it happens you may believe" (John 14:29), so that when it happens you will remember. Could we believe if we did not remember?

Much later in Saint John's life, when he was exiled to the Isle of Patmos presumably because of his faith and because of the ways his remembering shaped both his own life and the lives of numerous others, he continued to remember and to imagine. What he remembered then was the way that Jesus had been their dream, the divine center of their lives. Jesus had been all they wished for, all they hoped they could be. That's what John remembered and was unwilling to forget.

CONSIDER/ DISCUSS:

- Remember blessings. Be filled with wonder.
- Remember your own graciousness. Be grateful for grace.
- Remember hurts. Be forgiving and freeing.
- Remember your sins. Be humbled and thankful for mercy.

Dare to remember. It's where we begin to recognize the hand of God in our lives. It is the most radical thing we can do simply because it is of the Holy Spirit.

Spend a few minutes in quiet prayer. Ask God to show you one (or more) ways that you may be called to respond to this week's scriptures—

- in your relationship with God
- with family and friends
- at work, school, or church
- in the broader community

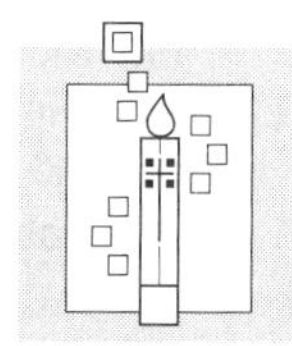

May 17, 2007

THE ASCENSION OF THE LORD

Many dioceses in the United States celebrate the Ascension on May 20, replacing the Seventh Sunday of Easter

Today's Focus: The Power to Save

We do not save ourselves. All we need do is look at our frail lives, something we do most every morning and every evening as we gaze into our mirrors or contemplate the work of our hands or the relationships of our lives. Indeed, no one of us makes it on our own. We are all in need of saving.

FIRST READING
Acts 1:1–11

In the first book, Theophilus, I dealt with all that Jesus did and taught until the day he was taken up, after giving instructions through the Holy Spirit to the apostles whom he had chosen. He presented himself alive to them by many proofs after he had suffered, appearing to them during forty days and speaking about the kingdom of God. While meeting with them, he enjoined them not to depart from Jerusalem, but to wait for "the promise of the Father about which you have heard me speak; for John baptized with water, but in a few days you will be baptized with the Holy Spirit."

When they had gathered together they asked him, "Lord, are you at this time going to restore the kingdom to Israel?" He answered them, "It is not for you to know the times or seasons that the Father has established by his own authority. But you will receive power when the Holy Spirit comes upon you, and you will be my witnesses in Jerusalem, throughout Judea and Samaria, and to the ends of the earth." When he had said this, as they were looking on, he was lifted up, and a cloud took him from their sight. While they were looking intently at the sky as he was going, suddenly two men dressed in white garments stood beside them. They said, "Men of Galilee, why are you standing there looking at the sky? This Jesus who has been taken up from you into heaven will return in the same way as you have seen him going into heaven."

PSALM RESPONSE
Psalm 47:6

God mounts his throne to shouts of joy: a blare of trumpets for the Lord.

SECOND READING
Ephesians 1: 17–23

Brothers and sisters: May the God of our Lord Jesus Christ, the Father of glory, give you a Spirit of wisdom and revelation resulting in knowledge of him. May the eyes of your hearts be enlightened, that you may know what is the hope that belongs to his call, what are the riches of glory in his inheritance among the holy ones, and what is the surpassing greatness of his power for us who believe, in accord with the exercise of his great might: which he worked in Christ, raising him from the dead and seating him at his right hand in the heavens, far above every principality, authority, power, and dominion, and every name that is named not only in this age but also in the one to come. And he put all things beneath his feet and gave him as head over all things to the church, which is his body, the fullness of the one who fills all things in every way.

– or –

SECOND READING
Hebrews 9:24–28; 10:19–23

Christ did not enter into a sanctuary made by hands, a copy of the true one, but heaven itself, that he might now appear before God on our behalf. Not that he might offer himself repeatedly, as the high priest enters each year into the sanctuary with blood that is not his own; if that were so, he would have had to suffer repeatedly from the foundation of the world. But now once for all he has appeared at the end of the ages to take away sin by his sacrifice. Just as it is appointed that men and women die once, and after this the judgment, so also Christ, offered once to take away the sins of many, will appear a second time, not to take away sin but to bring salvation to those who eagerly await him.

Therefore, brothers and sisters, since through the blood of Jesus we have confidence of entrance into the sanctuary by the new and living way he opened for us through the veil, that is, his flesh, and since we have "a great priest over the house of God," let us approach with a sincere heart and in absolute trust, with our hearts sprinkled clean from an evil conscience and our bodies washed in pure water. Let us hold unwaveringly to our confession that gives us hope, for he who made the promise is trustworthy.

GOSPEL
Luke 24:46–53

Jesus said to his disciples: "Thus it is written that the Christ would suffer and rise from the dead on the third day and that repentance, for the forgiveness of sins, would be preached in his name to all the nations, beginning from Jerusalem. You are witnesses of these things. And behold I am sending the promise of my Father upon you; but stay in the city until you are clothed with power from on high."

Then he led them out as far as Bethany, raised his hands, and blessed them. As he blessed them he parted from them and was taken up to heaven. They did him homage and then returned to Jerusalem with great joy, and they were continually in the temple praising God.

Understanding the Word

Luke is the author of both the first reading today and the Gospel. The Gospel ends with the ascension that took place on Easter Sunday. The Acts of the Apostles tells of the ascension that took place forty days later. "The ascension as the exaltation of Jesus as the risen Lord at the right hand of the Father took place immediately as part of the resurrection triumph, but his visible leave-taking of the community happened at some later time" (Jerome Kodell, OSB, "The Gospel According to Luke," *Collegeville Bible Commentary*, pp. 117–118).

At the time of his ascension Jesus gives an important commission to his followers. Matthew has these words of Christ: "[M]ake disciples of all nations" (28:19). Mark provides a similar commission, "Go into the whole world and proclaim the gospel to every creature" (16:15). Today's Gospel promises that "repentance, for the forgiveness of sins, would be preached in his name to all the nations" (Luke 24:47). Universal salvation is clearly the goal of Jesus.

As Jesus returns in glory to the Father, he reminds his followers that they are "witnesses of these things" (24:48). They are to be eyewitnesses and ministers of the word, cited by Luke as a source for his Gospel (1:2). In a key verse of the Acts of the Apostles Jesus says, "[Y]ou will receive power when the Holy Spirit comes upon you, and you will be my witnesses in Jerusalem, throughout Judea and Samaria, and to the ends of the earth" (Acts 1:8).

To support the work of his followers our Lord promises the conferral of the Holy Spirit in both the Gospel and the Acts of the Apostles. The Ascension marks the end of the Period of Jesus in salvation history. With the coming of the promised Spirit the third and final period will follow, the Period of the Church.

The infancy narrative of Luke had joy as a major theme. As the church begins its infancy, the disciples "returned to Jerusalem with great joy" (24:52). They had just been blessed by the risen Savior and given the promise of the Spirit—certainly reason for rejoicing!

Reflecting on the Word

There has been much in the pedophilia scandal of the Church that cries out for saving, but in the midst of it all one aspect disappointed and saddened us all, the realization that among the leadership of the Church those chosen for the role may be no more or less holy than the rest of us and just as much in need of saving. We had hoped for them to be somehow more than the rest of us, if for no other reason than that there would be someone who might at least show us how to be saved, so that we might have hope. Yet we came to realize that they and we are indeed in the same boat. They, like us, hide sins, draw back from doing what is painful, allow fear to overshadow trust. In short, they and we together are in need of being saved. So we need one another, simply because at various times and in various situations we as church call one another to the gospel, to compassion and justice and truth, to holiness.

The feast of the Ascension of the Lord is not the story of a helium-filled Jesus who is lifted higher and higher above this feeble planet of bumbling believers.

Rather it is the story of a Jesus who is revealed as the Christ, who reigns over the universe, whose vision is so much more than ours, not because he lives higher and sees all but because he lives in all and so transforms all. And so we, as sinful as we are, are sent out by him and empowered by him simply because he is with us as he promised he would be.

CONSIDER/ DISCUSS:

- What one quality in your mother or father, in addition to love, was a saving grace for you?
- Name five current Church leaders, cleric or lay, whom you would hold up as notable and exemplary.

Responding to the Word

Sometimes the power of Christ shows its face in the leadership of the Church, and sometimes that power shows its face amid the faithful. While none of us ever saves ourselves, it is through us that he who is Lord saves us all. It is his power, not ours—in leaders and believers alike.

Spend a few minutes in quiet prayer. Ask God to show you one (or more) ways that you may be called to respond to this week's scriptures—

- in your relationship with God
- with family and friends
- at work, school, or church
- in the broader community

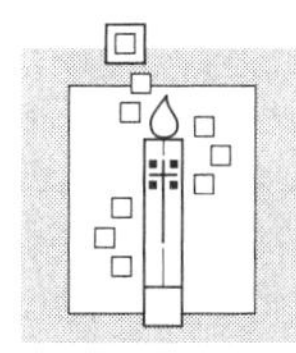

May 20, 2007

SEVENTH SUNDAY OF EASTER

Today's Focus: A Hunger to Be One with God

The Bible is a book about us. It's a book about God, too. It's about both—us and God and how the two happen to one another. So when John's Gospel says that Jesus and the Father are one, well, then that's what our lives are all about as well, precisely because that's what God is all about.

FIRST READING
Acts 7:55–60

Stephen, filled with the Holy Spirit, looked up intently to heaven and saw the glory of God and Jesus standing at the right hand of God, and Stephen said, "Behold, I see the heavens opened and the Son of Man standing at the right hand of God." But they cried out in a loud voice, covered their ears, and rushed upon him together. They threw him out of the city, and began to stone him. The witnesses laid down their cloaks at the feet of a young man named Saul. As they were stoning Stephen, he called out, "Lord Jesus, receive my spirit." Then he fell to his knees and cried out in a loud voice, "Lord, do not hold this sin against them"; and when he said this, he fell asleep.

PSALM RESPONSE
Psalm 97:1a, 9a

The Lord is king, the most high over all the earth.

SECOND READING
Revelation 22: 12–14, 16–17, 20

I, John, heard a voice saying to me: "Behold, I am coming soon. I bring with me the recompense I will give to each according to his deeds. I am the Alpha and the Omega, the first and the last, the beginning and the end."

Blessed are they who wash their robes so as to have the right to the tree of life and enter the city through its gates.

"I, Jesus, sent my angel to give you this testimony for the churches. I am the root and offspring of David, the bright morning star."

The Spirit and the bride say, "Come." Let the hearer say, "Come." Let the one who thirsts come forward, and the one who wants it receive the gift of life-giving water.

The one who gives this testimony says, "Yes, I am coming soon." Amen! Come, Lord Jesus!

GOSPEL
John 17:20–26

Lifting up his eyes to heaven, Jesus prayed, saying: "Holy Father, I pray not only for them, but also for those who will believe in me through their word, so that they may all be one, as you, Father, are in me and I in you, that they also may be in us, that the world may believe that you sent me. And I have given them the glory you gave me, so that they may be one, as we are one, I in them and you in me, that they may be brought to perfection as one, that the world may know that you sent me, and that you loved them even as you loved me. Father, they are your gift to me. I wish that where I am they also may be with me, that they may see my glory that you gave me, because you loved me before the foundation of the world. Righteous Father, the world also does not know you, but I know you, and they know that you sent me. I made known to them your name and I will make it known, that the love with which you loved me may be in them and I in them."

Understanding the Word

Today's Gospel from John is the remarkable conclusion of Jesus' Last Supper Discourse (chapters 14–17). It is especially meaningful for today's Christians since Jesus says, "I pray not only for them [the disciples at table], but also for those who will believe in me through their word" (John 17:20). What Jesus asks of the Father in prayer is "that they may all be one, as you, Father, are in me and I in you" (17:21). Jesus' prayer indicates clearly that this unity will come from God, but with the cooperation of the free will of his followers.

Unfortunately, the situation of Christianity today indicates that the followers of Jesus have not achieved unity. The Second Vatican Council spoke very strongly about this failure. "Certainly, such division openly contradicts the will of Christ, scandalizes the world, and damages the most holy cause, the preaching of the Gospel to every creature" (*Decree on Ecumenism*, 1).

Jesus had prayed that unity would bring his disciples to perfection in order that "the world may know that you sent me" (17:23). In his mind, unity would lead to effective proclamation of the gospel to the world. Jesus prayed to the Father for his followers, "that the love with which you loved me may be in them and I in them" (17:26). This indwelling love of the Father and the Son will support his followers in their efforts for unity in order to proclaim the gospel to the world.

Jesus also wants all his disciples to share in his glory in heaven. As the Son of God it was his will "that where I am they also may be with me, that they may see my glory that you gave me, because you loved me before the foundation of the world" (17:24). This sharing in the glory of Christ at his Second Coming (final eschatology) begins for the Christian already in this world (realized eschatology).

Jesus also notes that his work of making known the Father will continue through his death, resurrection, and ascension and through the ongoing work of the Holy Spirit. "[W]hen he [the Advocate] comes, the Spirit of truth, he will guide you to all truth" (16:13).

Reflecting on the Word

In recent years, there has been much interest in drugs that renew sexual potency. Some cynics have opined that it is no more than one more manifestation of our culture's obsession with pleasure. There may be that in the mix of things, but I also suspect there is something of the hunger for oneness with another at the heart of it all as well—consciously or unconsciously. The God whom we worship, who created and continues to create all things and make all things new, who is woven through all the events of our lives—in one way or another that God is finding a way to harmonize life. Indeed all of life longs to be united, not only our sexuality.

Consider our unrelenting efforts to find peace for the Middle East, for the puzzle of Iraq, for Afghanistan, all in the face of implacable opposition. True, it's all laced with our own self-interest as well, but so are our own personal lives, and they, too, are the work of our God. Bring back the moments of your life you'd like to live again. They too are all about being one: falling in love, family clustered around the Thanksgiving table, a quiet moment on a lake of transcendent solitude, the birth of your child, the divinely creative flow of inspiration and imagination.

The point is that we humans trip over ourselves in our eagerness and longing to be one. We seem driven to it, and it's all at the instigation of our God. It's the prayer of the Lord Jesus, "that they may be one, as we are one, I in them, and you in me, that they may be brought to perfection as one" (John 17:22–23).

CONSIDER/ DISCUSS:

- When have you felt most at one with another person or with creation? What triggered it? How and why was it holy?
- How has suffering played a role in those times of profound unity?

Responding to the Word

The urge to be one is there even when it's at the cost of great suffering, for it seldom happens without some dying. It's the way of love, and those who have ever made the journey know it to be so.

Spend a few minutes in quiet prayer. Ask God to show you one (or more) ways that you may be called to respond to this week's scriptures—

- in your relationship with God
- with family and friends
- at work, school, or church
- in the broader community

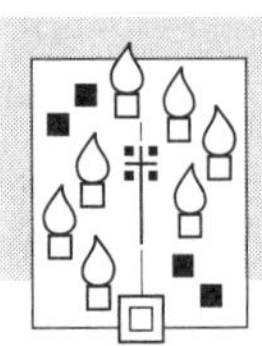

May 27, 2007

PENTECOST SUNDAY

Today's Focus: The Phlogiston of God

Wherever we wander, wherever we lay our heart, it's a struggle to be true to where the Spirit of God calls us, only usually we don't call it the Spirit of God. We say it's what we want to do with our lives, or our heart's desire, or our passion.

FIRST READING
Acts 2:1–11

When the time for Pentecost was fulfilled, they were all in one place together. And suddenly there came from the sky a noise like a strong driving wind, and it filled the entire house in which they were. Then there appeared to them tongues as of fire, which parted and came to rest on each one of them. And they were all filled with the Holy Spirit and began to speak in different tongues, as the Spirit enabled them to proclaim.

Now there were devout Jews from every nation under heaven staying in Jerusalem. At this sound, they gathered in a large crowd, but they were confused because each one heard them speaking in his own language. They were astounded, and in amazement they asked, "Are not all these people who are speaking Galileans? Then how does each of us hear them in his native language? We are Parthians, Medes, and Elamites, inhabitants of Mesopotamia, Judea and Cappadocia, Pontus and Asia, Phrygia and Pamphylia, Egypt and the districts of Libya near Cyrene, as well as travelers from Rome, both Jews and converts to Judaism, Cretans and Arabs, yet we hear them speaking in our own tongues of the mighty acts of God."

PSALM RESPONSE
Psalm 104:30

Lord, send out your Spirit, and renew the face of the earth.

SECOND READING
1 Corinthians 12: 3b–7, 12–13

Brothers and sisters: No one can say, "Jesus is Lord," except by the Holy Spirit. There are different kinds of spiritual gifts but the same Spirit; there are different forms of service but the same Lord; there are different workings but the same God who produces all of them in everyone. To each individual the manifestation of the Spirit is given for some benefit.

As a body is one though it has many parts, and all the parts of the body, though many, are one body, so also Christ. For in one Spirit we were all baptized into one body, whether Jews or Greeks, slaves or free persons, and we were all given to drink of one Spirit.

– or –

SECOND READING *Romans 8:8–17*

Brothers and sisters: Those who are in the flesh cannot please God. But you are not in the flesh; on the contrary, you are in the spirit, if only the Spirit of God dwells in you. Whoever does not have the Spirit of Christ does not belong to him. But if Christ is in you, although the body is dead because of sin, the spirit is alive because of righteousness. If the Spirit of the one who raised Jesus from the dead dwells in you, the one who raised Christ from the dead will give life to your mortal bodies also, through his Spirit that dwells in you. Consequently, brothers and sisters, we are not debtors to the flesh, to live according to the flesh. For if you live according to the flesh, you will die, but if by the Spirit you put to death the deeds of the body, you will live.

For those who are led by the Spirit of God are sons of God. For you did not receive a spirit of slavery to fall back into fear, but you received a Spirit of adoption, through whom we cry, "Abba, Father!" The Spirit himself bears witness with our spirit that we are children of God, and if children, then heirs, heirs of God and joint heirs with Christ, if only we suffer with him so that we may also be glorified with him.

GOSPEL *John 20:19–23*

On the evening of that first day of the week, when the doors were locked, where the disciples were, for fear of the Jews, Jesus came and stood in their midst and said to them, "Peace be with you." When he had said this, he showed them his hands and his side. The disciples rejoiced when they saw the Lord. Jesus said to them again, "Peace be with you. As the Father has sent me, so I send you." And when he had said this, he breathed on them and said to them, "Receive the Holy Spirit. Whose sins you forgive are forgiven them, and whose sins you retain are retained."

– or –

GOSPEL *John 14:15–16, 23b–26*

Jesus said to his disciples: "If you love me, you will keep my commandments. And I will ask the Father, and he will give you another Advocate to be with you always.

"Whoever loves me will keep my word, and my Father will love him, and we will come to him and make our dwelling with him. Those who do not love me do not keep my words; yet the word you hear is not mine but that of the Father who sent me.

"I have told you this while I am with you. The Advocate, the Holy Spirit whom the Father will send in my name, will teach you everything and remind you of all that I told you."

Understanding the Word

Pentecost was a major Jewish pilgrimage feast, recalling God's giving the Law to Moses. Awesome signs accompanied the appearance of Yahweh to Moses to establish the covenant. "Mount Sinai was all wrapped in smoke, for the LORD came down upon it in fire. The smoke rose from it as though from a furnace, and the whole mountain trembled violently" (Exodus 19:18). Similar signs appeared in the upper room on the Pentecost that we Christians celebrate. "[S]uddenly there came from the sky a noise like a strong driving wind, and it filled the entire house in which they were. Then there appeared to them tongues as of fire, which parted and came to rest on each one of them" (Acts 2:2–3).

Pentecost Sunday marks the birth of the church, the beginning of the New Covenant. As the Spirit came to these followers of Jesus, they were being commissioned to go out and proclaim the gospel. Their gift of tongues reversed the Tower of Babel scene (Genesis 11:1–9). There the one language was divided into many; on Pentecost the many languages represented were united into one by the intervention of God.

Saint Paul describes to the Romans today the effects of the Holy Spirit in the church. They are assured of final glorification with Jesus. "If the Spirit of the one who raised Jesus from the dead dwells in you, the one who raised Christ from the dead will give life to your mortal bodies also, through his Spirit that dwells in you" (Romans 8:11). To Saint Paul the only concern with eternal significance is whether one has the Spirit or not. The Apostle of the Gentiles assures the Romans, "For those who are led by the Spirit of God are [children] of God" (8:14).

Pentecost Sunday is extremely important for all Christians. The Holy Spirit gives life to the church and to all Christ's followers. Jesus had promised the coming of the Spirit during the Last Supper Discourse in John's Gospel. "I will ask the Father, and he will give you another Advocate to be with you always" (14:16). The Period of Jesus becomes the Period of the Church, the final period in salvation history with the permanent presence of the Holy Spirit.

Reflecting on the Word

In the Middle Ages, when science seemed to be stepsister to the arts, people thought that phlogiston was what made something burnable. The more phlogiston, the more readily flammable was the way they understood physics' inner workings. It explained why rocks did not burn and why straw readily did.

Though phlogiston has long been shelved, its theory is not so far removed from how the Spirit of God burns in our lives, nor is it far from the gifts that God's Spirit sets aflame in us. If some effort of ours glows with light and heat, it may be a sign of much Spirit, sort of like phlogiston. On the other hand, if in our effort to shine there's not even a spark, it's quite likely that that is not where the Spirit has settled into us. It might be better to pay attention then to some other aspect of life.

The struggle is to make sure that our imagined passion and where the Spirit of God wants us to be are one and the same so that the former does not cause us to stray from the latter. How does anyone know if they are where they should be? St. Paul says that the Spirit gives each of us our own dose of divine giftedness, our own spark with which to shine, but it's not given to us for our own glory or fun or feel-good self-image but for the good of others, for the community, for building up life. John's Gospel suggests one other such test—whether or not we're at peace. That, too, is the Spirit's gift.

CONSIDER/ DISCUSS:

- Name something that you are instinctively good at. How are you using it for the good of the community?
- Is there some longing that you need to relinquish simply because it's just not the gift you've been given?

Responding to the Word

As you and I go through life, we need to find out where the Spirit wants us to be. Often enough, however, it's not the same as where we would like to be, or sometimes even think we should be. It may be that at such times we're wrestling with the very Spirit of God.

Spend a few minutes in quiet prayer. Ask God to show you one (or more) ways that you may be called to respond to this week's scriptures—

- in your relationship with God
- with family and friends
- at work, school, or church
- in the broader community

Notes

Introduction to Ordinary Time II

Having celebrated the feast of Pentecost, the Church is now remembering liturgically that long period between Pentecost and the end of the world. The Gospel for the Thirty-third Sunday of this year will contain Jesus' reflections on the destruction of Jerusalem and the end of the world (Luke 21:5–19).

The Church will begin this liturgical period by celebrating the solemnity of the Most Holy Trinity, a new revelation given to the church by Jesus Christ. The following Sunday the liturgy remembers with gratitude the incredible gift of the Body and Blood of Christ, his continuing presence in our midst until the end of time.

The readings from the Gospel of Luke in the months ahead can be most helpful for one's spiritual life. Luke writes for Christians down through the ages, "so that you may realize the certainty of the teachings you have received" (Luke 1:4).

Prayer and the qualities of prayer will have a prominent place during this Ordinary Time. Jesus himself gives the example. "In those days he departed to the mountain to pray, and he spent the night in prayer to God" (Luke 6:12). The Our Father suggests confidence in prayer since we are addressing one who is our "Father" (11:2). Several parables of Christ teach the importance of persistence in prayer, the quality of prayer most stressed in Luke. The parable of the Pharisee and the tax collector makes it clear that humility is a critical attitude when praying (18:9–14). The account of the Samaritan leper who returns to give thanks to Jesus for his cure demonstrates that thanksgiving should also be a part of one's prayer life (17:11–19).

Jesus gives a wonderful teaching on God's willingness to forgive sins. Chapter 15 of Luke shows that God is not only willing to forgive, but that God will also forget the sins and rejoice with the penitent sinner (Luke 15:1–32). Jesus shows similar loving care for the poor and vulnerable, for anyone in need. In turn he uses the parables of the Good Samaritan (10:29–37) and the rich man and Lazarus (16:19–31) to insist that his followers must have love for all, despite any religious, racial, or economic differences.

The second or continuing reading in this final period of Year C will highlight several important New Testament letters. In Galatians Paul will defend the true teaching on justification in the face of false teachers. "If anyone preaches to you a gospel other than the one that you received, let that one be accursed!" (Galatians 1:9). Colossians will proclaim Jesus as "head of the body, the church" (Colossians 1:18). Hebrews is essentially a "message of encouragement" (Hebrews 13:22) for Christians in danger of becoming apostates. First and Second Timothy insist on teaching "the sound words of our Lord Jesus Christ" (1 Timothy 6:3) and provide practical advice for two of Paul's young disciples. Finally, 2 Thessalonians responds to mistaken concepts concerning the *parousia* (second coming) of Jesus.

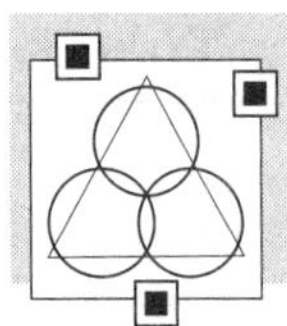

June 3, 2007

THE MOST HOLY TRINITY

Today's Focus: The Poetry of God

It sometimes seems that God may be a bit unsure whether our hearts can bear all that God wants to tell us in one sitting. So God says we'll hear it in bits and pieces, over the course of a lifetime. And God tells us not in words but in the happenings of our lives.

FIRST READING
Proverbs 8: 22–31

Thus says the wisdom of God:
"The LORD possessed me, the beginning of his ways,
  the forerunner of his prodigies of long ago;
from of old I was poured forth,
  at the first, before the earth.
When there were no depths I was brought forth,
  when there were no fountains or springs of water;
before the mountains were settled into place,
  before the hills, I was brought forth;
while as yet the earth and fields were not made,
  nor the first clods of the world.

"When the Lord established the heavens I was there,
  when he marked out the vault over the face of the deep;
when he made firm the skies above,
  when he fixed fast the foundations of the earth;
when he set for the sea its limit,
  so that the waters should not transgress his command;
then was I beside him as his craftsman,
  and I was his delight day by day,
playing before him all the while,
  playing on the surface of his earth;
  and I found delight in the human race."

PSALM RESPONSE
Psalm 8:2a

O Lord, our God, how wonderful your name in all the earth!

SECOND READING
Romans 5:1–5

Brothers and sisters: Therefore, since we have been justified by faith, we have peace with God through our Lord Jesus Christ, through whom we have gained access by faith to this grace in which we stand, and we boast in hope of the glory of God. Not only that, but we even boast of our afflictions, knowing that affliction produces endurance, and endurance, proven character, and proven character, hope, and hope does not disappoint, because the love of God has been poured out into our hearts through the Holy Spirit that has been given to us.

GOSPEL *John 16:12–15*

Jesus said to his disciples: "I have much more to tell you, but you cannot bear it now. But when he comes, the Spirit of truth, he will guide you to all truth. He will not speak on his own, but he will speak what he hears, and will declare to you the things that are coming. He will glorify me, because he will take from what is mine and declare it to you. Everything that the Father has is mine; for this reason I told you that he will take from what is mine and declare it to you."

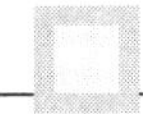

Understanding the Word

For some two thousand years belief in one God had been an essential teaching for the descendants of Abraham. Then when Jesus appeared on the scene it was revealed that while there is in fact one God, there are three persons in that God. Not surprisingly, it took the church some time to clarify its teachings concerning the Trinity.

Today's Gospel indicates how the early church and Christians would come to accept the mystery of the Holy Trinity. "But when he comes, the Spirit of truth, he will guide you to all truth" (John 16:13). The Spirit will not produce new revelation, but will clarify and continually apply the words and deeds of Jesus, including his teachings about the Trinity.

There are Trinitarian texts in the New Testament. Possibly the clearest text is in the Gospel of Matthew: "baptizing them [all nations] in the name of the Father, and of the Son, and of the holy Spirit" (Matthew 28:19). A familiar text from its use in the liturgy is found in 2 Corinthians, "The grace of the Lord Jesus Christ and the love of God and the fellowship of the holy Spirit be with all of you" (2 Corinthians 13:13).

Today's second reading (Romans 5:1–5) begins the second major part of this letter of Paul. He is outlining the wonderful results of justification: "peace with God through our Lord Jesus Christ" (5:1), and "hope of the glory of God" (5:2). Saint Paul makes clear that all these benefits for the believer are possible because "the love of God has been poured out into our hearts through the holy Spirit that has been given to us" (5:5). It is noteworthy that Paul mentions all three persons of the Trinity as he describes their connection with our justification and its great benefits.

Clearly no texts can make possible a human understanding of the Trinitarian mystery. But the church used the interpretation of these texts with the guidance of the Holy Spirit to proclaim the Triune God. Today's readings promise that the Spirit of truth sent by Christ will continue to enable Christians to develop a spiritual life based on the actions and teachings of Jesus.

Reflecting on the Word

Most of us do not like anyone messing with our poetry, whatever our form of poetry. Some people grow impatient with films that do not follow the story line of the original novel. Musicians take issue with interpretations of classic compositions. Children are upset with parents who change the ending of a bedtime tale or skip a scene or even a line. There are people passionate about those who dare to colorize early black-and-white films. How we do the poetry of religious ritual has caused people of faith to leave the Church. Christmas Midnight Mass rescheduled to 10:00 p.m. can and has brought Christmas to ruin. In short, "Don't mess with anyone's poetry."

Why all this on the feast of the Trinity? Because the scriptures paint God as a poet. If singers sing and dancers dance, if builders build and toddlers toddle, then poets poet, and God poets best of all. God poets with happenings instead of with words, as the reading from Proverbs attests. God poets with daydreams and fantasy and all sorts of pretend because when you're very young that's all you can hear. God poets with wisdom, the sort that takes many years to grow because sometimes people grow so old that that's all they have left—lots and lots of wisdom, and so that's what they understand best. God poets with love so that hardened hearts can be cracked open and hear a new song. God even poets with death, just so we'll be sure not to miss resurrection when it happens. Don't you see? God's a poet because there's no other way to tell us about it all. So don't mess with anybody's poetry.

CONSIDER/ DISCUSS:

- Pick a symbol for yourself of the God you believe in. Make it poetic. Maybe dew because God saturates all creation. Or music because God is the song in your life. Or wind because God can't really be controlled. What's your poetic symbol for God?
- If God speaks in bits and pieces, what is the most recent bit you have heard from God?
- Sometimes poetry is difficult to grasp. What about God can you not yet understand?

Responding to the Word

Because life is so awesome, God tells it in poetry, in glimpses of spirit as in Holy Spirit. Life is better understood as a poem than as a news report.

Spend a few minutes in quiet prayer. Ask God to show you one (or more) ways that you may be called to respond to this week's scriptures—

- in your relationship with God
- with family and friends
- at work, school, or church
- in the broader community

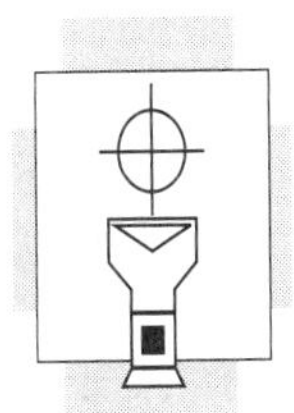

June 10, 2007

THE MOST HOLY BODY AND BLOOD OF CHRIST

Today's Focus: Making Eucharist Out of Our Lives

One of the curious perplexities of our lives seems to be that more comes forth from our want than from our abundance, more from our meager offerings of life and love than from those times when it seems we have much of both life and love.

FIRST READING *Genesis 14: 18–20*

In those days, Melchizedek, king of Salem, brought out bread and wine, and being a priest of God Most High, he blessed Abram with these words:

"Blessed be Abram by God Most High,
the creator of heaven and earth;
and blessed be God Most High,
who delivered your foes into your hand."

Then Abram gave him a tenth of everything.

PSALM RESPONSE *Psalm 110:4b*

You are a priest for ever, in the line of Melchizedek.

SECOND READING *1 Corinthians 11: 23–26*

Brothers and sisters: I received from the Lord what I also handed on to you, that the Lord Jesus, on the night he was handed over, took bread, and, after he had given thanks, broke it and said, "This is my body that is for you. Do this in remembrance of me." In the same way also the cup, after supper, saying, "This cup is the new covenant in my blood. Do this, as often as you drink it, in remembrance of me." For as often as you eat this bread and drink the cup, you proclaim the death of the Lord until he comes.

GOSPEL *Luke 9:11b–17*

Jesus spoke to the crowds about the kingdom of God, and he healed those who needed to be cured. As the day was drawing to a close, the Twelve approached him and said, "Dismiss the crowd so that they can go to the surrounding villages and farms and find lodging and provisions; for we are in a deserted place here." He said to them, "Give them some food yourselves." They replied, "Five loaves and two fish are all we have, unless we ourselves go and buy food for all these people." Now the men there numbered about five thousand. Then he said to his disciples, "Have them sit down in groups of about fifty." They did so and made them all sit down. Then taking the five loaves and the two fish, and looking up to heaven, he said the blessing over them, broke them, and gave them to the disciples to set before the crowd. They all ate and were satisfied. And when the leftover fragments were picked up, they filled twelve wicker baskets.

Understanding the Word

Today's reading from 1 Corinthians is the earliest literary account of the institution of the Eucharist, coming some ten years before any Gospel was composed. Writing from Ephesus about AD 55, Paul has many concerns, including the improper observance of the Eucharist. To counteract these situations, especially the divisions in the community, he writes this long letter. He insists that the proper understanding of the Eucharist will help bring unity and peace.

One special aspect of this narration is the fact that Jesus asks for remembrance of him after his words over both the bread and the wine. Remembrance of the Lord should remind the Corinthians that the Lord wanted them to manifest love for all with no exceptions. Jesus gives the perfect example. He will give his body for all and shed his blood for our salvation. In these few verses Paul uses "Lord" three times, the title connected with the resurrected Christ, the Son of God. Paul wants his converts to realize that the Eucharist is their way of meeting regularly with the Risen One, the source of spiritual strength given to all Christians throughout this final period of salvation history.

Jesus also introduces the concept of the new covenant, the new relationship between God and all people. "This cup is the new covenant in my blood" (1 Corinthians 11:25). He has in mind two Old Testament situations. Moses at the institution of the covenant said, "This is the blood of the covenant" (Exodus 24:8). The prophet Jeremiah wrote, "The days are coming, says the Lord, when I will make a new covenant with the house of Israel and the house of Judah" (Jeremiah 31:31).

The passage also has an eschatological thrust. Jesus says, "For as often as you eat this bread and drink the cup, you proclaim the death of the Lord until he comes" (1 Corinthians 11:26). Sharing in the Eucharist unites us to Jesus in this life, but also makes it possible for us to share in the glory of Jesus when he returns at the end of time.

Reflecting on the Word

Milwaukee's new art museum houses a collection of family photographs by Milton Rogovins—not of his family, but of thirty or forty families from a six-block area in the Lower West Side of Buffalo, New York. Arranged in triptychs, each family's story is poignantly told by a simple series of three family photographs taken over the span of twenty years.

In the end, beyond the thinning hair and thickening waists and fraying furniture, more than anything it is the weary eyes that tell the stories of these blue-collar, hard-working families, who seem to wonder how it was they ever came to find themselves in such a third and final photograph, as if they never could have dreamt it so. Yet each photograph also seems to suggest some foggy musing over how they must have been fed with so much more than simply gruel. I wonder, too, if that is not how parents of every age sometimes feel, when they feel that they've given all the love they have. And for some crazy reason it seems to be enough to keep everyone from starving for one more day.

It's at such times, too, that we become believers once again, or maybe for the first time. It's in moments when we didn't think we had enough to feed even ourselves that the little we had feeds however many thousands knocking at our door, with enough leftovers to fill baskets for at least a part of one more go-round—all from five loaves and two fish. And who would have thought it could be done? Which is why we come to faith, then: just because we never thought it could have been, yet still it was and is.

CONSIDER/ DISCUSS:

- When you hear the phrase "the body and blood of Christ," do you first think of the gifts upon the table or of those who have gathered around the table?
- When in your life has abundance come from meager input on your part? Was it coincidence or God or fate?

Responding to the Word

Like the Lord Jesus, what we are about is taking our simple lives in our hands, looking up to heaven with what we hold, blessing our lives, breaking them open, and giving them over to be shared—all of which is to say that what we are about is being eucharist for one another.

Spend a few minutes in quiet prayer. Ask God to show you one (or more) ways that you may be called to respond to this week's scriptures—

- in your relationship with God
- with family and friends
- at work, school, or church
- in the broader community

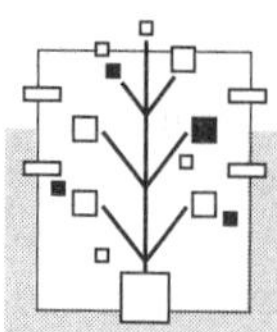

June 17, 2007

ELEVENTH SUNDAY IN ORDINARY TIME

Today's Focus: The Mystery of Mercy

Life is mysterious. It's been observed that the people we get angry at the most are also the people we love the most. Somehow, if we are fortunate, out of that mélange of mixed emotions and conflicting dynamics we learn how to give and receive love. Still, we don't always understand how.

FIRST READING
2 Samuel 12: 7–10, 13

Nathan said to David: "Thus says the LORD God of Israel: 'I anointed you king of Israel. I rescued you from the hand of Saul. I gave you your lord's house and your lord's wives for your own. I gave you the house of Israel and of Judah. And if this were not enough, I could count up for you still more. Why have you spurned the LORD and done evil in his sight? You have cut down Uriah the Hittite with the sword; you took his wife as your own, and him you killed with the sword of the Ammonites. Now, therefore, the sword shall never depart from your house, because you have despised me and have taken the wife of Uriah to be your wife.' " Then David said to Nathan, "I have sinned against the LORD." Nathan answered David: "The LORD on his part has forgiven your sin: you shall not die."

PSALM RESPONSE
Psalm 32:5c

Lord, forgive the wrong I have done.

SECOND READING
Galatians 2:16, 19–21

Brothers and sisters: We who know that a person is not justified by works of the law but through faith in Jesus Christ, even we have believed in Christ Jesus that we may be justified by faith in Christ and not by works of the law, because by works of the law no one will be justified. For through the law I died to the law, that I might live for God. I have been crucified with Christ; yet I live, no longer I, but Christ lives in me; insofar as I now live in the flesh, I live by faith in the Son of God who has loved me and given himself up for me. I do not nullify the grace of God; for if justification comes through the law, then Christ died for nothing.

In the shorter form of the reading, the passage in brackets is omitted.

GOSPEL
Luke 7:36—8:3 or 7:36–50

A Pharisee invited Jesus to dine with him, and he entered the Pharisee's house and reclined at table. Now there was a sinful woman in the city who learned that he was at table in the house of the Pharisee. Bringing an alabaster flask of ointment, she stood behind him at his feet weeping and began to bathe his feet with her tears. Then she wiped them with her hair, kissed them, and anointed them with the ointment. When the Pharisee who had invited him saw this he said to himself, "If this man were a prophet, he would know who and what sort of woman this is who is touching him, that she is a sinner." Jesus said to him in reply, "Simon, I have something to say to you." "Tell me, teacher," he said. "Two people were in debt to a certain creditor; one owed five hundred days' wages and the other owed fifty. Since they were unable to repay the debt, he forgave it for both. Which of them will love him more?" Simon said in reply, "The one, I suppose, whose larger debt was forgiven." He said to him, "You have judged rightly."

Then he turned to the woman and said to Simon, "Do you see this woman? When I entered your house, you did not give me water for my feet, but she has bathed them with her tears and wiped them with her hair. You did not give me a kiss, but she has not ceased kissing my feet since the time I entered. You did not anoint my head with oil, but she anointed my feet with ointment. So I tell you, her many sins have been forgiven because she has shown great love. But the one to whom little is forgiven, loves little." He said to her, "Your sins are forgiven." The others at table said to themselves, "Who is this who even forgives sins?" But he said to the woman, "Your faith has saved you; go in peace."

[Afterward he journeyed from one town and village to another, preaching and proclaiming the good news of the kingdom of God. Accompanying him were the Twelve and some women who had been cured of evil spirits and infirmities, Mary, called Magdalene, from whom seven demons had gone out, Joanna, the wife of Herod's steward Chuza, Susanna, and many others who provided for them out of their resources.]

Understanding the Word

The Gospel of Luke has been called the Gospel of Women. Today's Gospel reading provides strong reasons for that title. In two separate incidents women play a key role. Luke 7:36–50 relates the encounter of Jesus with a sinful woman. He is the guest of a Pharisee named Simon, who had not shown Jesus the normal gestures of respect for a guest, namely a kiss, washing the feet, and anointing the head with oil.

The woman of the story appears and performs all these gestures with great love. She "began to bathe his feet with her tears. Then she wiped them with her hair, kissed them, and anointed them with the ointment" (Luke 7:38).

The Pharisee sees Jesus as a teacher and suspects that he may be a prophet. But a true prophet would know that the woman is a sinner. Jesus responds by showing that he knows exactly who the woman is and also knows the very thoughts of his host. He then teaches a great lesson on love and forgiveness. The woman's signs of love show that she is a woman of faith, who realizes that God has forgiven her. She sees Jesus as God's agent and expresses her deep gratitude. The self-righteous Simon fails to realize his need for repentance and forgiveness.

The second part of today's Gospel (Luke 8:1–3) introduces the women from Galilee who accompany Jesus as he preaches "the good news of the kingdom of God" (8:1). Having been healed by Jesus, they will be his faithful followers, supporting him and the Twelve with their own resources. Jesus is showing his openness to women despite the contrary prevailing attitudes of that time. They will go with their Lord to Jerusalem and stand beneath the cross of Jesus (23:49) and will be the first to hear of the Resurrection (24:9–11).

Three of the women are mentioned by name: Mary Magdalene, Joanna, and Susanna. Father Joseph Fitzmyer notes that in the New Testament there is "no evidence whatsoever that the 'possession' of Mary Magdalene was the result of personal sinfulness" (*Anchor Bible*, "The Gospel According to Luke," vol. 28, p. 688). Joanna is the wife of Herod's steward, but nothing further is known of Susanna.

Reflecting on the Word

My father was a better father than I was a son. He worked hard and worried hard and put up with me hard. And as I look back on it now, I willingly took it all in.

By the time I was eighteen it was I who worked hard, mostly to keep my father at a distance, as sons so often do, because then I thought I had to find my own way through life and make my own mistakes and ford life's rivers with my own boat. So when he asked how things were going, I said, "Fine." And how was school? "Oh, school was school." And my friends? "Hadn't seen 'em."

It's probably true for most of us. Our fathers were better fathers than we were ever sons or daughters. And yet by some strange turn of grace we grew into people who have learned how to love, though often enough imperfectly, and into people who do suffer for others, though not without an occasional grimace or silent cringe.

Yet none of that happens very cleanly. It's messy and confusing and often enough cluttered with our own sin, and consequently with someone's forgiveness. Nevertheless, it is how David's heart was turned, because he had been forgiven much. And it is how Mary became an extravagant lover, because she was forgiven much. And it is how fathers and mothers teach us how to love, because we come to know their forgiveness. It's all an image of our God's forgiveness that Jesus came to proclaim, and so our hearts are moved to love.

CONSIDER/ DISCUSS:

- Remember a time when your father may have forgiven you. Thank your father, even if he is not present or no longer alive.
- How has forgiveness nurtured love in your life? How are you different because you have been forgiven?
- What is your estimation of how our society forgives?

Responding to the Word

The nudge to forgive finds itself felt in many nooks and crannies of our lives. Sometimes it is very obvious, but more often it means continuing to care about a person in spite of our feelings. It can be quite personal, but it can also be about issues and events in our society and community.

Spend a few minutes in quiet prayer. Ask God to show you one (or more) ways that you may be called to respond to this week's scriptures—

- in your relationship with God
- with family and friends
- at work, school, or church
- in the broader community

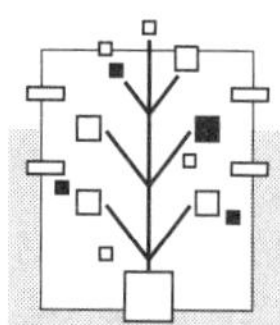

June 24, 2004

THE NATIVITY OF ST. JOHN THE BAPTIST

Today's Focus: The Divine Thread

Our lives hang by a thread, one common thread to which all else is tethered, a thread that holds it all together. Life unfolds more smoothly when we are able to recognize that thread and honor it.

FIRST READING
Isaiah 49:1–6

Hear me, O coastlands,
  listen, O distant peoples.
The Lord called me from birth,
  from my mother's womb he gave me my name.
He made of me a sharp-edged sword
  and concealed me in the shadow of his arm.
He made me a polished arrow,
  in his quiver he hid me.
You are my servant, he said to me,
  Israel, through whom I show my glory.

Though I thought I had toiled in vain,
  and for nothing, uselessly, spent my strength,
yet my reward is with the LORD,
  my recompense is with my God.
For now the LORD has spoken
  who formed me as his servant from the womb,
that Jacob may be brought back to him
  and Israel gathered to him;
and I am made glorious in the sight of the Lord,
  and my God is now my strength!
It is too little, he says, for you to be my servant,
  to raise up the tribes of Jacob,
    and restore the survivors of Israel;
I will make you a light to the nations,
  that my salvation may reach to the ends of the earth.

PSALM RESPONSE
Psalm 139:14a

I praise you for I am wonderfully made.

SECOND READING
Acts 13:22–26

In those days, Paul said: "God raised up David as their king; of him he testified, 'I have found David, son of Jesse, a man after my own heart; he will carry out my every wish.' From this man's descendants God, according to his promise, has brought to Israel a savior, Jesus. John heralded his coming by proclaiming a baptism of repentance to all the people of Israel; and as John was completing his course, he would say, 'What do you suppose that I am? I am not he. Behold, one is coming after me; I am not worthy to unfasten the sandals of his feet.'

"My brothers, children of the family of Abraham, and those others among you who are God-fearing, to us this word of salvation has been sent."

GOSPEL
Luke 1:57–66, 80

When the time arrived for Elizabeth to have her child she gave birth to a son. Her neighbors and relatives heard that the Lord had shown his great mercy toward her, and they rejoiced with her. When they came on the eighth day to circumcise the child, they were going to call him Zechariah after his father, but his mother said in reply, "No. He will be called John." But they answered her, "There is no one among your relatives who has this name." So they made signs, asking his father what he wished him to be called. He asked for a tablet and wrote, "John is his name," and all were amazed. Immediately his mouth was opened, his tongue freed, and he spoke blessing God. Then fear came upon all their neighbors, and all these matters were discussed throughout the hill country of Judea. All who heard these things took them to heart, saying, "What, then, will this child be?" For surely the hand of the Lord was with him.

The child grew and became strong in spirit, and he was in the desert until the day of his manifestation to Israel.

Understanding the Word

The birth of John the Baptist can truly be called a blessed event. It was a blessing for his mother, Elizabeth, because it removed the stigma of barrenness. It was a blessing for his father, Zechariah, because it led to healing of his muteness. But more importantly, it was a blessing for all of Israel, because John would prepare the way for Jesus, the "glory for your people Israel" (Luke 2:32). It was a blessing for all followers of Jesus since John also prepared the way for the "light for revelation to the Gentiles" (2:32).

This blessedness is clear from the name given Elizabeth's child in today's Gospel. The name John has the meaning "Yahweh has shown favor." As with the name Jesus, this name came to Zechariah through the intervention of the angel Gabriel (Luke 1:13), indicating the importance of the name. Jesus himself gives testimony to the fact that John lived up to his name. Jesus refers to the Baptist as "a burning and shining lamp" (John 5:35) and also says, "I tell you, among those born of women, no one is greater than John" (Luke 7:28).

Joy characterizes the birth of John as it also will the birth of Jesus. The angel promised Zechariah, "[Y]ou will have joy and gladness, and many will rejoice at his birth" (Luke 1:14). These words find fulfillment: "Her neighbors and relatives heard that the Lord had shown his great mercy toward her, and they rejoiced with her" (1:58). The angel of the Lord told the shepherds when Jesus was born, "I proclaim to you good news of great joy that will be for all the people" (2:10).

The circumcision, mentioned in today's Gospel (1:59) is important. Since the time of Abraham circumcision has been the sign of the covenant, indicating that one is joined to the people of Israel. Luke places great importance on this because he wants to show that both John and Jesus were definitely part of the people of Israel. In the Acts of the Apostles Luke will make clear that Christianity developed directly from Judaism.

Reflecting on the Word

One of the great Hasidic tales tells of the Rebbe Zushya on his deathbed. Reflecting upon his life, he began to lament to his friends gathered around him that he had not accomplished more than he had; how little it indeed all seemed. One of those present asked if he was perhaps afraid now of how God would judge him. The rebbe was about to say "Yes," but then thought a moment and said, "No, because when I appear before the Almighty, I will not be asked, 'Why were you not Moses?' I will only be asked, 'Why were you not Zushya?' "

There is indeed a thread that runs through each of our lives, a sort of Zushya thread that each of us must discover and to which each of us needs be faithful. In its own way it is the thread of that which we are called to be. In many ways it is so much more than a vocation, and still it may very well be the ultimate vocation that we must live out.

One's vocation may be to be married, or be a parent, or manage a business, or teach, or heal, or so many other worthy roles to live out. Yet within that calling is woven a thread. It may be to be a bridge builder among factions or one who listens and bears burdens or one who leads with wisdom and courage. That Zushya thread can be lived out in any vocation—in business or home care or school or whatever. Yet from the very beginning it is the thread upon which our entire life hangs—as it did for Isaiah and for John the Baptist and for Jesus, and for each of us as well.

CONSIDER/ DISCUSS:

- What is the thread that gives understanding and meaning to your life?
- At what point in your life did you begin to realize what the Zushya thread was for you?

Responding to the Word

There is a wholeness to life, a common thread woven through all that we are about. For each of us, then, the task is to live out what God has set for us to be, something so much more than appearances would suggest.

Spend a few minutes in quiet prayer. Ask God to show you one (or more) ways that you may be called to respond to this week's scriptures—

- in your relationship with God
- with family and friends
- at work, school, or church
- in the broader community

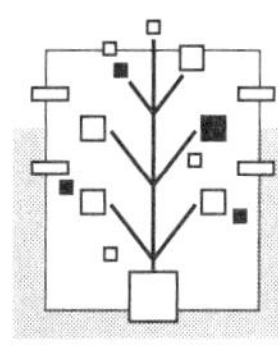

July 1, 2007

THIRTEENTH SUNDAY IN ORDINARY TIME

Today's Focus: To Live Deliberately

It matters to what and to whom we commit ourselves—whether or not we marry and if we do to whom, whether or not we have children, what it is to which we give over the energy of our labors, what dreams we allow ourselves to be driven by, and ultimately the extent to which we allow faith to shape our lives. It all matters.

FIRST READING
1 Kings 19:16b, 19–21

The LORD said to Elijah: "You shall anoint Elisha, son of Shaphat of Abel-meholah, as prophet to succeed you."

Elijah set out and came upon Elisha, son of Shaphat, as he was plowing with twelve yoke of oxen; he was following the twelfth. Elijah went over to him and threw his cloak over him. Elisha left the oxen, ran after Elijah, and said, "Please, let me kiss my father and mother goodbye, and I will follow you." Elijah answered, "Go back! Have I done anything to you?" Elisha left him, and taking the yoke of oxen, slaughtered them; he used the plowing equipment for fuel to boil their flesh, and gave it to his people to eat. Then Elisha left and followed Elijah as his attendant.

PSALM RESPONSE
Psalm 16:5a

You are my inheritance, O Lord.

SECOND READING
Galatians 5:1, 13–18

Brothers and sisters: For freedom Christ set us free; so stand firm and do not submit again to the yoke of slavery.

For you were called for freedom, brothers and sisters. But do not use this freedom as an opportunity for the flesh; rather, serve one another through love. For the whole law is fulfilled in one statement, namely, *You shall love your neighbor as yourself.* But if you go on biting and devouring one another, beware that you are not consumed by one another.

I say, then: live by the Spirit and you will certainly not gratify the desire of the flesh. For the flesh has desires against the Spirit, and the Spirit against the flesh; these are opposed to each other, so that you may not do what you want. But if you are guided by the Spirit, you are not under the law.

GOSPEL
Luke 9:51–62

When the days for Jesus' being taken up were fulfilled, he resolutely determined to journey to Jerusalem, and he sent messengers ahead of him. On the way they entered a Samaritan village to prepare for his reception there, but they would not welcome him because the destination of his journey was Jerusalem. When the disciples James and John saw this they asked, "Lord, do you want us to call down fire from heaven to consume them?" Jesus turned and rebuked them, and they journeyed to another village.

As they were proceeding on their journey someone said to him, "I will follow you wherever you go." Jesus answered him, "Foxes have dens and birds of the sky have nests, but the Son of Man has nowhere to rest his head."

And to another he said, "Follow me." But he replied, "Lord, let me go first and bury my father." But he answered him, "Let the dead bury their dead. But you, go and proclaim the kingdom of God." And another said, "I will follow you, Lord, but first let me say farewell to my family at home." To him Jesus said, "No one who sets a hand to the plow and looks to what was left behind is fit for the kingdom of God."

Understanding the Word

The Synoptic Gospels (Matthew, Mark, and Luke) compress the public life of Jesus into one year with just one trip to Jerusalem. The Gospel of John has three trips to that city and gives the basis for a three-year ministry of Jesus. The Synoptic Gospels follow the outline used by the early preachers of the gospel. The outline began with John the Baptist and the baptism of Jesus. Then after the ministry of Jesus in Galilee, the journey to Jerusalem followed, ending with the events of Holy Week.

In today's Gospel from Luke, the author uses strong prophetic language to indicate the determination of the Lord to go to Jerusalem, the city of his destiny. There he will complete the work given to him by the Father: his death, resurrection, and ascension. "When the days for Jesus' being taken up were fulfilled, he resolutely determined to journey to Jerusalem" (Luke 9:51). The long journey that follows gives Jesus the opportunity to teach his disciples so that they will become reliable and well-informed witnesses to him after the Ascension.

In today's Gospel, the residents of a Samaritan village reject Jesus because he is going to Jerusalem. There was a deep hatred between Jews and Samaritans at the time of Jesus. But he rebukes his followers for wanting to punish them. He will often make it clear that he came to save everyone, that universal salvation is his primary goal.

In the final episode of today's Gospel, Jesus demands a firm commitment from those who would be his followers. Even the filial obligation of burying one's parent must yield to the urgency of proclaiming the kingdom of God. His difficult statement "Let the dead bury their dead" (9:60) means that those who are spiritually dead, who do not accept Jesus, should bury those who are physically dead. He then turns to the man who had offered to follow him, saying, "But you, go and proclaim the kingdom of God" (9:60). In today's first reading Elisha gives an example of being willing to leave his former way of life to share in the prophetic mission of Elijah.

Reflecting on the Word

The preamble of our Constitution states what we as a nation intend to be about.

"We the people of the United States, in order to form a more perfect union, establish justice, insure domestic tranquility, provide for the common defence, promote the general welfare, and secure the blessings of liberty to ourselves and our posterity, do ordain and establish this Constitution for the United States of America." In stating what we as a nation propose as our tasks, we are proclaiming that to which we intend to commit ourselves. Indeed, one knows who one is by one's commitments.

Somewhere in the course of our personal lives each of us comes to face the question of commitment, to its risks and its unknowns. Some, out of fear, turn away. Others, because they seek comfort, refuse the challenge. Still others, too enamored of the banquet of choices before them, never decide and so never commit. Finally there are also those who step into the swirling darkness and say yes, simply because they realize only too well that if they do not, a life of any significance will be less likely from that very moment onward.

It is what drove Henry David Thoreau to Walden, in search of a purpose for which to live. "I went to the woods because I wished to live deliberately, to front only the essential facts of life, and see if I could not learn what it had to teach, and not when I came to die, discover that I had not lived. I did not wish to live what was not life, living is so dear, nor did I wish to practise resignation, unless it was quite necessary. I wanted to live deep and suck out all the marrow of life, to live so sturdily and Spartan-like as to put to rout all that was not life" (*Walden*, 1854).

CONSIDER/ DISCUSS:

- Make a list of your commitments, the ones that entail a cost on your part. Do you like what you see? Is anything missing? Should any be discarded?
- In what ways and to what extent are you committed to God? To the Lord Jesus? To the call of faith?

Responding to the Word

What we commit ourselves to matters. Conversely, looking back with longing dilutes the present and consequently the future as well. As believers, it is the vision of Jesus that continually shapes our present and future without disparaging our past.

Spend a few minutes in quiet prayer. Ask God to show you one (or more) ways that you may be called to respond to this week's scriptures—

- in your relationship with God
- with family and friends
- at work, school, or church
- in the broader community

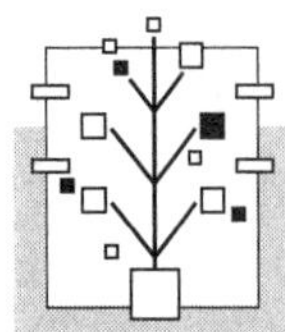

July 8, 2007

FOURTEENTH SUNDAY IN ORDINARY TIME

Today's Focus: A Restless Itch

There seems to be an instinct sewn into the fabric of who we are that moves us outward. Some folks need to be a success. Others need to make a difference. Still others need to mix it up in life. Something there will not leave us content.

FIRST READING
Isaiah 66: 10–14c

Thus says the LORD:
Rejoice with Jerusalem and be glad because of her,
all you who love her;
exult, exult with her,
all you who were mourning over her!
Oh, that you may suck fully
of the milk of her comfort,
that you may nurse with delight
at her abundant breasts!
For thus says the LORD:
Lo, I will spread prosperity over Jerusalem like a river,
and the wealth of the nations like an overflowing torrent.
As nurslings, you shall be carried in her arms,
and fondled in her lap;
as a mother comforts her child,
so will I comfort you;
in Jerusalem you shall find your comfort.

When you see this, your heart shall rejoice
and your bodies flourish like the grass;
the LORD's power shall be known to his servants.

PSALM RESPONSE
Psalm 66:1

Let all the earth cry out to God with joy.

SECOND READING
Galatians 6: 14–18

Brothers and sisters: May I never boast except in the cross of our Lord Jesus Christ, through which the world has been crucified to me, and I to the world. For neither does circumcision mean anything, nor does uncircumcision, but only a new creation. Peace and mercy be to all who follow this rule and to the Israel of God.

From now on, let no one make troubles for me; for I bear the marks of Jesus on my body.

The grace of our Lord Jesus Christ be with your spirit, brothers and sisters. Amen.

In the shorter form of the reading, the passage in brackets is omitted.

GOSPEL *Luke 10:1–12, 17–20 or 10:1–9*

At that time the Lord appointed seventy-two others whom he sent ahead of him in pairs to every town and place he intended to visit. He said to them, "The harvest is abundant but the laborers are few; so ask the master of the harvest to send out laborers for his harvest. Go on your way; behold, I am sending you like lambs among wolves. Carry no money bag, no sack, no sandals; and greet no one along the way. Into whatever house you enter, first say, 'Peace to this household.' If a peaceful person lives there, your peace will rest on him; but if not, it will return to you. Stay in the same house and eat and drink what is offered to you, for the laborer deserves his payment. Do not move about from one house to another. Whatever town you enter and they welcome you, eat what is set before you, cure the sick in it and say to them, 'The kingdom of God is at hand for you.' [Whatever town you enter and they do not receive you, go out into the streets and say, 'The dust of your town that clings to our feet, even that we shake off against you.' Yet know this: the kingdom of God is at hand. I tell you, it will be more tolerable for Sodom on that day than for that town."

The seventy-two returned rejoicing, and said, "Lord, even the demons are subject to us because of your name." Jesus said, "I have observed Satan fall like lightning from the sky. Behold, I have given you the power to 'tread upon serpents' and scorpions and upon the full force of the enemy and nothing will harm you. Nevertheless, do not rejoice because the spirits are subject to you, but rejoice because your names are written in heaven."]

Understanding the Word

As Jesus proceeds to Jerusalem, he sends seventy(-two) disciples in pairs to prepare the way for him by preaching and healing (manuscript evidence for Luke's Gospel is evenly divided between seventy and seventy-two). Recall that Yahweh gives some of the spirit of Moses to seventy elders (see Numbers 11:16–17). Here Jesus endows his disciples with his authority and power to heal. He wants them not only to work in the abundant harvest, but also to pray for more laborers.

In chapter nine Jesus sends out the Twelve in a similar fashion (Luke 9:1–6). The sending of the seventy(-two) has a stronger sense of urgency and rejection. Because of the urgency, the disciples are not to be distracted by material things or ordinary greetings. They are to concentrate on their work of proclaiming peace to households. Peace is an important word in the Bible, often associated by Luke with salvation. The Hebrew background stresses completion, perfection found in God and all God's blessings.

There will be rejection, but the proclaiming must continue: "The kingdom of God is at hand for you" (10:9). Sodom is given as a terrible example of an immoral city that treated immigrants cruelly and was destroyed by God (see Genesis 19:1–29). A similar fate awaits those towns that refuse to accept the disciples sent by Jesus. In doing so, they reject also Jesus and the Father who sent him.

As the disciples return, they rejoice that they were able to expel demons because of Jesus' name. Jesus commends the effectiveness of their work by saying, "I have observed Satan fall like lightning from the sky" (10:18). This replacement of the dominion of Satan and the forces of evil by the kingdom of God is a good description of Jesus' mission. Jesus promises even greater power over evil. However, the real reason for joy is not that power, but "because your names are written in heaven" (10:20). The concept of a heavenly registry is an Old Testament theme. "At that time your people shall escape, everyone who is found written in the book" (Daniel 12:1).

Reflecting on the Word

As it happened, they were both named Thomas (the name means "twin"), though the older went by Tom and the younger by Thomas. Their only tangible link was that they both knew me, but beyond that I'm fairly sure neither ever knew the other or the other's story.

Tom, the elder Thomas, was married to Sue. They married right after college and soon thereafter began a family, a boy and two girls. By the time I met Sue and Tom, their family had been pushed from the nest, so it was just the two of them again. They retired, and that's where the story tells a tale. In retirement Sue was content to enjoy life. Having endured the struggles of raising a family, she simply wanted to move to sunny Florida, play golf, and gather with friends. Tom, on the other hand, was restless. He wasn't ready to back away from making a difference, as he put it. He wanted to be involved in life and in people's growth. In the end that difference generated too much heat between the two of them. The tension ended their marriage in divorce.

Thomas, the younger one, came to me thinking he might want to be a priest. He wasn't certain, but as a college sophomore he looked at his life and said to me, "I want to make a difference with my life. I want to die for something and not just live."

Two Thomases, one story. Both felt an impulse to enter into life and change it. Whether they would succeed mattered little to either. They simply needed to offer others a possibility for life. That instinct of theirs is how God sends people into the world and makes life flourish.

CONSIDER/ DISCUSS:

- When have you felt pushed to make a difference? Toward what does your restlessness drive you?
- The Gospels do not insist that we change anyone or convert them. They simply ask us to be the presence of peace. How comfortable are you with that?

Responding to the Word

Like the disciples sent out by Jesus, life cannot help but burst outward. If it goes flat, like a bottle of soda long opened, something seems not right about it at all.

Spend a few minutes in quiet prayer. Ask God to show you one (or more) ways that you may be called to respond to this week's scriptures—

- in your relationship with God
- with family and friends
- at work, school, or church
- in the broader community

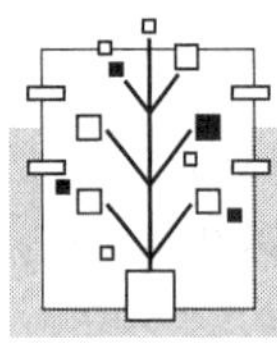

July 15, 2007

FIFTEENTH SUNDAY IN ORDINARY TIME

Today's Focus: The Mystery of Human Motivation

We humans are indeed a mysterious lot. We wonder why others do what they do, and even find ourselves perplexed over our own behavior. Where does it all come from, we wonder?

FIRST READING
Deuteronomy 30: 10–14

Moses said to the people: "If only you would heed the voice of the LORD, your God, and keep his commandments and statutes that are written in this book of the law, when you return to the LORD, your God, with all your heart and all your soul.

"For this command that I enjoin on you today is not too mysterious and remote for you. It is not up in the sky, that you should say, 'Who will go up in the sky to get it for us and tell us of it, that we may carry it out?' Nor is it across the sea, that you should say, 'Who will cross the sea to get it for us and tell us of it, that we may carry it out?' No, it is something very near to you, already in your mouths and in your hearts; you have only to carry it out."

PSALM RESPONSE
Psalm 69:33 or Psalm 19:9a

Turn to the Lord in your need, and you will live.

Your words, Lord, are spirit and life.

SECOND READING
Colossians 1: 15–20

Christ Jesus is the image of the invisible God,
  the firstborn of all creation.
For in him were created all things in heaven and on earth,
  the visible and the invisible,
  whether thrones or dominions or principalities or powers;
  all things were created through him and for him.
He is before all things,
  and in him all things hold together.
He is the head of the body, the church.
He is the beginning, the firstborn from the dead,
  that in all things he himself might be preeminent.
For in him all the fullness was pleased to dwell,
  and through him to reconcile all things for him,
  making peace by the blood of his cross
  through him, whether those on earth or those in heaven.

GOSPEL
Luke 10:25–37

There was a scholar of the law who stood up to test Jesus and said, "Teacher, what must I do to inherit eternal life?" Jesus said to him, "What is written in the law? How do you read it?" He said in reply,

You shall love the Lord, your God,
with all your heart,
with all your being,

with all your strength,
and with all your mind,
and your neighbor as yourself.

He replied to him, "You have answered correctly; do this and you will live."

But because he wished to justify himself, he said to Jesus, "And who is my neighbor?" Jesus replied, "A man fell victim to robbers as he went down from Jerusalem to Jericho. They stripped and beat him and went off leaving him half-dead. A priest happened to be going down that road, but when he saw him, he passed by on the opposite side. Likewise a Levite came to the place, and when he saw him, he passed by on the opposite side. But a Samaritan traveler who came upon him was moved with compassion at the sight. He approached the victim, poured oil and wine over his wounds and bandaged them. Then he lifted him up on his own animal, took him to an inn, and cared for him. The next day he took out two silver coins and gave them to the innkeeper with the instruction, 'Take care of him. If you spend more than what I have given you, I shall repay you on my way back.' Which of these three, in your opinion, was neighbor to the robbers' victim?" He answered, "The one who treated him with mercy." Jesus said to him, "Go and do likewise."

Understanding the Word

In today's Gospel Jesus is pleased that the scholar of the law understands the key role of love of God and neighbor. Jesus then uses the parable of the Good Samaritan to stress that this love of neighbor can have no exceptions.

This Sunday's second reading teaches much about the right of Christ to demand that love of God and neighbor. The New Testament does not have a book of hymns like the psalms of the Old Testament, but does have beautiful, theologically informative hymns scattered among its various books. There is the wonderful Prologue of the Gospel of John (1:1–18), the christological hymn in Philippians (2:6–11), and today's hymn about the preeminence of Jesus (Colossians 1:15–20). This hymn is truly outstanding in its teachings about Christ and is probably from the liturgy of the early church.

The Letter to the Colossians intends to counteract some false teachings in the local community. While these false teachings are not completely understood by biblical scholars, it does appear that they were undermining the work of Jesus. Accepting and following Jesus was, according to the false teachers, not sufficient for salvation. In that context, the hymn declares emphatically the pre-existence of Jesus, his preeminence in both creation and redemption, and his role as head of the church. The wisdom literature of the Old Testament has influenced the writing of this hymn. Proverbs 3:19 provides an example, "The Lord by wisdom founded the earth, / established the heavens by understanding."

Jesus is called the image of God, a perfect reflection of the Father. He is God's agent in causing and sustaining all of creation. He deserves, therefore, to be called "the firstborn of all creation" (Colossians 1:15). He is also declared emphatically to be "the firstborn from the dead" (1:18) and "the head of the body, the church" (1:18). Jesus then is also preeminent in the work of reconciliation. Having the fullness of God, he achieved this reconciliation by shedding his blood on the cross.

As creator, Jesus Christ affects "all things in heaven and on earth" (1:16). As reconciler, he brings peace, salvation for "those on earth or those in heaven" (1:20).

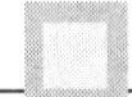

Reflecting on the Word

Lawrence Kohlberg was a psychologist and professor at Harvard University. He studied human behavior and motivation and observed a typical progression in moral behavior through six different stages.

At stage one we respond to the threat of punishment. We perform good acts because if we do not, we will suffer the consequences. This is why we slow down when we see a squad car monitoring traffic. At stage two we are motivated by a reward—like a raise in salary or a nicer home. Stage three suggests that we are motivated by public opinion and what people think of us. Kohlberg referred to it as the good boy/girl stage. Stage four, the motivating influence is law, our duty to society and good order. Kohlberg believed most people do not move beyond level three or four. At stage five a person is motivated by a sense of social responsibility for others. The world needs to be a better place, and we need to contribute to it. At stage six a person's motivation is totally and fully internalized. Now a person feels free to move outside the law or public opinion for the sake of doing good for others, for the sake of true and legitimate love. That alone matters and may even end in martyrdom. Kohlberg said that we call these people saints, and that few ever attain this level of motivation.

What Kohlberg's theory suggests is that as we become more mature, the motivating principle for our behavior is more and more internalized. More and more we assume individual responsibility for who we are and for the world in which we live.

CONSIDER/ DISCUSS:

- What motivates your behavior? Which of Kohlberg's stages best describes you?
- Can you trace shifts through life in the growth of your behavioral motivation? Can you recall when these shifts took place?
- Consider the Gospel's parable. At what stage of moral growth might each of the three passersby have been?

Responding to the Word

We are never who we were, but always in the process of becoming. Deep within us something calls us into being more fully human, always in the image of Jesus.

Spend a few minutes in quiet prayer. Ask God to show you one (or more) ways that you may be called to respond to this week's scriptures—

- in your relationship with God
- with family and friends
- at work, school, or church
- in the broader community

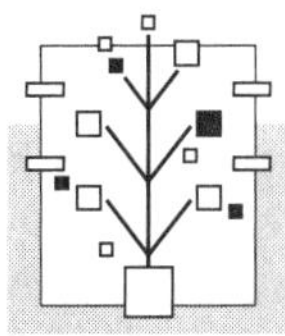

July 22, 2007

SIXTEENTH SUNDAY IN ORDINARY TIME

Today's Focus: On the Winds of Change

Most of us like to keep life as it is. Change can be unsettling, especially too much of it. Yet change also brings new perspectives and opens us to becoming what we never would have dreamed.

FIRST READING
Genesis 18: 1–10a

The LORD appeared to Abraham by the terebinth of Mamre, as he sat in the entrance of his tent, while the day was growing hot. Looking up, Abraham saw three men standing nearby. When he saw them, he ran from the entrance of the tent to greet them; and bowing to the ground, he said: "Sir, if I may ask you this favor, please do not go on past your servant. Let some water be brought, that you may bathe your feet, and then rest yourselves under the tree. Now that you have come this close to your servant, let me bring you a little food, that you may refresh yourselves; and afterward you may go on your way." The men replied, "Very well, do as you have said."

Abraham hastened into the tent and told Sarah, "Quick, three measures of fine flour! Knead it and make rolls." He ran to the herd, picked out a tender, choice steer, and gave it to a servant, who quickly prepared it. Then Abraham got some curds and milk, as well as the steer that had been prepared, and set these before the three men; and he waited on them under the tree while they ate.

They asked Abraham, "Where is your wife Sarah?" He replied, "There in the tent." One of them said, "I will surely return to you about this time next year, and Sarah will then have a son."

PSALM RESPONSE
Psalm 15:1a

He who does justice will live in the presence of the Lord.

SECOND READING
Colossians 1: 24–28

Brothers and sisters: Now I rejoice in my sufferings for your sake, and in my flesh I am filling up what is lacking in the afflictions of Christ on behalf of his body, which is the church, of which I am a minister in accordance with God's stewardship given to me to bring to completion for you the word of God, the mystery hidden from ages and from generations past. But now it has been manifested to his holy ones, to whom God chose to make known the riches of the glory of this mystery among the Gentiles; it is Christ in you, the hope for glory. It is he whom we proclaim, admonishing everyone and teaching everyone with all wisdom, that we may present everyone perfect in Christ.

GOSPEL
Luke 10:38–42

Jesus entered a village where a woman whose name was Martha welcomed him. She had a sister named Mary who sat beside the Lord at his feet listening to him speak. Martha, burdened with much serving, came to him and said, "Lord, do you not care that my sister has left me by myself to do the serving? Tell her to help me." The Lord said to her in reply, "Martha, Martha, you are anxious and worried about many things. There is need of only one thing. Mary has chosen the better part and it will not be taken from her."

Understanding the Word

"Understanding the Word" presumes the importance of hearing and comprehending the word of God. In today's Gospel Jesus commends Mary for choosing to be his disciple and hear from him the word of God. He says, "Mary has chosen the better part and it will not be taken from her" (Luke 10:42). "Implied in the phrase 'the word of God' is an address by the revealing and saving God to human beings from whom a response of faith is sought" (Joseph A. Fitzmyer, SJ, "The Gospel According to Luke," *Anchor Bible*, vol. 28, p. 157).

Jesus is continuing his journey to Jerusalem, but stops in the village of Bethany, the home of his friends Mary, Martha, and Lazarus. The Gospel of John also refers to these friends (John 11:1; 12:1–3). Bethany is near Jerusalem, the goal of Jesus' journey. Luke later mentions Bethany as Jesus approaches the Mount of Olives (Luke 19:29).

Jesus truly appreciated the concern of Martha for his physical needs, but preferred the attention to him and his word shown by Mary. She realized that "[t]here is need of only one thing" (10:42), to be a disciple of Jesus. It was quite unusual at that time for a woman to be a disciple of a Jewish teacher. Mary "sat beside the Lord at his feet, listening to him speak" (10:39) as a disciple would. In the Acts of the Apostles Paul says, "At the feet of Gamaliel I was educated strictly in our ancestral law" (Acts 22:3). The fact that Jesus accepts Mary as a disciple highlights another theme of the Gospel of Luke, namely the great concern of Jesus for women.

The Christian reader of Luke's Gospel is being told that Jesus does expect acts of loving concern for one's neighbor as exemplified by the Good Samaritan in last Sunday's Gospel (Luke 10:29–37). But this incident in Bethany reminds everyone that it is essential to find one's strength for a Christ-like life by imitating Mary, who drew close to Jesus and heard from him the word of God. That word is the basic message of Jesus for the world, a very important theme for Luke.

Reflecting on the Word

God's future for us seems to hinge upon the unexpected. Consider the story of Abraham and Sarah. What we are seems to depend upon the tendentious nature of Abraham's offer of hospitality to some wandering strangers who come upon him at a desert oasis. They are weary and bedraggled and eagerly accept his kindness, and in return they promise a son to this aged and skeptical couple. The promise comes true and nine months later the couple births Isaac, through whom the Hebrew nation unfolds, of which Jesus was a member, to whom as his disciples we claim allegiance.

Today's Gospel is still another tale of unexpected turns, not because Martha was abandoned in the kitchen, or was unimportant, or because her sister, Mary, seemed more spiritual, but because it became apparent that a woman could sit at the feet of a master as readily as a man. Such a thing was both unexpected and unsettling.

We can hardly be inattentive to the unexpected in our lives. Such moments may be the very soupspoon of God stirring our lives into some new cuisine. The unplanned job relocation at a time when life finally seems settled, the child who comes late in life (as it did for Abraham and Sarah), the unpredicted mental illness of a spouse or child, the needed care for an aging parent, changing parish dynamics, shifting financial winds, the unfolding homosexual orientation of a child or sibling, addiction and the treatment it calls for, doubts in one's faith, prayer that no longer satisfies—all so unexpected. It may all be a hint of God's imagination, of the way God brings us to holiness and grace, and of the nature of God's kingdom.

CONSIDER/ DISCUSS:

- When has the unexpected become for you a treasured turn of events?
- When you consider accepting the unexpected, of which virtue are you most in need?

Responding to the Word

It would seem that God thrives on the unexpected. Or else God uses the unexpected as a stirring spoon in the soup pot of life. Either way, there is a sense in which the unexpected has a quality of the divine about it.

Spend a few minutes in quiet prayer. Ask God to show you one (or more) ways that you may be called to respond to this week's scriptures—

- in your relationship with God
- with family and friends
- at work, school, or church
- in the broader community

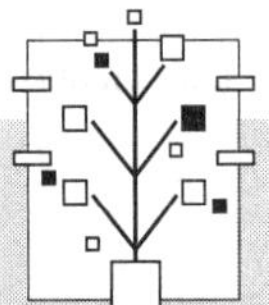

July 29, 2007

SEVENTEENTH SUNDAY IN ORDINARY TIME

Today's Focus: Of Wanting and Getting

We tend to be curious and wily creatures who want much from life, and yet we seldom seem to know what it is we really seek. So we keep on wanting, mostly because our insides keep on longing and aching and searching.

FIRST READING
Genesis 18: 20–32

In those days, the LORD said: "The outcry against Sodom and Gomorrah is so great, and their sin so grave, that I must go down and see whether or not their actions fully correspond to the cry against them that comes to me. I mean to find out."

While Abraham's visitors walked on farther toward Sodom, the LORD remained standing before Abraham. Then Abraham drew nearer and said: "Will you sweep away the innocent with the guilty? Suppose there were fifty innocent people in the city; would you wipe out the place, rather than spare it for the sake of the fifty innocent people within it? Far be it from you to do such a thing, to make the innocent die with the guilty so that the innocent and the guilty would be treated alike! Should not the judge of all the world act with justice?" The LORD replied, "If I find fifty innocent people in the city of Sodom, I will spare the whole place for their sake." Abraham spoke up again: "See how I am presuming to speak to my Lord, though I am but dust and ashes! What if there are five less than fifty innocent people? Will you destroy the whole city because of those five?" He answered, "I will not destroy it, if I find forty-five there." But Abraham persisted, saying "What if only forty are found there?" He replied, "I will forbear doing it for the sake of the forty." Then Abraham said, "Let not my Lord grow impatient if I go on. What if only thirty are found there?" He replied, "I will forbear doing it if I can find but thirty there." Still Abraham went on, "Since I have thus dared to speak to my Lord, what if there are no more than twenty?" The LORD answered, "I will not destroy it, for the sake of the twenty." But he still persisted: "Please, let not my Lord grow angry if I speak up this last time. What if there are at least ten there?" He replied, "For the sake of those ten, I will not destroy it."

PSALM RESPONSE
Psalm 138:3a

Lord, on the day I called for help, you answered me.

SECOND READING
Colossians 2: 12–14

Brothers and sisters: You were buried with him in baptism, in which you were also raised with him through faith in the power of God, who raised him from the dead. And even when you were dead in transgressions and the uncircumcision of your flesh, he brought you to life along with him, having forgiven us all our transgressions; obliterating the bond against us, with its legal claims, which was opposed to us, he also removed it from our midst, nailing it to the cross.

GOSPEL
Luke 11:1–13

Jesus was praying in a certain place, and when he had finished, one of his disciples said to him, "Lord, teach us to pray just as John taught his disciples." He said to them, "When you pray, say:

Father, hallowed be your name,
your kingdom come.
Give us each day our daily bread
and forgive us our sins
for we ourselves forgive everyone in debt to us,
and do not subject us to the final test."

And he said to them, "Suppose one of you has a friend to whom he goes at midnight and says, 'Friend, lend me three loaves of bread, for a friend of mine has arrived at my house from a journey and I have nothing to offer him,' and he says in reply from within, 'Do not bother me; the door has already been locked and my children and I are already in bed. I cannot get up to give you anything.' I tell you, if he does not get up to give the visitor the loaves because of their friendship, he will get up to give him whatever he needs because of his persistence.

"And I tell you, ask and you will receive; seek and you will find; knock and the door will be opened to you. For everyone who asks, receives; and the one who seeks, finds; and to the one who knocks, the door will be opened. What father among you would hand his son a snake when he asks for a fish? Or hand him a scorpion when he asks for an egg? If you then, who are wicked, know how to give good gifts to your children, how much more will the Father in heaven give the Holy Spirit to those who ask him?"

Understanding the Word

The great love of the Father for his children and the importance of persistent, confident prayer on the part of those children are the highlights of today's Gospel. The selection opens with Luke's form of the Our Father. God is addressed as Abba, a child's word for father, expressing the family closeness between God and us all.

Luke's version of the Lord's Prayer has five petitions. The Christian looks to God for the fulfillment of all five. God is asked to reveal the holiness of the divine name and to bring the kingdom to fulfillment. "Thus says the Lord God: Not for your sakes do I act, house of Israel, but for the sake of my holy name" (Ezekiel 36:22). Christ will carry on this important work of the Father with the expectation that his followers will also cooperate in this work.

The Father is then asked to provide the children with some basic needs, namely food, forgiveness, and freedom from the test. The Greek word *epiousios* can be translated as "daily," as it is in the New American Bible, but it can also mean necessary or future bread. It is the only use of the word in the Bible and leads to difficulty in interpretation.

Forgiveness of sins is necessary for all. But Jesus indicates that we also must be willing to forgive. Forgiveness of sins plays a large role in Luke's Gospel when, for example, John proclaims "a baptism of repentance for the forgiveness of sins" (Luke 3:3).

In the Old Testament and in the New there is talk of a "test." Whether a test in this lifetime regarding apostasy, for example, or the final eschatological test, Jesus teaches us to pray that we do not undergo that test. Later, he warns his apostles, "Get up and pray that you may not undergo the test" (Luke 22:46).

In the rest of today's Gospel (Luke 11:5–13) Jesus reminds the listeners of the Father's love, infinitely surpassing the love of any human father. God will answer prayers that are persistent and confident in a way that is best for each person, even giving the greatest gift, the Holy Spirit.

Reflecting on the Word

Coming to God with our wants and desires does not seem especially out of character for us, especially with God telling us to come, as this week's Gospel would suggest.

Yet we can also find ourselves wondering if praying for something really increases the likelihood of it coming about. Does praying to find a job or sell a house or make a safe journey or find a lost object help to make them happen? Well, you say, it doesn't hurt. Yes, but does it help?

On the one hand the fruitfulness of such prayer is attested to by numerous accounts as well as by the scriptures of this weekend. On the other hand folks have vigorously quoted other scriptures that assure us that God knows our needs even before we ask and demonstrate the foolhardiness of thinking we will win a hearing by the sheer multiplication of words. Not every basketball free throw preceded by a sign of the cross swishes through.

This Sunday's Gospel, however, adds an interesting note. After lengthy encouragement to look to God to hear and answer our prayers, Jesus concludes, "If you then, who are wicked, know how to give good gifts to your children, how much more will the Father in heaven give the Holy Spirit to those who ask him?" (Luke 11:13). Suddenly it becomes a quest for the Holy Spirit. We had come looking for health or needed funds or good grades or a new job, and the promise becomes God's Spirit.

CONSIDER/ DISCUSS:

- What sort of expectations do you bring to your prayer? Why do you pray?
- At what point in your life did how you pray change? Why?

Responding to the Word

In promising the Holy Spirit, Saint Luke's Jesus responds to our most basic needs. If we hunger for deep joy, or to become gentle or kind or generous, Luke's Jesus promises that the Father will give it.

Spend a few minutes in quiet prayer. Ask God to show you one (or more) ways that you may be called to respond to this week's scriptures—

- in your relationship with God
- with family and friends
- at work, school, or church
- in the broader community

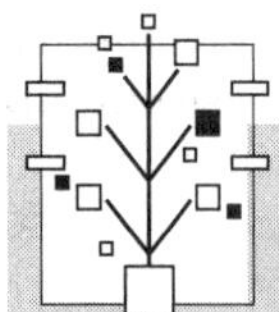

August 5, 2007

EIGHTEENTH SUNDAY IN ORDINARY TIME

Today's Focus: The Wise Use of Money

There are aspects of life that some of us always seem to be messing up. Relationships come to mind. Our use of power is another. And our sexuality. You can undoubtedly name others. Using them well can be a challenge. The wise use of money is another one that this week's scriptures call us to deal with.

FIRST READING
Ecclesiastes 1:2; 2:21–23

Vanity of vanities, says Qoheleth,
vanity of vanities! All things are vanity!

Here is one who has labored with wisdom and knowledge and skill, and yet to another who has not labored over it, he must leave property. This also is vanity and a great misfortune. For what profit comes to man from all the toil and anxiety of heart with which he has labored under the sun? All his days sorrow and grief are his occupation; even at night his mind is not at rest. This also is vanity.

PSALM RESPONSE
Psalm 90:1

If today you hear his voice, harden not your hearts.

SECOND READING
Colossians 3: 1–5, 9–11

Brothers and sisters: If you were raised with Christ, seek what is above, where Christ is seated at the right hand of God. Think of what is above, not of what is on earth. For you have died, and your life is hidden with Christ in God. When Christ your life appears, then you too will appear with him in glory.

Put to death, then, the parts of you that are earthly: immorality, impurity, passion, evil desire, and the greed that is idolatry. Stop lying to one another, since you have taken off the old self with its practices and have put on the new self, which is being renewed, for knowledge, in the image of its creator. Here there is not Greek and Jew, circumcision and uncircumcision, barbarian, Scythian, slave, free; but Christ is all and in all.

GOSPEL
Luke 12:13–21

Someone in the crowd said to Jesus, "Teacher, tell my brother to share the inheritance with me." He replied to him, "Friend, who appointed me as your judge and arbitrator?" Then he said to the crowd, "Take care to guard against all greed, for though one may be rich, one's life does not consist of possessions."

Then he told them a parable. "There was a rich man whose land produced a bountiful harvest. He asked himself, 'What shall I do, for I do not have space to store my harvest?' And he said, 'This is what I shall do: I shall tear down my barns and build larger ones.

There I shall store all my grain and other goods and I shall say to myself, "Now as for you, you have so many good things stored up for many years, rest, eat, drink, be merry!"' But God said to him, 'You fool, this night your life will be demanded of you; and the things you have prepared, to whom will they belong?' Thus will it be for all who store up treasure for themselves but are not rich in what matters to God."

Understanding the Word

In today's second reading Saint Paul reminds the Colossians that by baptism they "were raised with Christ" and should "seek what is above" (Colossians 3:1). Paul adds a long list of vices that they must avoid. Prominent in the list is "greed that is idolatry" (3:5). Greed becomes idolatrous because it replaces God with possessions as an idol to be worshipped.

Today's Gospel from Luke serves as an excellent commentary on the words of Saint Paul. When someone asks Jesus to be an arbiter with his brother he refuses to become involved, principally because he realizes that greed is motivating the man's request.

The danger of greed is clearly taught in the parable of the rich fool. The rich man makes provisions for a self-centered life of pleasure. God, however, demands his soul just as he is beginning to carry out his plan. One must understand that the end of this life is unpredictable. The kingdom of God will be eternal. A wise person, therefore, will become "rich in what matters to God" (Luke 12:21). Jesus is not condemning possessions and prudent planning as such, but wants the kingdom of God to have priority in a person's life, manifested by a willingness to share with the poor and vulnerable.

Father Joseph Fitzmyer, SJ has an excellent comment on today's Gospel. "It is much more important to be than to have—to be one who listens to God's word and acts on it than to live in an unnecessary abundance of wealth" ("The Gospel According to Luke," *Anchor Bible*, vol. 28A, p. 969).

Reflecting on the Word

For the disciple of Jesus one issue seems to be how to cultivate an attitude toward money as a means and not as an end. People whom I've come to consider on the way to some sort of holiness all seem to have a healthy attitude about money. They seem to be able to deal with it yet all the while keeping it in balance with the rest of life. So I asked around.

Tithing seems to be a frequent way of maintaining some sort of balance—ten percent off the top of one's income. People who tithe seem to remember the poor in more than a token way.

Some folks said they don't use credit cards precisely to keep them from spending sprees. Others spoke to the question of owning stocks. Some refuse to do so simply because they know it would become one more anxiety in their life. Another refused to allow herself to read the stock market page of the newspaper, lest she become anxious about her investments.

A middle-aged priest said that at the end of every calendar year he emptied his checking and savings accounts. He said he thought it good to begin each year at zero. Now, he is a priest and so has some good job security, but I also wonder if anyone else empties their bank accounts at the end of the year. Another person said he had decided what a responsible amount of savings would be for retirement and other needs. Everything over and above he gives away.

Someone else decided to live by needs rather than by wants and tried to be attentive to her inclination to shift items from the latter category to the former. She felt it worked for her.

CONSIDER/ DISCUSS:

- How do you keep money from becoming an overriding concern in your life?
- Whom do you know who has a healthy "biblical" attitude toward the use of money?

Responding to the Word

It doesn't really matter how we keep a balance about money or how we make sure we use money wisely as disciples. What matters is that we do so, if for no other reason than to make sure that we care for the weakest among us, and to make sure we keep trust in our God and not in ourselves.

Spend a few minutes in quiet prayer. Ask God to show you one (or more) ways that you may be called to respond to this week's scriptures—

- in your relationship with God
- with family and friends
- at work, school, or church
- in the broader community

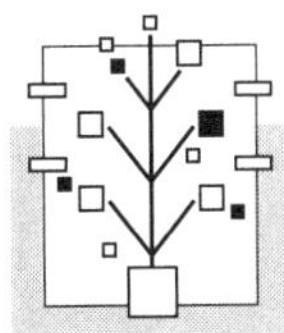

August 12, 2007

NINETEENTH SUNDAY IN ORDINARY TIME

Today's Focus: Autobiography or Biography?

For the most part we prefer to write our own storyline. Surprises tend to be too unsettling. Being the author of our own life assures us of controlling the ending lest our comedy become a tragedy.

FIRST READING
Wisdom 18:6–9

The night of the passover was known beforehand to our fathers,
that, with sure knowledge of the oaths in which they put their faith,
they might have courage.
Your people awaited the salvation of the just
and the destruction of their foes.
For when you punished our adversaries,
in this you glorified us whom you had summoned.
For in secret the holy children of the good were offering sacrifice
and putting into effect with one accord the divine institution.

PSALM RESPONSE
Psalm 33:12b

Blessed the people the Lord has chosen to be his own.

In the shorter form of the reading, the passage in brackets is omitted.

SECOND READING
Hebrews 11: 1–2, 8–19 or 11:1–2, 8–12

Brothers and sisters: Faith is the realization of what is hoped for and evidence of things not seen. Because of it the ancients were well attested.

By faith Abraham obeyed when he was called to go out to a place that he was to receive as an inheritance; he went out, not knowing where he was to go. By faith he sojourned in the promised land as in a foreign country, dwelling in tents with Isaac and Jacob, heirs of the same promise; for he was looking forward to the city with foundations, whose architect and maker is God. By faith he received power to generate, even though he was past the normal age—and Sarah herself was sterile—for he thought that the one who had made the promise was trustworthy. So it was that there came forth from one man, himself as good as dead, descendants as numerous as the stars in the sky and as countless as the sands on the seashore.

[All these died in faith. They did not receive what had been promised but saw it and greeted it from afar and acknowledged themselves to be strangers and aliens on earth, for those who speak thus show that they are seeking a homeland. If they had been thinking of the land from which they had come, they would have had opportunity to return. But now they desire a better homeland, a heavenly one. Therefore, God is not ashamed to be called their God, for he has prepared a city for them.

By faith Abraham, when put to the test, offered up Isaac, and he who had received the promises was ready to offer his only son, of whom it was said, "Through Isaac descendants shall bear your name." He reasoned that God was able to raise even from the dead, and he received Isaac back as a symbol.]

In the shorter form of the reading, the passages in brackets are omitted.

GOSPEL
Luke 12:32–48
or 12:35–40

Jesus said to his disciples: ["Do not be afraid any longer, little flock, for your Father is pleased to give you the kingdom. Sell your belongings and give alms. Provide money bags for yourselves that do not wear out, an inexhaustible treasure in heaven that no thief can reach nor moth destroy. For where your treasure is, there also will your heart be.]

"Gird your loins and light your lamps and be like servants who await their master's return from a wedding, ready to open immediately when he comes and knocks. Blessed are those servants whom the master finds vigilant on his arrival. Amen, I say to you, he will gird himself, have them recline at table, and proceed to wait on them. And should he come in the second or third watch and find them prepared in this way, blessed are those servants. Be sure of this: if the master of the house had known the hour when the thief was coming, he would not have let his house be broken into. You also must be prepared, for at an hour you do not expect, the Son of Man will come."

[Then Peter said, "Lord, is this parable meant for us or for everyone?" And the Lord replied, "Who, then, is the faithful and prudent steward whom the master will put in charge of his servants to distribute the food allowance at the proper time? Blessed is that servant whom his master on arrival finds doing so. Truly, I say to you, the master will put the servant in charge of all his property. But if that servant says to himself, 'My master is delayed in coming,' and begins to beat the menservants and the maidservants, to eat and drink and get drunk, then that servant's master will come on an unexpected day and at an unknown hour and will punish the servant severely and assign him a place with the unfaithful. That servant who knew his master's will but did not make preparations nor act in accord with his will shall be beaten severely; and the servant who was ignorant of his master's will but acted in a way deserving of a severe beating shall be beaten only lightly. Much will be required of the person entrusted with much, and still more will be demanded of the person entrusted with more."]

Jesus imparts two critical lessons to his followers in today's Gospel. Since the Father has given the kingdom to the disciples, Jesus wants their hearts to be with the kingdom, their treasure, and not with possessions. In a loving way he calls them "little flock" (12:32) and urges using possessions as alms.

The other important teaching of Jesus is the absolute necessity of preparing for his second coming, for the eschatological judgment. The fact of that coming, the *parousia*, is definite, but the time is uncertain. Therefore, says Christ, be watchful; be faithful!

"You also must be prepared, for at an hour you do not expect, the Son of Man will come" (Luke 12:40). "Son of Man" is the title Jesus uses most frequently for himself, and others never used it. He applies it during his public ministry: "Just as Jonah became a sign to the Ninevites, so will the Son of Man be to this generation" (Luke 11:30); in his suffering: "The Son of Man must suffer greatly and be rejected by the elders, the chief priests, and the scribes, and be killed and on the third day be raised" (Luke 9:22); and in his glorious return at the end of time, as in 12:40 above.

In response to Peter's question "Lord, is this parable meant for us or for everyone?" (12:41), Jesus makes it clear that watchfulness for the Second Coming applies to all, but especially to the leaders of the Christian communities. Should such a leader use the delay in the *parousia* to misuse his power, the master "will punish [him] severely and assign him a place with the unfaithful" (12:46). This is a warning to all Christians to be faithful throughout this period until the Second Coming. The greater the gifts, the greater the responsibility (12:48).

Vigilance similar to that of the faithful servants will be rewarded. Christ even says that the master "will gird himself, have them recline at table, and proceed to wait on them" (12:37). Service, therefore, becomes the sign of true authority, the example for all Christian leaders. "I am among you as the one who serves" (22:27).

Reflecting on the Word

It's tempting to wish that our faith in God would enable us to have an unfailing trust that God will take us to where we want to be. It would free us from diddling with decisions, vacillating and second-guessing. Only that wouldn't be faith because it would be our own script we'd have God carrying out.

Faith in God surrenders the script. It also surrenders the outcome, which is why Abraham, when asked by God to pack up kin and belongings and move to another land, did just that without knowing where or how he'd eventually settle in. And much later, like the unpredictable thread of a good novel, Abraham's story finds him and Sarah with child when they are 100 and 90 years old. A decade or so later, Abraham again finds himself without any sensible or sane understanding of the storyline as he leads young Isaac up a sacrificial mountain to what would seem to be a failure of God's promise to Abraham to father countless generations. Once more God rewrites the ending. Throughout Abraham's life it is God's script that Abraham lives out, not his own.

Faith is unpredictable, like good novels that twist and turn and keep us in suspense. If novels are well written, they keep us up long into the night. On the other hand, we like our lives quite the opposite. The appearance of the unpredictable tends to unsettle and undo our living. We presume that good lives, unlike a good novel, are interesting and engaging but always knowledgably focused and without unwarranted surprises. And so we expect good novels and good lives to be like the tracks of the railroad—parallel, but never touching or crossing lest someone or something be derailed.

CONSIDER/ DISCUSS:

- Make two lists of memorable personal events, those that eventually brought you to good and desirable places and those that did not. What observations or conclusions might you make about your listings?
- Do you wish you had been more controlling or less controlling of your life?

Responding to the Word

Growth and change are always the result of conflict, of clashing visions that force adaptation. This is not to say that God writes tragedies and suffering into the script, but only that God uses all the unfolding twists and turns of the plot to bring the story to a divine conclusion.

Spend a few minutes in quiet prayer. Ask God to show you one (or more) ways that you may be called to respond to this week's scriptures—

- in your relationship with God
- with family and friends
- at work, school, or church
- in the broader community

August 15, 2007

THE ASSUMPTION OF THE BLESSED VIRGIN MARY

Today's Focus: Fields of Life

To celebrate the Assumption is to celebrate a God who lifts us all out of our everyday deaths and ultimately out of our final death as well, and so into life—in the image of Mary.

FIRST READING
Revelation 11: 19a; 12:1–6a, 10ab

God's temple in heaven was opened, and the ark of his covenant could be seen in the temple.

A great sign appeared in the sky, a woman clothed with the sun, with the moon beneath her feet, and on her head a crown of twelve stars. She was with child and wailed aloud in pain as she labored to give birth. Then another sign appeared in the sky; it was a huge red dragon, with seven heads and ten horns, and on its heads were seven diadems. Its tail swept away a third of the stars in the sky and hurled them down to the earth. Then the dragon stood before the woman about to give birth, to devour her child when she gave birth. She gave birth to a son, a male child, destined to rule all the nations with an iron rod. Her child was caught up to God and his throne. The woman herself fled into the desert where she had a place prepared by God.

Then I heard a loud voice in heaven say:
"Now have salvation and power come,
and the kingdom of our God
and the authority of his Anointed One."

PSALM RESPONSE
Psalm 45:10bc

The queen stands at your right hand, arrayed in gold.

SECOND READING
1 Corinthians 15: 20–27

Brothers and sisters: Christ has been raised from the dead, the firstfruits of those who have fallen asleep. For since death came through man, the resurrection of the dead came also through man. For just as in Adam all die, so too in Christ shall all be brought to life, but each one in proper order: Christ the firstfruits; then, at his coming, those who belong to Christ; then comes the end, when he hands over the kingdom to his God and Father, when he has destroyed every sovereignty and every authority and power. For he must reign until he has put all his enemies under his feet. The last enemy to be destroyed is death, for "he subjected everything under his feet."

GOSPEL
Luke 1:39–56

Mary set out and traveled to the hill country in haste to a town of Judah, where she entered the house of Zechariah and greeted Elizabeth. When Elizabeth heard Mary's greeting, the infant leaped in her womb, and Elizabeth, filled with the Holy Spirit, cried out in a loud voice and said, "Blessed are you among women, and blessed is the fruit of your womb. And how does this happen to me, that the mother of my Lord should come to me? For at the moment the sound of your greeting reached my ears, the infant in my womb leaped for joy. Blessed are you who believed that what was spoken to you by the Lord would be fulfilled."

And Mary said:

"My soul proclaims the greatness of the Lord;
  my spirit rejoices in God my Savior
  for he has looked upon his lowly servant
From this day all generations will call me blessed:
  the Almighty has done great things for me,
  and holy is his Name.
  He has mercy on those who fear him
  in every generation.
He has shown the strength of his arm,
  and has scattered the proud in their conceit.
He has cast down the mighty from their thrones,
  and has lifted up the lowly.
He has filled the hungry with good things,
  and the rich he has sent away empty.
He has come to the help of his servant Israel
  for he has remembered his promise of mercy,
  the promise he made to our fathers,
  to Abraham and his children for ever."

Mary remained with her about three months and then returned to her home.

Understanding the Word

When Pope Pius XII formally defined the doctrine of the Assumption of Mary in 1950, he made a reference to the text that is today's first reading. The Holy Father pointed out that theologians "have recognized the Assumption of the Virgin Mother of God as something signified, not only in various figures of the Old Testament, but also in that Woman clothed with Sun, whom John the Apostle contemplated on the Island of Patmos" (Pope Pius XII, *Munificentissimus Deus*, 27).

Apocalyptic writing, as found in Revelation, is difficult to interpret. It was used extensively in Judaism between 200 BC and AD 200. Revelation is the only example of that type of writing in the New Testament. The "woman clothed with the sun" in today's reading (Revelation 12:1) refers primarily to the church; but as Demetrius R. Dumm, OSB writes, "The woman, whose son is snatched up to heaven and who is pursued by the dragon, represents the new Israel, the Christian Church, but the image may also be applied to Mary in her symbolic identification with the community of believers" (*The Collegeville Pastoral Dictionary of Biblical Theology*, p. 595).

Today's second reading has these significant words from Saint Paul, "In Christ shall all be brought to life, but each one in proper order: Christ the firstfruits; then, at his coming, those who belong to Christ" (1 Corinthians 15:22–23). The doctrine of the Assumption of Mary stresses the special place of Mary, his mother. She is certainly the first of all those who belong to Christ, since "having completed the course of her earthly life, [she] was assumed body and soul into heavenly glory" (*Munificentissimus Deus*, 44).

In today's Gospel Elizabeth says of Mary, "Blessed are you among women and blessed is the fruit of your womb" (Luke 1:42). She also calls Mary "the mother of my Lord," referring to Mary as the Mother of God since Lord is the Greek form for Yahweh. According to Pope Pius XII, the theologians "saw, in the mystery of the Assumption, the fulfillment of that most perfect grace granted to the Blessed Virgin and the special blessing that countered the curse of Eve" (*Munificentissimus Deus*, 27).

Reflecting on the Word

In the film *Field of Dreams* it is 1988. Ray Kinsella hears a voice instructing him to build a baseball diamond in his cornfield. "If you build it, they will come," he is told. So he does, and Shoeless Joe Jackson and the Chicago Black Sox show up—the eight White Sox players banned from baseball for throwing the 1919 World Series. The players walk out of the August cornfield and onto Kinsella's baseball diamond as if they were walking out of the realm of death just to play the field. After the game Terrance Mann, Kinsella's skeptical friend, chooses to return with them into the past and so follows them into the rows of swaying corn stalks. He disappears back into the very death from which the Black Sox had first come. It was his choice, and Terrance Mann did it fully conscious of what he was leaving behind.

Believers, too, choose to walk into the unknown, not unlike Terrance Mann, though often with more trepidation. After all, life can be a surrender, every day, to a God who guides more than we control, whose wisdom is more than we know. For us who live in the fields of life it is a daily assertion of God's reign over our lives, always a loss of control and a surrender to the unknown. It is what makes each and every death so unsettling. Yet it is with faith that we are able to say yes to what we do not know because we trust in a God who fills our hungers and lifts us up even when we are lowly and in fear.

CONSIDER/ DISCUSS:

- When was the last time you consciously chose to walk into the unknown, trusting that you would find life?
- Life comes through the dying, not simply after. When has your dying brought about fuller life for you or someone else?

Responding to the Word

In celebrating the Assumption of the Blessed Virgin Mary our souls, too, proclaim the greatness of the Lord, simply because it is the Almighty who does great things for us, just as Mary once proclaimed about her life.

Spend a few minutes in quiet prayer. Ask God to show you one (or more) ways that you may be called to respond to this week's scriptures—

- in your relationship with God
- with family and friends
- at work, school, or church
- in the broader community

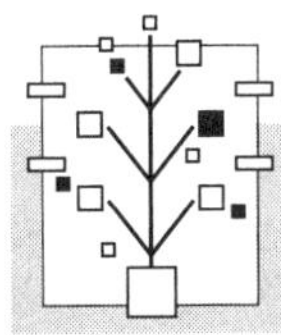

August 19, 2007

TWENTIETH SUNDAY IN ORDINARY TIME

Today's Focus: Standing Alone

As much as the coming fall urges us back into living with greater intensity, somewhere along life's way there comes an even more poignant time when each of us must decide what we stand for in life, what is worth caring about and struggling for, even weeping over.

FIRST READING
Jeremiah 38: 4–6, 8–10

In those days, the princes said to the king: "Jeremiah ought to be put to death; he is demoralizing the soldiers who are left in this city, and all the people, by speaking such things to them; he is not interested in the welfare of our people, but in their ruin." King Zedekiah answered: "He is in your power"; for the king could do nothing with them. And so they took Jeremiah and threw him into the cistern of Prince Malchiah, which was in the quarters of the guard, letting him down with ropes. There was no water in the cistern, only mud, and Jeremiah sank into the mud.

Ebed-melech, a court official, went there from the palace and said to him: "My lord king, these men have been at fault in all they have done to the prophet Jeremiah, casting him into the cistern. He will die of famine on the spot, for there is no more food in the city." Then the king ordered Ebed-melech the Cushite to take three men along with him, and draw the prophet Jeremiah out of the cistern before he should die.

PSALM RESPONSE
Psalm 40:14b

Lord, come to my aid!

SECOND READING
Hebrews 12:1–4

Brothers and sisters: Since we are surrounded by so great a cloud of witnesses, let us rid ourselves of every burden and sin that clings to us and persevere in running the race that lies before us while keeping our eyes fixed on Jesus, the leader and perfecter of faith. For the sake of the joy that lay before him he endured the cross, despising its shame, and has taken his seat at the right of the throne of God. Consider how he endured such opposition from sinners, in order that you may not grow weary and lose heart. In your struggle against sin you have not yet resisted to the point of shedding blood.

GOSPEL
Luke 12:49–53

Jesus said to his disciples: "I have come to set the earth on fire, and how I wish it were already blazing! There is a baptism with which I must be baptized, and how great is my anguish until it is accomplished! Do you think that I have come to establish peace on the earth? No, I tell you, but rather division. From now on a household of five will be divided, three against two and two against three; a father will be divided against his son and a son against his father, a mother against her daughter and a daughter against her mother, a mother-in-law against her daughter-in-law and a daughter-in-law against her mother-in-law."

Understanding the Word

As Jesus continues on his way to Jerusalem and the events of his passion, he speaks of the challenges facing him and all of his followers. He begins by saying, "I have come to set the earth on fire, and how I wish it were already blazing!" (Luke 12:49). Fire can be a symbol of the Holy Spirit, but here it seems to refer rather to the fire of judgment, a biblical concept. "But who will endure the day of his [messenger of the covenant] coming? / And who can stand when he appears? / For he is like the refiner's fire, / or like the fuller's lye" (Malachi 3:2). John the Baptist says of Jesus, "He will baptize you with the holy Spirit and fire" (Luke 3:16).

Jesus next speaks of a "baptism with which I must be baptized" (Luke 12:50). Again, while some see this as a reference to baptism in the Spirit, it seems more plausible that Jesus is referring to his mission, which will culminate in Jerusalem. He is in anguish until his mission from the Father is completed.

The person and ministry of Jesus the prophet will be the source of division. It is not that he wants division. He speaks of establishing division on the earth rather than peace in the sense that he permits every person to choose freely for or against him. Jesus clearly came to bring peace; the angels announce at his coming. "Glory to God in the highest and on earth peace to those on whom his favor rests" (Luke 2:14). Unfortunately, many freely choose to reject this true peace of Jesus and division results, even within families.

Today's first reading highlights the prophet Jeremiah. He caused division among the people, as did Jesus. "All in all, no one in the history of Israel was more like Jesus than Jeremiah . . . Jesus was rejected by his own people; so was Jeremiah . . . Jesus was scourged, imprisoned, and put on trial for his life; so was Jeremiah" (Peter F. Ellis, "Jeremiah/Baruch," *Collegeville Bible Commentary*, 14, p. 6). Every follower of the Lord must make the free decision to accept him. That acceptance demands assigning the highest priority to love of God and neighbor in one's daily life.

Reflecting on the Word

By now just about all of summer has been unwrapped and spent. As the season drains away and summer's light dims, so too grows the realization that the busy work of life must soon be taken up in earnest once more. Once more the realization returns that life calls us seriously to particular autumn cares. No matter how fearful or challenging, each of us must follow that inner voice or else sense that life will have become less.

Such was the story of Jeremiah, who found himself prophet to the Hebrew people. He sensed an inner call to speak God's word against the nation's political alliances and against the king's penchant to trust in military machines. As a result Jeremiah found himself tossed into a well. Yet he remained committed.

It is also the story of Jesus, who came with truth as a walking stick and the kingdom as seeds of life to be scattered and sown. He also knew full well that few would walk where he would walk or choose to feed on what he would sow. Yet he would not back away from what he was about.

Such a willingness to stretch ourselves into the unknown is part of that mysterious list of things that make us human. At such times we walk in the shadow of Jesus as he leads us into new ways of being human. Seldom, if ever, is it without struggle or even pain, yet it is then that we begin to gain a fuller sense of who we truly are, and it is then that through us God brings the world to something new.

CONSIDER/ DISCUSS:

- Over what issue do you find yourself standing alone?
- Why do you choose to do so? How would life be different if you did not stand by such a conviction?

Responding to the Word

Each of us must choose to step into some unknown, guided by our God-given vision of what our lives must be about, a vision to which others are often blind. At these moments one can feel both most alone and most alive.

Spend a few minutes in quiet prayer. Ask God to show you one (or more) ways that you may be called to respond to this week's scriptures—

- in your relationship with God
- with family and friends
- at work, school, or church
- in the broader community

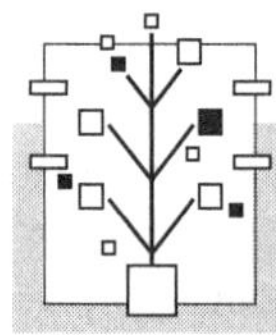

August 26, 2007

TWENTY-FIRST SUNDAY IN ORDINARY TIME

Today's Focus: A Door into Darkness

Jacques Cousteau once commented that adolescence is the best time of our life because that is when all of life's doors stand open before us. Once we begin walking through some doors, he noted, others close. So which door we walk through matters.

FIRST READING
Isaiah 66:18-21

Thus says the LORD: I know their works and their thoughts, and I come to gather nations of every language; they shall come and see my glory. I will set a sign among them; from them I will send fugitives to the nations: to Tarshish, Put and Lud, Mosoch, Tubal and Javan, to the distant coastlands that have never heard of my fame, or seen my glory; and they shall proclaim my glory among the nations. They shall bring all your brothers and sisters from all the nations as an offering to the LORD, on horses and in chariots, in carts, upon mules and dromedaries, to Jerusalem, my holy mountain, says the LORD, just as the Israelites bring their offering to the house of the LORD in clean vessels. Some of these I will take as priests and Levites, says the LORD.

PSALM RESPONSE
Mark 16:15

Go out to all the world and tell the good news.

SECOND READING
Hebrews 12: 5–7, 11–13

Brothers and sisters, You have forgotten the exhortation addressed to you as children:

"My son, do not disdain the discipline of the Lord
or lose heart when reproved by him;
for whom the Lord loves, he disciplines;
he scourges every son he acknowledges."

Endure your trials as "discipline"; God treats you as sons. For what "son" is there whom his father does not discipline? At the time, all discipline seems a cause not for joy but for pain, yet later it brings the peaceful fruit of righteousness to those who are trained by it.

So strengthen your drooping hands and your weak knees. Make straight paths for your feet, that what is lame may not be disjointed but healed.

GOSPEL
Luke 13:22–30

Jesus passed through towns and villages, teaching as he went and making his way to Jerusalem. Someone asked him, "Lord, will only a few people be saved?" He answered them, "Strive to enter through the narrow gate, for many, I tell you, will attempt to enter but will not be strong enough. After the master of the house has arisen and locked the door, then will you stand outside knocking and saying, 'Lord, open the door for us.' He will say to you in reply, 'I do not know where you are from.' And you will say, 'We ate and drank in your company and you taught in our streets.' Then he will say to you, 'I do not know where you are from. Depart from me, all you evildoers!' And there will be wailing and grinding of teeth when you see Abraham, Isaac, and Jacob and all the prophets in the kingdom of God and you yourselves cast out. And people will come from the east and the west and from the north and the south and will recline at table in the kingdom of God. For behold, some are last who will be first, and some are first who will be last."

Understanding the Word

In today's Gospel Jesus calls upon his followers for a true *metanoia*, a reformation of life. The Greek word means "a change of mind." This involves setting clear priorities in one's life—a life reformed, reshaped so that God is at the center. Earlier in the chapter Jesus is explicit. "But I tell you, if you do not repent [reform your lives], you will all perish" (Luke 13:3).

Luke reminds the reader that Jesus is continuing his journey to Jerusalem. He takes the occasion of this journey to instruct his disciples on critical issues, such as the need for reformation of one's life. This reformation calls for total commitment to Christ. He makes clear that a superficial knowledge will not suffice—"We ate and drank in your company and you taught in our streets" (13:26). The struggle to enter the narrow door implies that the proper reformation of life is urgent, that it requires total dedication to Jesus. He is the Lord, the master, who has control over the door to salvation.

Jesus also warns his contemporaries that if they do not reform, the Gentiles, who will come from the four corners of the globe, will replace them in the future. Today's first reading has Yahweh proclaiming, "I come to gather nations of every language; they shall come and see my glory" (Isaiah 66:18). The new, reconstituted Israel will be open to both Jews and Gentiles who will truly reform their lives.

Christ will say to those who did not reform their lives, "Depart from me, all you evildoers!" (Luke 13:27). Having rejected Jesus and his salvation, they will experience "wailing and grinding of teeth" (13:28).

The kingdom of God is portrayed here as a banquet, a frequent biblical image. (Isaiah 25:6, for example, promises, "On this mountain the LORD of hosts / will provide for all peoples / A feast of rich food and choice wines.") There will be great rejoicing at this banquet. There Jewish patriarchs and prophets, wonderful examples of reformation of life, will be joined by the saved from every nation, both Jew and Gentile.

Reflecting on the Word

The gift of options and choices can be both a blessing and a curse. How does one know the right door? How does one decide? Today's Gospel admonishes us to enter through the narrow one, yet what does that mean? Is it the least attractive? The most difficult? The one without any fun on the other side? The one no one else chooses? The one that sets us apart? Which is the narrow door?

The psychologist Carl Jung posited that each of us has a shadow side to our personality. There are those aspects of who we are that we would prefer to keep in the dark. In part that shadow is a composite of all that we would prefer to not be. It holds our angers and greed and instincts for revenge, our laziness and lusts and boastful pride.

Our shadows also hold our failed ideals—the ideal parent or spouse or disciple of Jesus. None of us ever quite measures up, and most of us would rather keep that fact against the back wall of our darkest closet. The doors to such closets are very narrow indeed.

It is, however, only by entering such darknesses and coming to recognize and admit who we truly are that we also come to discover God standing in the midst of our weakest selves. So, advises Jesus, do enter through the narrow door. Don't back away from your most honest self. Recognize who you are, in the light and in the dark, lest no one recognize you when you knock for entrance into the kingdom.

CONSIDER/ DISCUSS:

- What aspect of who you are is the most difficult to accept?
- What is your community's shadow? The Church's shadow?

Responding to the Word

Crossing the doorway into one's shadow side is a journey everyone makes, not only believers. People come journeying from the east and the west, from the north and the south, believers and those not yet so. To know the journey ahead of time, however, is a most saving grace.

Spend a few minutes in quiet prayer. Ask God to show you one (or more) ways that you may be called to respond to this week's scriptures—

- in your relationship with God
- with family and friends
- at work, school, or church
- in the broader community

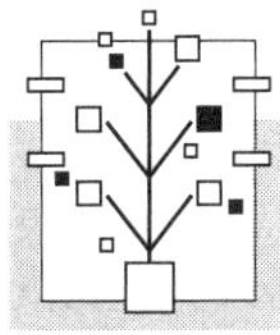

September 2, 2007

TWENTY-SECOND SUNDAY IN ORDINARY TIME

Today's Focus: Elusive Humility

Though most of us do seek happiness, nothing guarantees that God made us to be happy on this side of the great divide we call death. Nevertheless, we sometimes come to expect happiness, even demand it as if we had some sort of right to it. Perhaps we should be seeking humility first.

FIRST READING
Sirach 3:17–18, 20, 28–29

My child, conduct your affairs with humility,
and you will be loved more than a giver of gifts.
Humble yourself the more, the greater you are,
and you will find favor with God.
What is too sublime for you, seek not,
into things beyond your strength search not.
The mind of a sage appreciates proverbs,
and an attentive ear is the joy of the wise.
Water quenches a flaming fire,
and alms atone for sins.

PSALM RESPONSE
Psalm 68:11b

God, in your goodness, you have made a home for the poor.

SECOND READING
Hebrews 12: 18–19, 22–24a

Brothers and sisters: You have not approached that which could be touched and a blazing fire and gloomy darkness and storm and a trumpet blast and a voice speaking words such that those who heard begged that no message be further addressed to them. No, you have approached Mount Zion and the city of the living God, the heavenly Jerusalem, and countless angels in festal gathering, and the assembly of the firstborn enrolled in heaven, and God the judge of all, and the spirits of the just made perfect, and Jesus, the mediator of a new covenant, and the sprinkled blood that speaks more eloquently than that of Abel.

GOSPEL
Luke 14:1, 7–14

On a sabbath Jesus went to dine at the home of one of the leading Pharisees, and the people there were observing him carefully.

He told a parable to those who had been invited, noticing how they were choosing the places of honor at the table. "When you are invited by someone to a wedding banquet, do not recline at table in the place of honor. A more distinguished guest than you may have been invited by him, and the host who invited both of you may approach you and say, 'Give your place to this man,' and then you would proceed with embarrassment to take the lowest place. Rather, when you are invited, go and take the lowest place so that when the host comes to you he may say, 'My friend, move up to a higher position.' Then you will enjoy the esteem of your companions at the table. For everyone who exalts himself will be humbled, but the one who humbles himself will be exalted." Then he said to the host who invited him, "When you hold a lunch or a dinner, do not invite your friends or your brothers or your relatives or your wealthy neighbors, in case they may invite you back and you have repayment. Rather, when you hold a banquet, invite the poor, the crippled, the lame, the blind; blessed indeed will you be because of their inability to repay you. For you will be repaid at the resurrection of the righteous."

Understanding the Word

The second reading today is from the Letter to the Hebrews. It is in fact a written homily, a "message of encouragement" (Hebrews 13:22) rather than a letter like those of St. Paul. The purpose of the homily is to keep Christians from abandoning their faith, from becoming apostates. While there are many questions concerning such issues as its authorship and recipients, this letter contains wonderful teaching about Jesus and his relationship to the old covenant. It asserts that Christ is especially the Word of the Father, God's final revelation. He is also the priest of the new covenant. In contrast to the sacrifices of the old covenant, Christ's single offering removes sin once and for all.

Today's passage from the last section of Hebrews brings together the principal themes of the book. The reader is presented with the strong contrast between the Mosaic covenant and the new covenant of Jesus. Gloom, darkness, and prohibited access to God characterize the beginning of the old covenant (see Exodus 19:16–25).

The Christian covenant, by contrast, is presented as a joyful experience. God is present with Jesus. The Father and the Son are approachable. The angels, the saints of the old covenant, the assembly of Christians all join in this joyful experience on Mount Zion, the heavenly Jerusalem. Though many Christians are still on earth, the author portrays them as with Jesus since they have already known his graces, his saving action. They share, therefore, in realized eschatology, an important theme in the Gospel of John.

Verse 24 highlights the role of Jesus as priest of the new covenant, saving us by shedding his blood. The blood of Abel calls for vengeance (Genesis 4:10), but the blood of Christ calls for confidence (Hebrews 10:19).

God is there on Mount Zion as "judge of all" (Hebrews 12:23). Though the covenant of Jesus is infinitely superior to the old covenant, there will be judgment, accountability for one's actions. The author of Hebrews is therefore imploring all Christians to remain faithful to Christ, not to become apostates.

Reflecting on the Word

Life is about so much more than being happy. Happiness is more a by-product than a goal. It takes humility to be able to live that way, acknowledging that neither you nor I are the center of the universe. None of us is—not of the universe, not of this planet earth, maybe not even of our own lives. Knowing that, and living it as well, is what humility is about. Humility is . . .

. . . understanding that something is not amiss in another person simply because he or she does not like you.

. . . accepting the fact that another's preference for a McDonald's cheeseburger versus your preference for *osso bucco* (or even knowing what it is) does not put the two of you on different planes of human worth.

. . . being willing to clean not only your own bathroom, but someone else's bathroom as well.

. . . respecting the opinion of a teenager when you yourself are over 60; or being a teenager who appreciates the wisdom of someone who is much older.

. . . realizing that someone of the opposite political persuasion may be more intelligent, or compassionate, or insightful, or even more holy—and being at peace with that fact.

All of that and much more is the hidden underside of the virtue of humility, for no one of us is the axis on which worlds spin.

In the end, such an attitude of humility toward life and its patrons affects our comings and goings, the paths that we walk and the tables at which we sit. In fact, it has already begun. It happens at the Lord's table, where all are welcome.

CONSIDER/ DISCUSS:

- What is your working definition of humility? How do you try to embody it in your life?
- With whom would you least enjoy sitting at table? Is there a way in which they show the face of God to you? Is there anyone for whom they are a blessing?

Responding to the Word

When the simple and the wise, the old and the young, the rich and the needy, the healthy and the weak all mingle and feast side by side, then the kingdom will have been realized.

Spend a few minutes in quiet prayer. Ask God to show you one (or more) ways that you may be called to respond to this week's scriptures—

- in your relationship with God
- with family and friends
- at work, school, or church
- in the broader community

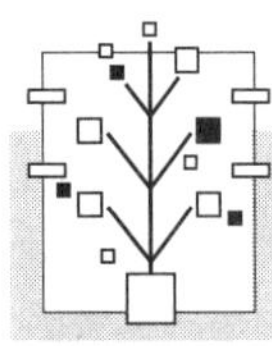

September 9, 2007

TWENTY-THIRD SUNDAY IN ORDINARY TIME

Today's Focus: The Price of Holy

These days we've turned the calendar page on summer for another year, even if September 21 is yet to come. Summer has been left behind, and with it all its cotton candy picnics and parades of fireworks and beaches. Over the years we've left enough of life behind as well—not only our summers.

FIRST READING
Wisdom 9: 13–18b

Who can know God's counsel,
  or who can conceive what the LORD intends?
For the deliberations of mortals are timid,
  and unsure are our plans.
For the corruptible body burdens the soul
  and the earthen shelter weighs down the mind
    that has many concerns.
And scarce do we guess the things on earth,
  and what is within our grasp we find with difficulty;
  but when things are in heaven, who can search them out?
Or who ever knew your counsel, except you had given wisdom
  and sent your holy spirit from on high?
And thus were the paths of those on earth made straight.

PSALM RESPONSE
Psalm 90:1

In every age, O Lord, you have been our refuge.

SECOND READING
Philemon 9–10, 12–17

I, Paul, an old man, and now also a prisoner for Christ Jesus, urge you on behalf of my child Onesimus, whose father I have become in my imprisonment; I am sending him, that is, my own heart, back to you. I should have liked to retain him for myself, so that he might serve me on your behalf in my imprisonment for the gospel, but I did not want to do anything without your consent, so that the good you do might not be forced but voluntary. Perhaps this is why he was away from you for a while, that you might have him back forever, no longer as a slave but more than a slave, a brother, beloved especially to me, but even more so to you, as a man and in the Lord. So if you regard me as a partner, welcome him as you would me.

GOSPEL *Luke 14:25–33*

Great crowds were traveling with Jesus, and he turned and addressed them, "If anyone comes to me without hating his father and mother, wife and children, brothers and sisters, and even his own life, he cannot be my disciple. Whoever does not carry his own cross and come after me cannot be my disciple. Which of you wishing to construct a tower does not first sit down and calculate the cost to see if there is enough for its completion? Otherwise, after laying the foundation and finding himself unable to finish the work the onlookers should laugh at him and say, 'This one began to build but did not have the resources to finish.' Or what king marching into battle would not first sit down and decide whether with ten thousand troops he can successfully oppose another king advancing upon him with twenty thousand troops? But if not, while he is still far away, he will send a delegation to ask for peace terms. In the same way, anyone of you who does not renounce all his possessions cannot be my disciple."

Understanding the Word

Saint Paul's letter to Philemon, from which today's second reading is taken, has only twenty-five verses, but contains important teaching concerning the effects of baptism. Paul begins with greetings "to Philemon, our beloved and our co-worker, to Apphia our sister, to Archippus our fellow soldier, and to the church at your house" (Philemon 1–2). In the early period of the church the followers of Jesus assembled for liturgical celebrations at the homes of fellow Christians.

The practical purpose of this short letter is to ensure a truly Christian welcome for Onesimus, Philemon's runaway slave. Paul speaks of "my child Onesimus, whose father I have become in my imprisonment" (10). Since Onesimus by his baptism has become a Christian, Paul expects Philemon to receive the runaway slave as a brother in Christ. Paul refers to the new relationship by his teaching that all baptized persons are "in the Lord" (16), brothers and sisters of Jesus Christ. In the letter to the Galatians Paul spells out this point: "There is neither Jew nor Greek, there is neither slave nor free person, there is not male and female; for you are all one in Christ Jesus" (Galatians 3:28). This teaching will eventually undermine the institution of slavery.

Paul goes further, asking Philemon to return Onesimus to him for the important ministry of the gospel (13). He indicates his close relationship to the runaway slave by referring to him as "my own heart" (12). The Greek word translated "heart" is "a term that conveys such depth that, with this personal identification with Onesimus, Paul expresses one of the closest possible bonds of love that can unite one person with another" (Judith M. Ryan, "Philemon," *Sacra Pagina*, p. 236).

Despite this closeness with Onesimus, Paul, while clearly exerting moral pressure, respects Philemon's free will. "I did not want to do anything without your consent, so that the good you do might not be forced but voluntary" (14). Paul even sees a providential purpose in the separation of Onesimus from Philemon "for a while." Now Philemon has him back "forever" as a brother in Christ (15).

Reflecting on the Word

It's said that we never really grow up until both of our parents have died. I suspect that most who have had to walk that path recognize some truth there. So when the Gospel advises us to turn our back on father and mother and family and even on ourselves—maybe it's not about rejecting but about becoming able to live the gospel more maturely, about releasing our grip on the past and growing up. Maybe letting go of childish things is the cost and also the wisdom of the God who waits patiently for us.

One of life's tasks, it seems, is to learn the balancing act between loving without possessiveness and relinquishing without indifference or abandonment. In truth, perhaps we never really learn to balance the two. We mostly lean in the direction opposite where we are at the time, until we suspect we may have leaned too far and switch directions. It's a wisdom we come to that's worthwhile for parenting but also for marriage and one's profession and growing old and just about everything else that life serves up.

This balancing is also at the heart of faith and discipleship. It's how we come to recognize the hand of God in our lives, by living in such a way that God has the freedom to rearrange the pieces and so bring us to fuller life. It's the wisdom that teaches us how to be a disciple but also the sort of discipleship that brings us to wisdom. It's also the light shining forth in today's reading from the book of Wisdom.

CONSIDER/ DISCUSS:

- What or who has been the most painful "letting go" you have had to face?
- How have you grown from the times you have had to "let go"? Have they brought you to any sort of wisdom?

Responding to the Word

"Renounce your possessions," the Gospel insists. We can't say that we always have. Rather, it seems that we've often done more accumulating than renouncing. And yet each accumulation may have made room for one more way of being made new as the disciples we all are called to become.

Spend a few minutes in quiet prayer. Ask God to show you one (or more) ways that you may be called to respond to this week's scriptures—

- in your relationship with God
- with family and friends
- at work, school, or church
- in the broader community

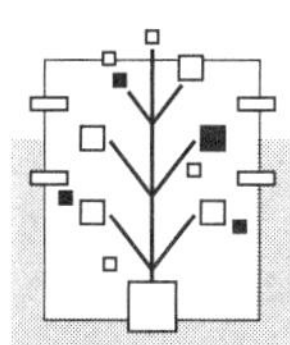

September 16, 2007

TWENTY-FOURTH SUNDAY IN ORDINARY TIME

Today's Focus: Lost and Found

Sometimes life finds us when we didn't know we were lost. We can be like toddlers wandering off into a countryside exploding with amazing discoveries, even straying obliviously to the edge of calamity, and then snatched back into life and love without realizing we'd walked away.

FIRST READING
Exodus 32: 7–11, 13–14

The LORD said to Moses, "Go down at once to your people, whom you brought out of the land of Egypt, for they have become depraved. They have soon turned aside from the way I pointed out to them, making for themselves a molten calf and worshiping it, sacrificing to it and crying out, 'This is your God, O Israel, who brought you out of the land of Egypt!' I see how stiff-necked this people is," continued the LORD to Moses. "Let me alone, then, that my wrath may blaze up against them to consume them. Then I will make of you a great nation."

But Moses implored the LORD, his God, saying, "Why, O LORD, should your wrath blaze up against your own people, whom you brought out of the land of Egypt with such great power and with so strong a hand? Remember your servants Abraham, Isaac, and Israel, and how you swore to them by your own self, saying, 'I will make your descendants as numerous as the stars in the sky; and all this land that I promised, I will give your descendants as their perpetual heritage.' " So the LORD relented in the punishment he had threatened to inflict on his people.

PSALM RESPONSE
Luke 15:18

I will rise and go to my father.

SECOND READING
1 Timothy 1: 12–17

Beloved: I am grateful to him who has strengthened me, Christ Jesus our Lord, because he considered me trustworthy in appointing me to the ministry. I was once a blasphemer and a persecutor and arrogant, but I have been mercifully treated because I acted out of ignorance in my unbelief. Indeed, the grace of our Lord has been abundant, along with the faith and love that are in Christ Jesus. This saying is trustworthy and deserves full acceptance: Christ Jesus came into the world to save sinners. Of these I am the foremost. But for that reason I was mercifully treated, so that in me, as the foremost, Christ Jesus might display all his patience as an example for those who would come to believe in him for everlasting life. To the king of ages, incorruptible, invisible, the only God, honor and glory forever and ever. Amen.

In the shorter form of the reading, the passage in brackets is omitted.

GOSPEL
Luke 15:1–32 or 15:1–10

Tax collectors and sinners were all drawing near to listen to Jesus, but the Pharisees and scribes began to complain, saying, "This man welcomes sinners and eats with them." So to them he addressed this parable. "What man among you having a hundred sheep and losing one of them would not leave the ninety-nine in the desert and go after the lost one until he finds it? And when he does find it, he sets it on his shoulders with great joy and, upon his arrival home, he calls together his friends and neighbors and says to them, 'Rejoice with me because I have found my lost sheep.' I tell you, in just the same way there will be more joy in heaven over one sinner who repents than over ninety-nine righteous people who have no need of repentance.

"Or what woman having ten coins and losing one would not light a lamp and sweep the house, searching carefully until she finds it? And when she does find it, she calls together her friends and neighbors and says to them, 'Rejoice with me because I have found the coin that I lost.' In just the same way, I tell you, there will be rejoicing among the angels of God over one sinner who repents."

[Then he said, "A man had two sons, and the younger son said to his father, 'Father give me the share of your estate that should come to me.' So the father divided the property between them. After a few days, the younger son collected all his belongings and set off to a distant country where he squandered his inheritance on a life of dissipation. When he had freely spent everything, a severe famine struck that country, and he found himself in dire need. So he hired himself out to one of the local citizens who sent him to his farm to tend the swine. And he longed to eat his fill of the pods on which the swine fed, but nobody gave him any. Coming to his senses he thought, 'How many of my father's hired workers have more than enough food to eat, but here am I, dying from hunger. I shall get up and go to my father and I shall say to him, "Father, I have sinned against heaven and against you. I no longer deserve to be called your son; treat me as you would treat one of your hired workers." ' So he got up and went back to his father. While he was still a long way off, his father caught sight of him, and was filled with compassion. He ran to his son, embraced him and kissed him. His son said to him, 'Father, I have sinned against heaven and against you; I no longer deserve to be called your son.' But his father ordered his servants, 'Quickly bring the finest robe and put it on him; put a ring on his finger and sandals on his feet. Take the fattened calf and slaughter it. Then let us celebrate with a feast, because this son of mine was dead, and has come to life again; he was lost, and has been found.' Then the celebration began. Now the older son had been out in the field and, on his way back, as he neared the house, he heard the sound of music and dancing. He called one of the servants and asked what this might mean. The servant said to him, 'Your brother has returned and your father has slaughtered the fattened calf because he has him back safe and sound.' He became angry, and when he refused to enter the house, his father came out and pleaded with him. He said to his father in reply, 'Look, all these years I served you and not once did I disobey your orders; yet you never gave me even a young goat to feast on with my friends. But when your son returns, who swallowed up your property with prostitutes, for him you slaughter the fattened calf.' He said to him, 'My son, you are here with me always; everything I have is yours. But now we must celebrate and rejoice, because your brother was dead and has come to life again; he was lost and has been found.' "]

Understanding the Word

Today's Gospel is an amazing teaching on the unconditional love of God for all. God's children are more important to God than anything they may have done. Jesus welcomes the tax collectors and sinners, the marginalized of his day. The self-righteous Pharisees and scribes are upset and say, "This man [a pejorative expression in the Greek text] welcomes sinners and eats with them" (Luke 15:2).

Jesus' response here, as always, is that he cares for sinners because his Father loves everyone. The three parables all present God as not only looking for the sinner, but also accepting the sinner back with great rejoicing. God not only forgives and forgets, but also does it with great joy! In the final verse today the father, symbolizing God, says, "We must celebrate and rejoice" (15:32).

The shepherd rejoicing over his sheep that was lost and then found and the woman who recovers her lost coin represent God, who pursues sinners and tries to bring them back so that there can be "rejoicing among the angels of God over one sinner who repents" (15:10).

The third parable portrays a loving father dealing with two children who have different problems. But the principal point is that the father has great love for both his sons. One important difference in this parable is the fact that the son who left his father has free will. After his departure and life of dissolution, he ends up tending pigs. Since the Jewish people consider pigs unclean, this occupation represents the worst moral degradation. But he does repent freely and returns. The compassionate father "ran to his son, embraced him and kissed him" (15:20).

When the elder son, representing the Pharisees and scribes, becomes aware of the banquet prepared for his brother, he is angry. But the father comes out to him and invites him into the banquet. Jesus stops there with the parable. The invitation is there for the Pharisees and scribes to enter God's kingdom and rejoice with the repentant sinners. The decision is up to them!

Reflecting on the Word

Writing, it seems, is mostly about waiting, though most of us tend to think of it as a pen-in-hand sort of thing, or a fingers-on-the-keyboard activity. Eventually it does come to that, but much of the time before can be spent waiting. Some would say it's waiting for the muse to show, or imagination to kick in, or for the idea to float free.

Anyone who has ever tried to do some writing—a description of what it's like to fall in love or a piece of poetry or an attempt to share the meandering path of a soul's journey—knows that such writing takes a great deal of waiting before it can happen, if indeed it ever happens at all. And sometimes when it does happen, it feels more like being found than it does like succeeding.

Many of the inner pieces of our lives seem to be like that. Discovering one's calling, falling in love, faith and the conversion that gives rise to it, recognizing the gifts sewn into the hems and cuffs of our lives—they all seem to find us rather than the other way around. Sometimes it's even in spite of our own efforts. Sometimes they feel like the very work and intention of the Divine One.

The scriptures are filled with stories of God doing the finding, even when we didn't know we'd been lost. That's the way it is with us and God—so often being found without even asking.

CONSIDER/ DISCUSS:

- What event in your life has given you the sense of being found? What has been pure gift, without any effort on your part?
- On the one hand, why bother being good if God will find us and free us from our sin anyway? On the other hand, if we can extricate ourselves from our sin, why do we need the Lord Jesus?

Responding to the Word

God does seem to find us, and also finds a life calling for us, and finds love for us, and finds meaning for us, and even finds a way out of our sin for us—even when we didn't know we needed to be found.

Spend a few minutes in quiet prayer. Ask God to show you one (or more) ways that you may be called to respond to this week's scriptures—

- in your relationship with God
- with family and friends
- at work, school, or church
- in the broader community

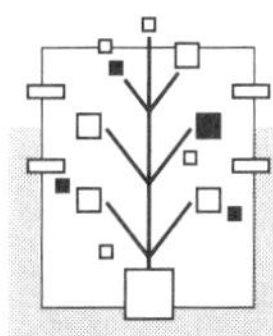

September 23, 2007

TWENTY-FIFTH SUNDAY IN ORDINARY TIME

Today's Focus: The "Sly" Side of God

It's been said that God writes straight with crooked lines. Sometimes what seems unfortunate turns out to be a blessing. We find ourselves wondering what to accept in life and what to resist.

FIRST READING
Amos 8:4–7

Hear this, you who trample upon the needy
  and destroy the poor of the land!
"When will the new moon be over," you ask,
  "that we may sell our grain,
  and the sabbath, that we may display the wheat?
We will diminish the ephah,
  add to the shekel,
  and fix our scales for cheating!
We will buy the lowly for silver,
  and the poor for a pair of sandals;
  even the refuse of the wheat we will sell!"
The LORD has sworn by the pride of Jacob:
  Never will I forget a thing they have done!

PSALM RESPONSE
Psalm 113:1a, 7b

Praise the Lord, who lifts up the poor.

SECOND READING
1 Timothy 2: 1–8

Beloved: First of all, I ask that supplications, prayers, petitions, and thanksgivings be offered for everyone, for kings and for all in authority, that we may lead a quiet and tranquil life in all devotion and dignity. This is good and pleasing to God our savior, who wills everyone to be saved and to come to knowledge of the truth.

  For there is one God.
  There is also one mediator between God and men,
  the man Christ Jesus,
  who gave himself as ransom for all.

This was the testimony at the proper time. For this I was appointed preacher and apostle—I am speaking the truth, I am not lying—, teacher of the Gentiles in faith and truth.

It is my wish, then, that in every place the men should pray, lifting up holy hands, without anger or argument.

In the shorter form of the reading, the passage in brackets is omitted.

GOSPEL
Luke 16:1–13
or 16:10–13

Jesus said to his disciples, ["A rich man had a steward who was reported to him for squandering his property. He summoned him and said, 'What is this I hear about you? Prepare a full account of your stewardship, because you can no longer be my steward.' The steward said to himself, 'What shall I do, now that my master is taking the position of steward away from me? I am not strong enough to dig and I am ashamed to beg. I know what I shall do so that, when I am removed from the stewardship, they may welcome me into their homes.' He called in his master's debtors one by one. To the first he said, 'How much do you owe my master?' He replied, 'One hundred measures of olive oil.' He said to him, 'Here is your promissory note. Sit down and quickly write one for fifty.' Then to another the steward said, 'And you, how much do you owe?' He replied, 'One hundred kors of wheat.' The steward said to him, 'Here is your promissory note; write one for eighty.' And the master commended that dishonest steward for acting prudently.

"For the children of this world are more prudent in dealing with their own generation than are the children of light. I tell you, make friends for yourselves with dishonest wealth, so that when it fails, you will be welcomed into eternal dwellings.] The person who is trustworthy in very small matters is also trustworthy in great ones; and the person who is dishonest in very small matters is also dishonest in great ones. If, therefore, you are not trustworthy with dishonest wealth, who will trust you with true wealth? If you are not trustworthy with what belongs to another, who will give you what is yours? No servant can serve two masters. He will either hate one and love the other, or be devoted to one and despise the other. You cannot serve both God and mammon."

Understanding the Word

Today's Gospel is part of a chapter that speaks to the right use of material possessions by Jesus' followers. The parable, unique to Luke, encourages prudence and resolute action on the part of the disciples.

The parable is not easy to understand. It may be helpful to realize the economics behind it. A manager working for a wealthy landowner handled his material and financial possessions. When he made a loan of his master's property, the interest was added to the principal and only the total amount appeared on the contract. The interest could be very high despite the prohibition against usury in the Old Testament (Exodus 22:24). The interest or commission belonged to the manager. When this manager realized that he was losing his position because of past dishonesty, he made a prudent decision to give up his commission to his master's debtors. He wanted to assure security and a home when he would soon be dismissed. This action was not immoral or illegal because the commission belonged to him.

The landlord praised the manager for his prudence, but did not approve his previous wrongdoing (see Luke 16:1). The point that Jesus makes is that his followers should be equally prudent when responding to him and to his demand for repentance. They would thereby earn an eternal home in heaven. Jesus was concerned because "the children of this world are more prudent in dealing with their own generation than are the children of light" (16:8).

After this application of the parable, the Gospel gives several independent sayings of Jesus concerning the use of wealth. Jesus wants his followers to use money to assist the needy and thereby assure their salvation (16:9). Daily fidelity is also expected of Christians (16:10–12). He calls wealth "dishonest" (16:9) because it often leads human beings to put wealth before God. Jesus says one must choose God or mammon (16:13). Mammon is personified as a false god attracting persons away from the true and only God. Jesus demands that we serve God, an honorable activity for every person, and not mammon, an enslaving and degrading activity. Saint Paul speaks of a greedy person, for example, as an idolater (Ephesians 5:5).

Reflecting on the Word

The conversation took place years ago. The couple had come to arrange for a celebration of their golden wedding anniversary. So we sat and talked, and they shared their story of how young they were when they married, and of the three children they had had in the first four years—a daughter and then two sons. They laughed in retrospect at their struggles and arguments. Finally they talked about their fourth child, a son, born when the other three were in their late teens and almost twenty. The pregnancy was not a pleasant time, they explained. This child was seen as an intrusion on their plans for the future. They found themselves needing to work through resentments and some canceling of dreams. But in the end, they said, when the time came for the birth, they were able to welcome their fourth child with love.

Now thirty years later it was this third son who was taking care of them in their old age. The husband had had a mild stroke that left him unable to negotiate life as freely as before, and she was plagued by arthritis. But it was this youngest son who lived with them and watched over them and loved them as they had loved him.

Sometimes God is like the steward in the Gospel, this fellow who slyly finds a way to make things turn out in the end, who will use any means available to make life survivable. This may not be the usual take on this passage, but parables are often about how God moves in our lives. Sometimes the Gospel writers add their own endings to make them fit their own message, and this seems to me what Luke did in this parable. So then perhaps God is the steward, the sly one who juggles the books to make life balance out. And that may be why Jesus commends the steward (even though we keep referring to him as unjust). Maybe he was just sly, kind of sneaky, but for a good purpose, as God seems to have been with the elderly couple who came to tell me their story.

CONSIDER/ DISCUSS:

- What in your life began as a burden but turned out to be a blessing?
- If God is a sly trickster of sorts, why do you suppose that is?

Responding to the Word

Much of life seems not to follow established rules or logical procedures. Sometimes the most we can do is go along with it, wondering whether it is chance or misfortune or the "sly" hand of God. Yet we can learn the difference if we look through the eyes of faith.

Spend a few minutes in quiet prayer. Ask God to show you one (or more) ways that you may be called to respond to this week's scriptures—

- in your relationship with God
- with family and friends
- at work, school, or church
- in the broader community

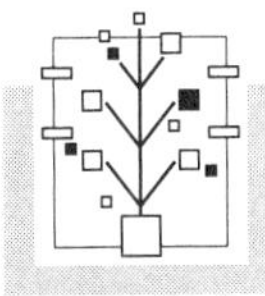

September 30, 2007

TWENTY-SIXTH SUNDAY IN ORDINARY TIME

Today's Focus: The Day the Sky Fell

How do we know what we do not know? How do we know what we are blind to or deaf to? How do we know what we're missing in life because we've grown insensitive? It seems we seldom change unless we are hit over the head.

FIRST READING
Amos 6:1a, 4–7

Thus says the LORD the God of hosts:
Woe to the complacent in Zion!
Lying upon beds of ivory,
  stretched comfortably on their couches,
they eat lambs taken from the flock,
  and calves from the stall!
Improvising to the music of the harp,
  like David, they devise their own accompaniment.
They drink wine from bowls
  and anoint themselves with the best oils;
  yet they are not made ill by the collapse of Joseph!
Therefore, now they shall be the first to go into exile,
  and their wanton revelry shall be done away with.

PSALM RESPONSE
Psalm 146:1b

Praise the Lord, my soul!

SECOND READING
1 Timothy 6: 11–16

But you, man of God, pursue righteousness, devotion, faith, love, patience, and gentleness. Compete well for the faith. Lay hold of eternal life, to which you were called when you made the noble confession in the presence of many witnesses. I charge you before God, who gives life to all things, and before Christ Jesus, who gave testimony under Pontius Pilate for the noble confession, to keep the commandment without stain or reproach until the appearance of our Lord Jesus Christ that the blessed and only ruler will make manifest at the proper time, the King of kings and Lord of lords, who alone has immortality, who dwells in unapproachable light, and whom no human being has seen or can see. To him be honor and eternal power. Amen.

GOSPEL
Luke 16:19–31

Jesus said to the Pharisees: "There was a rich man who dressed in purple garments and fine linen and dined sumptuously each day. And lying at his door was a poor man named Lazarus, covered with sores, who would gladly have eaten his fill of the scraps that fell from the rich man's table. Dogs even used to come and lick his sores. When the poor man died, he was carried away by angels to the bosom of Abraham. The rich man also died and was buried, and from the netherworld, where he was in torment, he raised his eyes and saw Abraham far off and Lazarus at his side. And he cried out,

'Father Abraham, have pity on me. Send Lazarus to dip the tip of his finger in water and cool my tongue, for I am suffering torment in these flames.' Abraham replied, 'My child, remember that you received what was good during your lifetime while Lazarus likewise received what was bad; but now he is comforted here, whereas you are tormented. Moreover, between us and you a great chasm is established to prevent anyone from crossing who might wish to go from our side to yours or from your side to ours.' He said, 'Then I beg you, father, send him to my father's house, for I have five brothers, so that he may warn them, lest they too come to this place of torment.' But Abraham replied, 'They have Moses and the prophets. Let them listen to them.' He said, 'Oh no, father Abraham, but if someone from the dead goes to them, they will repent.' Then Abraham said, 'If they will not listen to Moses and the prophets, neither will they be persuaded if someone should rise from the dead.' "

Understanding the Word

The Gospel of Luke deserves the title "Gospel of Social Justice." Today's reading is a perfect example of Luke's concern for the poor and vulnerable. The rich man dresses and banquets in splendid fashion every day. Lazarus, a poor man, lies at the door of the rich man covered with sores and eager to eat even the scraps from the rich man's table.

Then there is a startling reversal of fortunes. Lazarus dies and merits a place of honor with Abraham; the rich man at his death is confined to the torments of the netherworld. Abraham insists that the chasm between the two main characters in this parable is unbridgeable. The rich man and his brothers did not respond to the need for repentance, another important theme of Luke.

The rich man "cried out, 'Father Abraham, have pity on me' " (Luke 16:24), but to be a true child of Abraham requires more than being a genetic descendant. One must imitate the truly living faith of Abraham manifested by good deeds. Having refused mercy to Lazarus, the rich man nevertheless asks pity from Abraham.

It is important to note that it is the improper use of wealth that is the problem here. Both the Old Testament and Jesus demanded the preferential option for the poor and vulnerable. "The needy will never be lacking in the land; that is why I command you to open your hand to your poor and needy kinsman in your country" (Deuteronomy 15:11). In his description of the Last Judgment Jesus calls lack of concern for the poor and needy lack of concern for him (Matthew 25:31–46).

Jesus addressed this parable to the Pharisees, "who loved money, heard all these things and sneered at him" (Luke 16:14). However, Luke wants every generation of Christians to take to heart the lesson of this parable. Followers of Jesus must reach out to the poor.

As a footnote, the Christian reader will also see an allusion to Christ's death and resurrection in Abraham's statement that the brothers would not repent even if "someone should rise from the dead" (16:31).

Reflecting on the Word

"The sky is falling! The sky is falling!" cried Chicken Little. It turned out to be only a pea.

When on September 11, 2001 the two towers of the World Trade Center came crashing down, they were not the sky, but for many they seemed to be the very pillars that held the sky braced and arched over this nation's largest city. That evening people across our nation gathered in churches and synagogues and mosques to pray, drawn like metal shavings to some magnetic power beyond themselves. Yet what was it that drew us? It did not seem to be fear, not guilt or regret for past behavior either. Yet we came, dazed perhaps, or driven, certainly seeking something for which no one had words.

Perhaps we came because each of us had become sharply aware of something to which we had grown dulled—that we are not in control of our lives. On that day the chasm between where we live and where we hoped to live seemed unbridgeable, and we wondered how or when it had happened.

It may have been that our quest for the good life had brought us to the point where we seemed no longer to need even God. Perhaps we no longer even wanted to need God; we enjoyed our self-sufficiency so much that even wanting to need seemed foreign and strange. If that is the chasm—that we have become incapable of recognizing the beauty of being in need and dependent—maybe that is why any of us came that night, because we had a glimmer of the other side, of recognizing the need to need.

CONSIDER/ DISCUSS:

- On September 11 and the days following, why did you pray?
- What have you become more conscious of, more aware of, since that day?
- How do you remain conscious of and sensitive to the presence of the poor? Of Lazarus among us?

Responding to the Word

As long as we're still alive, as long as we can glimpse what it looks like to need the Lord, then there is still hope; then the chasm has not yet become so wide that we cannot go back. Then Lazarus is still a brother and not simply a beggar we pass; then the very presence of God can still shine in our hearts.

Spend a few minutes in quiet prayer. Ask God to show you one (or more) ways that you may be called to respond to this week's scriptures—

- in your relationship with God
- with family and friends
- at work, school, or church
- in the broader community

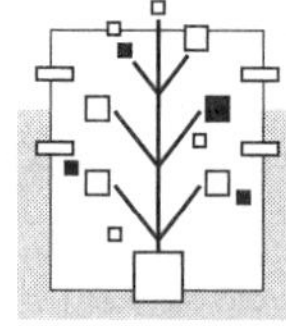

October 7, 2007

TWENTY-SEVENTH SUNDAY IN ORDINARY TIME

Today's Focus: Dreams Matter

In Shakespeare's The Tempest, *the magician Prospero reflects upon life and where it goes and the gods and goddesses and spirits who weave it all. Toward the end he muses that "we are such stuff as dreams are made on, and our little life is rounded with a sleep."*

FIRST READING
Habakkuk 1: 2–3; 2:2–4

How long, O LORD? I cry for help
but you do not listen!
I cry out to you, "Violence!"
but you do not intervene.
Why do you let me see ruin;
why must I look at misery?
Destruction and violence are before me;
there is strife, and clamorous discord.
Then the LORD answered me and said:
Write down the vision clearly upon the tablets,
so that one can read it readily.
For the vision still has its time,
presses on to fulfillment, and will not disappoint;
if it delays, wait for it,
it will surely come, it will not be late.
The rash one has no integrity;
but the just one, because of his faith, shall live.

PSALM RESPONSE
Psalm 95:8

If today you hear his voice, harden not your hearts.

SECOND READING
2 Timothy 1: 6–8, 13–14

Beloved: I remind you to stir into flame the gift of God that you have through the imposition of my hands. For God did not give us a spirit of cowardice but rather of power and love and self-control. So do not be ashamed of your testimony to our Lord, nor of me, a prisoner for his sake; but bear your share of hardship for the gospel with the strength that comes from God.

Take as your norm the sound words that you heard from me, in the faith and love that are in Christ Jesus. Guard this rich trust with the help of the Holy Spirit that dwells within us.

GOSPEL
Luke 17:5–10

The apostles said to the Lord, "Increase our faith." The Lord replied, "If you have faith the size of a mustard seed, you would say to this mulberry tree, 'Be uprooted and planted in the sea,' and it would obey you.

"Who among you would say to your servant who has just come in from plowing or tending sheep in the field, 'Come here immediately and take your place at table'? Would he not rather say to him, 'Prepare something for me to eat. Put on your apron and wait on me while I eat and drink. You may eat and drink when I am finished'? Is he grateful to that servant because he did what was commanded? So should it be with you. When you have done all you have been commanded, say, 'We are unprofitable servants; we have done what we were obliged to do.' "

Understanding the Word

In today's first reading the prophet Habakkuk says, "The just one, because of his faith, shall live" (Habakkuk 2:4). In today's Gospel the apostles request of Jesus, "Increase our faith" (Luke 17:5). Faith becomes the key issue in this selection from Luke.

Jesus tells the apostles that their faith is not even the size of a mustard seed. He uses hyperbole concerning the mulberry tree to make his point, namely that even the tiniest seed of faith can produce wonderful results. The Greek text makes it clear that the apostles do not have even that small amount of faith. An increase is definitely needed.

Christian faith is essentially the response of human beings to God's revelation in the person of Jesus and his ministry. Everyone must realize that faith itself is a gift from God, not something one can earn. That is the point of today's short parable and its application. The master-slave relationship at that time is reflected in the harsh details of the parable. The slave cannot expect gratitude for doing his duty.

Jesus uses the parable to teach that his disciples also do not earn faith. He expects that good works by his followers will come out of their living faith. But faith and the works that result are a gift of God. Saint Paul is very helpful on this point. "For by grace you have been saved through faith, and this is not from you; it is the gift of God; it is not from works, so no one may boast" (Ephesians 2:8–9).

Faith and the good works of the Christian, therefore, are the gift of God. Every follower of Jesus must be grateful rather than boastful. The sign of a truly living faith is seen in loving acts of justice and charity. The Letter of James reinforces that teaching: "So also faith of itself, if it does not have works, is dead" (James 2:17). The history of the apostles after Pentecost indicates that the Lord definitely did increase their faith, a faith that produced the beginnings of the church.

Reflecting on the Word

With faith we are inclined to think that there is nothing we cannot do, that faith is the stuff from which we can create any future. All we need is a seed's worth of faith, and we can uproot mulberry trees, or if not mulberry trees at least uproot the chaos in our lives. Yet that sort of mindset places faith in ourselves and in our own vision and not in God's. The faith of the Gospels is a giving over of ourselves to God's dream for us. That is also the dutiful servant of this week's Gospel parable, the one who trusts that the divine vision can and does bring forth life, and so does what the servant is obliged to do, under obligation to some inner dream that pushes the servant and us to action.

Consider the persistence of that dream. In spite of human sin, people still long to lead good lives. In spite of war, nations seek the ways of peace together. Faith continues to be passed on from generation to generation. Beauty and art rise like cream to feed our souls. Despite the lure of riches we insist that the poor be cared for and the weak not be abandoned. We relentlessly look for ways to break down barriers between peoples. We demand that justice prevail, that right not be determined by might, and that all people have access to those resources necessary for life. We continue to explore how we might heal broken lives and battered spirits. We nurture children and refuse to abandon the aged. We foster freedom among nations, protect the environment, and seek ways out of poverty for those mired in its muck. Indeed dreams matter. They are how God transforms us.

CONSIDER/ DISCUSS:

- As a person of faith, what do you expect from your faith? What do you expect from God?
- On a scale of 1 to 10, where do you place your trust that God's vision does and will come to fruition?

Good Questions

Responding to the Word

God moves us to wherever God needs us to be. Amazingly, it does not take a great master plan to give God such an opening. Luke insists that a mustard seed's worth of faith is enough to let God do what God does best. And so it happens.

Spend a few minutes in quiet prayer. Ask God to show you one (or more) ways that you may be called to respond to this week's scriptures—

- in your relationship with God
- with family and friends
- at work, school, or church
- in the broader community

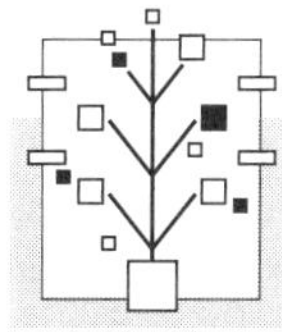

October 14, 2007

TWENTY-EIGHTH SUNDAY IN ORDINARY TIME

Today's Focus: Remembering with Gratitude

Gerald Stern, himself a poet, once said that it is the poet's job to remember. He was right, I think, but I also think that it's the task of all art to help us remember. Without art, without music or dance or film or novels, life grows empty.

FIRST READING
2 Kings 5: 14–17

Naaman went down and plunged into the Jordan seven times at the word of Elisha, the man of God. His flesh became again like the flesh of a little child, and he was clean of his leprosy.

Naaman returned with his whole retinue to the man of God. On his arrival he stood before Elisha and said, "Now I know that there is no God in all the earth, except in Israel. Please accept a gift from your servant."

Elisha replied, "As the LORD lives whom I serve, I will not take it"; and despite Naaman's urging, he still refused. Naaman said: "If you will not accept, please let me, your servant, have two mule-loads of earth, for I will no longer offer holocaust or sacrifice to any other god except to the LORD."

PSALM RESPONSE
Psalm 98:2b

The Lord has revealed to the nations his saving power.

SECOND READING
2 Timothy 2: 8–13

Beloved: Remember Jesus Christ, raised from the dead, a descendant of David: such is my gospel, for which I am suffering, even to the point of chains, like a criminal. But the word of God is not chained. Therefore, I bear with everything for the sake of those who are chosen, so that they too may obtain the salvation that is in Christ Jesus, together with eternal glory. This saying is trustworthy:

If we have died with him
  we shall also live with him;
if we persevere
  we shall also reign with him.
But if we deny him
  he will deny us.
If we are unfaithful
  he remains faithful,
  for he cannot deny himself.

GOSPEL *Luke 17:11–19*

As Jesus continued his journey to Jerusalem, he traveled through Samaria and Galilee. As he was entering a village, ten lepers met him. They stood at a distance from him and raised their voices, saying, "Jesus, Master! Have pity on us!" And when he saw them, he said, "Go show yourselves to the priests." As they were going they were cleansed. And one of them, realizing he had been healed, returned, glorifying God in a loud voice; and he fell at the feet of Jesus and thanked him. He was a Samaritan. Jesus said in reply, "Ten were cleansed, were they not? Where are the other nine? Has none but this foreigner returned to give thanks to God?" Then he said to him, "Stand up and go; your faith has saved you."

Understanding the Word

Today's readings highlight the hardships, but also the cure of two lepers, Naaman of Aram and the unnamed Samaritan. Both men are non-Jews, a lesson to the reader that God's love is universal. The Samaritan had a double problem. In addition to being a leper, he could experience bitter racial hatred on the part of the Jews. Lepers had to stay outside the camp and cry out to warn passersby (see Leviticus 13:45–46). Both men seek help. Naaman approaches the prophet Elisha and the Samaritan is part of a group of ten lepers who call out, "Jesus, Master! Have pity on us!" (Luke 17:13).

Naaman and the Samaritan carry out the instructions from Elisha and Jesus. Healing then follows through the intervention of the prophet of the Old Testament and Jesus, the prophet of the New Testament. Faith is the result of the miraculous healings. Naaman declares, "I will no longer offer holocaust or sacrifice to any other god except to the LORD" (2 Kings 5:17). Jesus assures the Samaritan, "[Y]our faith has saved you" (Luke 17:19).

The key teaching of Jesus here is that faith is essential for his followers, a faith that gives glory to God and thanksgiving to Jesus. The Samaritan "returned, glorifying God in a loud voice; and he fell at the feet of Jesus and thanked him" (17:15–16). The Samaritan here becomes the great example of faith, just as the Good Samaritan earlier in Luke's Gospel (10:29–37) is recognized even in our dictionaries as the model for unselfish love of neighbor.

Today's story of the healing of ten lepers also has the strong theme of thankfulness. All ten were healed, but only one, a "foreigner" (17:18), showed his gratitude. Jesus was concerned and asked, "Where are the other nine?" (17:17). It is important to call out to Jesus for help, as the Samaritan did; but one should also make prayers of thanksgiving a part of one's spiritual life, as the Samaritan did.

Reflecting on the Word

In the days that followed the horror of death that cascaded from the collapsing towers of the World Trade Center, most of us found ourselves trying to untangle our emotional snarl of anger and grief and fear and desire for revenge. Somewhere in the fog of those days a friend reminded me how important it is not to allow our anger and hunger for revenge to obscure our spirit's very human need for beauty. More than revenge, what our spirits need is everything that lifts us up to life's wonder and awe—not so that we forget the horror but that we remember life's beauty.

It is at that point, the point of remembering, that gratitude also begins. More than anything, we need people in our lives who cast beauty upon us. We need them so that we remember what life is really called to be, or else we will forget, and that will be the ultimate tragedy.

In Jewish culture it took ten individuals to make a community. So when the ten lepers cast their plea for pity like a fish net over Jesus passing by, it was an outcast community of fringe dwellers who remembered the beauty of life and love and longed to be drawn back into its mainstream, physically as well as socially. In the end the healing with which they were blessed moved the non-Jew, the Samaritan, to return not only with an armful of gratitude for the new life but also with a new way of looking at the powers of life. His gratitude moved him to faith.

CONSIDER/ DISCUSS:

- For you, which comes first, the chicken or the egg? Are you grateful because of your faith or are you a believer because you have gratitude? When has that shift taken place in your life?
- Remember a time when you were able to be the way to gratitude in the heart of another. Then realize you may also have been their doorway to faith.

Responding to the Word

Gratitude moves us to faith, and remembering moves us to that gratitude. That's why we need to treasure those whose gift of beauty helps us to remember. They nudge us into faith.

Spend a few minutes in quiet prayer. Ask God to show you one (or more) ways that you may be called to respond to this week's scriptures—

- in your relationship with God
- with family and friends
- at work, school, or church
- in the broader community

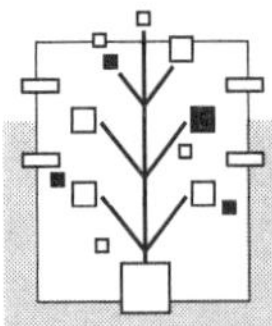

October 21, 2007

TWENTY-NINTH SUNDAY IN ORDINARY TIME

Today's Focus: Life's Knocking

Though we may at times miss the life about us, we find hope in the promise that it's not God who is inattentive and indifferent—it's us. Still, life keeps knocking on our door.

FIRST READING
Exodus 17: 8–13

In those days, Amalek came and waged war against Israel. Moses, therefore, said to Joshua, "Pick out certain men, and tomorrow go out and engage Amalek in battle. I will be standing on top of the hill with the staff of God in my hand." So Joshua did as Moses told him: he engaged Amalek in battle after Moses had climbed to the top of the hill with Aaron and Hur. As long as Moses kept his hands raised up, Israel had the better of the fight, but when he let his hands rest, Amalek had the better of the fight. Moses' hands, however, grew tired; so they put a rock in place for him to sit on. Meanwhile Aaron and Hur supported his hands, one on one side and one on the other, so that his hands remained steady till sunset. And Joshua mowed down Amalek and his people with the edge of the sword.

PSALM RESPONSE
Psalm 121:2

Our help is from the Lord, who made heaven and earth.

SECOND READING
2 Timothy 3:14 — 4:2

Beloved: Remain faithful to what you have learned and believed, because you know from whom you learned it, and that from infancy you have known the sacred Scriptures, which are capable of giving you wisdom for salvation through faith in Christ Jesus. All Scripture is inspired by God and is useful for teaching, for refutation, for correction, and for training in righteousness, so that one who belongs to God may be competent, equipped for every good work.

I charge you in the presence of God and of Christ Jesus, who will judge the living and the dead, and by his appearing and his kingly power: proclaim the word; be persistent whether it is convenient or inconvenient; convince, reprimand, encourage through all patience and teaching.

GOSPEL
Luke 18:1–8

Jesus told his disciples a parable about the necessity for them to pray always without becoming weary. He said, "There was a judge in a certain town who neither feared God nor respected any human being. And a widow in that town used to come to him and say, 'Render a just decision for me against my adversary.' For a long time the judge was unwilling, but eventually he thought, 'While it is true that I neither fear God nor respect any human being, because this widow keeps bothering me I shall deliver a just decision for her lest she finally come and strike me.' " The Lord said, "Pay attention to what the dishonest judge says. Will not God then secure the rights of his chosen ones who call out to him day and night? Will he be slow to answer them? I tell you, he will see to it that justice is done for them speedily. But when the Son of Man comes, will he find faith on earth?"

Understanding the Word

Saint Paul met Timothy at Lystra on his second missionary journey. Paul writes to Timothy, "I yearn to see you again, recalling your tears, so that I may be filled with joy, as I recall your sincere faith that first lived in your grandmother Lois and in your mother Eunice and that I am confident lives also in you" (2 Timothy 1:4–5). Timothy became a very important part of the life and ministry of Paul. He often traveled with the apostle and was given important missions. "I hope, in the Lord Jesus, to send Timothy to you soon, so that I too may be heartened by hearing news of you" (Philippians 2:19).

Today's second reading from 2 Timothy is an exhortation to Timothy to be faithful to his ministry at Ephesus. He was given charge of the Christian community in that important city. Paul encourages Timothy to remain faithful to his Christian instruction and also to the "sacred Scriptures, which are capable of giving you wisdom for salvation through faith in Christ Jesus," (2 Timothy 3:15).

The following verse is extremely important for the Church's teaching on biblical inspiration, the fact that God is the principal author of every book of the Bible, working with human co-authors. This text (3:16) is quoted in the *Dogmatic Constitution on Divine Revelation*, n.11, Vatican Council II. "Since all that the inspired authors or sacred writers assert must be considered as asserted by the Holy Spirit, one should affirm that the books of Scripture teach firmly, faithfully and without error the truth that God decided to put down in the sacred writings for our salvation's sake. Thus, 'all scripture is inspired by God and is useful for teaching, for refutation, for correction, and for training in righteousness.' "

A second important teaching on inspiration is found in 2 Peter, "[N]o prophecy ever came through human will; but rather human beings moved by the holy Spirit spoke under the influence of God" (2 Peter 1:21). The Holy Spirit inspires every book of the Bible and gives to believers the word of God in human language.

Reflecting on the Word

My house shares a back yard with four college students. Ryan is one of them. Every morning the first thing Ryan does is go out the back door with a bagful of nuts and feed the squirrels. They hang out in our apple tree the way teenagers hang out around malls. One of the squirrels has become particularly bold and now waits expectantly for Ryan right at the back door. Lately the squirrel won't go away, no matter the time of day, no matter who's in the back yard. The squirrel just won't leave, nuts or no nuts, people or no people. Because it's become pesky, I now ignore the squirrel most of the time. Though Ryan doesn't, I do. Nevertheless, the squirrel is slowly getting my attention. Over the course of my lifetime, God is getting my attention, too.

People tend to hear this week's Gospel parable about the widow who keeps knocking on the judge's door as a story about God who eventually gives in to the widow. I think it's more a story about me eventually giving in to God. I hope God's not offended by being compared to a squirrel, but God is much more like the squirrel (or the widow) than like the judge. God's the one who does the pleading, it seems to me. While the parable seems to say, "Don't lose heart; God will eventually hear and answer," perhaps it's really saying, "Don't lose heart; God will not give up knocking on your door."

CONSIDER/ DISCUSS:

- What was the occasion for the last time when you gave in to God?
- Which door of your life has God been knocking on recently?

Responding to the Word

The good news is that God refuses to lose heart with us, like the widowed woman who refuses to quit knocking. Neither will turn away and go home, not from the judge's barred and silent door or from ours. Just like the squirrel.

Spend a few minutes in quiet prayer. Ask God to show you one (or more) ways that you may be called to respond to this week's scriptures—

- in your relationship with God
- with family and friends
- at work, school, or church
- in the broader community

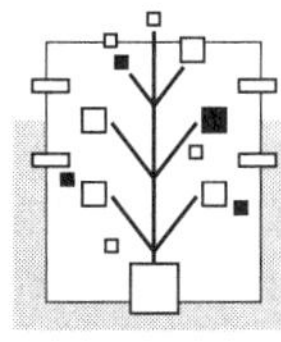

October 28, 2007

THIRTIETH SUNDAY IN ORDINARY TIME

Today's Focus: Jekyll and Hyde

It's almost un-American to think of ourselves as anything other than self-sufficient. The more successful we are, the better we feel about ourselves. In our quiet moments, however, a different "self" emerges.

FIRST READING
Sirach 35: 12–14, 16–18

The LORD is a God of justice,
who knows no favorites.
Though not unduly partial toward the weak,
yet he hears the cry of the oppressed.
The Lord is not deaf to the wail of the orphan,
nor to the widow when she pours out her complaint.
The one who serves God willingly is heard;
his petition reaches the heavens.
The prayer of the lowly pierces the clouds;
it does not rest till it reaches its goal,
nor will it withdraw till the Most High responds,
judges justly and affirms the right,
and the Lord will not delay.

PSALM RESPONSE
Psalm 34:7a

The Lord hears the cry of the poor.

SECOND READING
2 Timothy 4: 6–8, 16–18

Beloved: I am already being poured out like a libation, and the time of my departure is at hand. I have competed well; I have finished the race; I have kept the faith. From now on the crown of righteousness awaits me, which the Lord, the just judge, will award to me on that day, and not only to me, but to all who have longed for his appearance.

At my first defense no one appeared on my behalf, but everyone deserted me. May it not be held against them! But the Lord stood by me and gave me strength, so that through me the proclamation might be completed and all the Gentiles might hear it. And I was rescued from the lion's mouth. The Lord will rescue me from every evil threat and will bring me safe to his heavenly kingdom. To him be glory forever and ever. Amen.

GOSPEL
Luke 18:9–14

Jesus addressed this parable to those who were convinced of their own righteousness and despised everyone else. "Two people went up to the temple area to pray; one was a Pharisee and the other was a tax collector. The Pharisee took up his position and spoke this prayer to himself, 'O God, I thank you that I am not like the rest of humanity—greedy, dishonest, adulterous—or even like this tax collector. I fast twice a week, and I pay tithes on my whole income.' But the tax collector stood off at a distance and would not even raise his eyes to heaven but beat his breast and prayed, 'O God, be merciful to me a sinner.' I tell you, the latter went home justified, not the former; for whoever exalts himself will be humbled, and the one who humbles himself will be exalted."

Understanding the Word

Today's first reading from the book of Sirach sets the stage for the parable of Jesus to follow. "The prayer of the lowly pierces the clouds" (Sirach 35:17). Today's Gospel is a perfect example of how the prayer of the humble effects justification. "In a sense this passage joins those of chapter 15 as one of the great Lucan parables of mercy—about God's mercy shown to a sinner who stands before him and acknowledges his own worthlessness" (Joseph A. Fitzmyer, "The Gospel According to Luke," *Anchor Bible*, vol. 28 A, p. 1184).

Earlier in the Gospel Jesus declared, "I have not come to call the righteous to repentance but sinners" (Luke 5:32). The Pharisee and tax collector are types of the self-righteous and the sinner. Clearly not all Pharisees are self-righteous, but as a group they have become the model of that attitude. The man in the parable lists his virtues, justifying himself before God. For example, he goes farther than the Mosaic law demands in fasting and tithing. But he has disdain for the tax collector and "the rest of humanity—greedy, dishonest, adulterous" (18:11).

By contrast the tax collector also appears before God in the temple with all the signs of true repentance. He "would not even raise his eyes to heaven but beat his breast and prayed, 'O God, be merciful to me a sinner' " (18:13). He leaves judgment to God. Jesus as the Son of God declares the tax collector justified.

Luke wants his Christian readers to learn the lesson from the parable. Humility is required, not self-exaltation. All followers of Jesus should approach him with the tax collector's humble and contrite prayer of petition, "O God, be merciful to me a sinner" (18:13). The book of Sirach can also provide a final insight into today's teaching: "Nor will it [the prayer of the lowly] withdraw till the Most High responds, / judges justly and affirms the right" (Sirach 35:18), exactly as Jesus did in today's parable.

Reflecting on the Word

Last night while we all slept the killing frost came upon us, just as we knew it would. So this morning the colors are a bit less so, and the morning chill knows it's won. The tomato plants are limp, too, and the palette of summer's flowers has surrendered to autumn's hardier hues. It's not the same this morning.

That's what the killing frost does to our lives. It slips in while we sleep. In some ways, I suppose, that is why we're like the Pharisee of this week's Gospel. He was a very good man, he really was. He just didn't know that the killing frost had slowly settled into his life. He never felt the ice in the garden of his soul.

In other ways, we're like the tax collector. He knew the killing frost had come, but was unsure about whether God would really be merciful to him, a sinner. He was losing hope—that soul quality that recognizes that while we can't make it by ourselves, God can and does do for us what we cannot.

Maybe that's how both of them were so much alike—two men who lived without hope, one because he didn't think he needed it, and the other because he doubted that it was available to him. Or maybe not. Maybe the tax collector did have hope; after all, the last line of the Gospel says he went home justified.

CONSIDER/ DISCUSS:

- Has a killing frost ever settled into your life without you realizing it? How did you respond? How do you wish you had responded?
- Have you ever lived with hopelessness? What was your response? What brought you back to hope?

Responding to the Word

If we're honest with ourselves, we are both sinful and graced. And it's good to admit to both. None of us is ever completely one or the other. We are both, and neither side is self-sufficient or without hope.

Spend a few minutes in quiet prayer. Ask God to show you one (or more) ways that you may be called to respond to this week's scriptures—

- in your relationship with God
- with family and friends
- at work, school, or church
- in the broader community

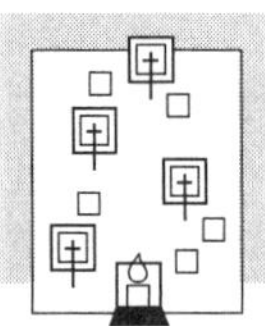

November 1, 2007

THE SOLEMNITY OF ALL SAINTS

Today's Focus: An Instinct for Holiness

Though we tend to see holiness as something that sets one apart, Saint Paul points out that what makes one holy is the same as what makes one fully human. In some ways holiness is bred in our bones.

FIRST READING
Revelation 7: 2–4, 9–14

I, John, saw another angel come up from the East, holding the seal of the living God. He cried out in a loud voice to the four angels who were given power to damage the land and the sea, "Do not damage the land or the sea or the trees until we put the seal on the foreheads of the servants of our God." I heard the number of those who had been marked with the seal, one hundred and forty-four thousand marked from every tribe of the Israelites.

After this I had a vision of a great multitude, which no one could count, from every nation, race, people, and tongue. They stood before the throne and before the Lamb, wearing white robes and holding palm branches in their hands. They cried out in a loud voice:

"Salvation comes from our God, who is seated on the throne,
and from the Lamb."

All the angels stood around the throne and around the elders and the four living creatures. They prostrated themselves before the throne, worshiped God, and exclaimed:

"Amen. Blessing and glory, wisdom and thanksgiving,
honor, power, and might
be to our God forever and ever. Amen."

Then one of the elders spoke up and said to me, "Who are these wearing white robes, and where did they come from?" I said to him, "My lord, you are the one who knows." He said to me, "These are the ones who have survived the time of great distress; they have washed their robes and made them white in the blood of the Lamb."

PSALM RESPONSE
Psalm 24:6

Lord, this is the people that longs to see your face.

SECOND READING
1 John 3:1–3

Beloved: See what love the Father has bestowed on us that we may be called the children of God. Yet so we are. The reason the world does not know us is that it did not know him. Beloved, we are God's children now; what we shall be has not yet been revealed. We do know that when it is revealed we shall be like him, for we shall see him as he is. Everyone who has this hope based on him makes himself pure, as he is pure.

GOSPEL *Matthew 5:1–12a*

When Jesus saw the crowds, he went up the mountain, and after he had sat down, his disciples came to him. He began to teach them, saying:

"Blessed are the poor in spirit,
  for theirs is the kingdom of heaven.
Blessed are they who mourn,
  for they will be comforted.
Blessed are the meek,
  for they will inherit the land.
Blessed are they who hunger and thirst for righteousness,
  for they will be satisfied.
Blessed are the merciful,
  for they will be shown mercy.
Blessed are the clean of heart,
  for they will see God.
Blessed are the peacemakers,
  for they will be called children of God.
Blessed are they who are persecuted for the sake of righteousness,
  for theirs is the kingdom of heaven.
Blessed are you when they insult you and persecute you and utter
  every kind of evil against you falsely because of me.
Rejoice and be glad,
  for your reward will be great in heaven."

Understanding the Word

The solemnity of All Saints is very meaningful to all followers of Jesus. We celebrate the uncountable numbers of people, some our own family and friends, who have successfully won a place before the throne of God. Today's first reading from the Revelation of John is perfect for the occasion. It contains two visions: one that evokes life on this earth with its problems, and one that anticipates the eternal happiness of heaven.

In the first vision, people are being sealed by God. The image is that of a ruler who uses his signet ring to mark something as his property. God's seal marks the Christian as a member of God's kingdom. One hundred forty-four thousand are sealed from every tribe of the Israelites. The church was seen as the new Israel, the continuation of the people of the old covenant. The number symbolizes the vast multitude of those on earth facing the "great distress" (Revelation 7:14). In the book of Ezekiel the faithful are marked with an X to save them from God's punishment (Ezekiel 9:4–6). Here the seal is not for protection from evil, but to impart God's strength for dealing with the trials of life. At the time the author of Revelation was thinking especially of fierce Roman persecutions.

The second vision depicts of the throne of God and the Lamb surrounded by those who have successfully survived the tribulations. John speaks of "a great multitude, which no one could count, from every nation, race, people, and tongue" (Revelation 7:9). Their white robes and the palm branches indicate their victory. After their hymn attributing the victory to God and the Lamb (a favorite title for Jesus Christ in Revelation), the heavenly beings respond, "Amen. Blessing and glory, wisdom and thanksgiving, honor, power, and might be to our God forever and ever. Amen" (7:12).

One of the elders informs John that those wearing the white robes are "the ones who have survived the time of great distress; they have washed their robes and made them white in the blood of the Lamb" (7:14). Not only the martyrs, but also all those who remain faithful despite adversities, all the saints, will enjoy eternal happiness before the throne of God and the Lamb.

Reflecting on the Word

Instincts are strange and curious things. They come in various shapes and sizes and impulses. They are all quite natural—sometimes frighteningly so, and for the most part they are quite common, though some not so much as others. Self defense, sexual drives, hunger and thirst—those find a home in all of us. But others can be quite exceptional—the way Frank Sinatra could spin a song or Michelangelo could use color or Bill Gates continues to build the computer industry. Mastery of a technique alone is never quite as successful as someone who is gifted with an uncommon instinct.

Some folks seem to have an instinct for holiness, more so than the rest of us. Then holiness is unmistakable. Yet in some ways we all share in a bit of holiness, holiness of the sort highlighted in the Beatitudes. It's fairly common to root for the underdog, which can be likened to mourning or grieving for the oppressed. And we do try to make and keep peace—between our kids, with our spouse, among those with whom we work. Moreover, we know that insisting on having our own way, which is the opposite of being humble or meek, is not going to win friends and influence others. Those are all instincts of holiness, God-given as Saint John points out in today's first reading. He says that "salvation comes from our God . . . and from the Lamb" (Revelation 7:10). So we really can't take credit for our goodness, because the instinct for it seems to be God's doing.

CONSIDER/ DISCUSS:

- Do you have a favorite saint, one canonized and held up as a model for holiness by the Church? What feature of that person's story makes it so attractive to you?
- What instinct for holiness most frequently stirs your spirit? What is your response?

Responding to the Word

There are those who seem to have an instinct for goodness far beyond the rest of us. We find ourselves calling them saints, both those named officially and those written on our hearts. Still, at some point they, too, had to say "yes" to that instinct and respond to it. Perhaps our own saintliness will lie in the way we respond to the instinct that God has given to each of us.

Spend a few minutes in quiet prayer. Ask God to show you one (or more) ways that you may be called to respond to this week's scriptures—

- in your relationship with God
- with family and friends
- at work, school, or church
- in the broader community

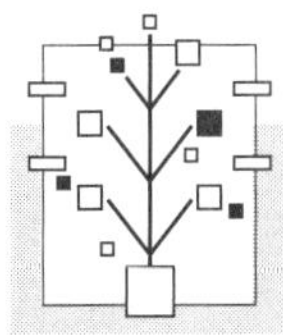

November 4, 2007

THIRTY-FIRST SUNDAY IN ORDINARY TIME

Today's Focus: Life Is a Fish Tank

We are inclined to insist that sinners repent, that they change their ways and don goodness and virtue. However, few of us change unless we first come to recognize how our current state of affairs inhibits greater happiness and fulfillment. It is that "coming to see" that seems to be the work of some force other than ourselves.

FIRST READING
Wisdom 11:22 — 12:2

Before the LORD the whole universe is as a grain
from a balance
or a drop of morning dew come down upon the earth.
But you have mercy on all, because you can do all things;
and you overlook people's sins that they may repent.
For you love all things that are
and loathe nothing that you have made;
for what you hated, you would not have fashioned.
And how could a thing remain, unless you willed it;
or be preserved, had it not been called forth by you?
But you spare all things, because they are yours,
O LORD and lover of souls,
for your imperishable spirit is in all things!
Therefore you rebuke offenders little by little,
warn them and remind them of the sins
they are committing,
that they may abandon their wickedness
and believe in you, O LORD!

PSALM RESPONSE
Psalm 145:1

I will praise your name forever, my king and my God.

SECOND READING
2 Thessalonians 1:11 — 2:2

Brothers and sisters: We always pray for you, that our God may make you worthy of his calling and powerfully bring to fulfillment every good purpose and every effort of faith, that the name of our Lord Jesus may be glorified in you, and you in him, in accord with the grace of our God and Lord Jesus Christ.

We ask you, brothers and sisters, with regard to the coming of our Lord Jesus Christ and our assembling with him, not to be shaken out of your minds suddenly, or to be alarmed either by a "spirit," or by an oral statement, or by a letter allegedly from us to the effect that the day of the Lord is at hand.

GOSPEL
Luke 19:1–10

At that time, Jesus came to Jericho and intended to pass through the town. Now a man there named Zacchaeus, who was a chief tax collector and also a wealthy man, was seeking to see who Jesus was; but he could not see him because of the crowd, for he was short in stature. So he ran ahead and climbed a sycamore tree in order to see Jesus, who was about to pass that way. When he reached the place, Jesus looked up and said, "Zacchaeus, come down quickly, for today I must stay at your house." And he came down quickly and received him with joy. When they all saw this, they began to grumble, saying, "He has gone to stay at the house of a sinner." But Zacchaeus stood there and said to the Lord, "Behold, half of my possessions, Lord, I shall give to the poor, and if I have extorted anything from anyone I shall repay it four times over." And Jesus said to him, "Today salvation has come to this house because this man too is a descendant of Abraham. For the Son of Man has come to seek and to save what was lost."

Understanding the Word

Today's Gospel begins with a reminder of Jesus' continuing journey to Jerusalem: "Jesus came to Jericho" (Luke 19:1). There Zacchaeus, a "chief tax collector and also a wealthy man" (19:2), was willing to climb a sycamore tree to see Jesus. Neither his position as an official nor his riches kept him from appearing undignified. Jesus rewarded his efforts by inviting himself to Zacchaeus' house. There is grumbling, as there often is when Jesus associates with persons judged to be sinners.

Zacchaeus responds to the grumbling by assuring Jesus that he is making good use of his wealth. He gives half to the poor. Should he unintentionally extort anything, he repays four-fold. The Greek verbs for "give" and "repay" can be translated either as present tense or future tense. If future—"I shall give" and "I shall repay," as translated in the New American Bible—then Zacchaeus would have realized that he was a sinner and promised to repent. The scholars are divided but the present tense seems preferable—"I give" and "I repay." Zacchaeus becomes the great example of the proper use of material possessions. The rich man gave none of his resources to help the poor and suffering Lazarus (16:19–31). The rich official walks away from Jesus' call to follow him because of his wealth (18:18–23). Zacchaeus, by way of contrast, is extremely generous with his possessions, practicing proper stewardship.

Jesus says to Zacchaeus, "Today I *must* stay at your house" (19:5, emphasis added). This necessity is part of God's plan for the Son. Jesus also assures his host that he has brought salvation to the house because Zacchaeus is "a descendant of Abraham" (19:9).

The incident ends with an important statement by Jesus concerning his work as savior. "For the Son of Man has come to seek and to save what was lost" (19:10). The words recall the great prophecy of Ezekiel, "The lost I will seek out, the strayed I will bring back . . . shepherding them rightly" (34:16).

Reflecting on the Word

There is a fish tank in our dining room. Over the course of the past year some of the fish have passed on to the Great Aquarium in the Sky, leaving but one gold angelfish and a couple of clown loches. It was time to replenish the tank, and so I brought home three black angelfish. That was the beginning of a sort of aquatic Armageddon. The lone gold angel (territorial by nature) began policing and protecting its place in the tank. Immediately the three black angels were herded into a corner and seldom left it, either out of fear from intimidation or simply from good fish sense.

It was in many ways the initiation of a process of transformation for the gold angel. Bit by bit over the course of the ensuing weeks the black angels ventured out of the corner. With a sense of boundaries thinning and finally fading, they sparred and flirted. Less and less the gold angel asserted itself. More and more the black angels ventured into middle space. It seemed that the gold angel was either tiring of its defensive tasks or growing acclimated to life with newcomers.

The story of the fish tank is in many ways our story. One morning we awake to the buzz of our alarm and to the new day much as we have done every other day, except that on this day, by the time we bring it to a close we will have found ourselves in a totally new and different world—a bit like the gold angelfish, but more like Zaccheus of this week's Gospel as we read it in the New American Bible translation ("I shall give" and "I shall repay"). Something happens, whether by happenstance or intention, whether by grace or by sin, but from that day on we are pushed into looking at life and seeing it in a different fashion.

CONSIDER/ DISCUSS:

- What do you see now as destructive of wholeness in your life that you did not always see?
- What have you found to be helpful while waiting for others to see?

Responding to the Word

What takes place in our lives is seldom of our own choosing, yet it can bring us to someplace new. It may be the story of the gold angelfish, but much beyond that it is the story of God bringing us to a new place in life, just as Jesus did with Zaccheus.

Spend a few minutes in quiet prayer. Ask God to show you one (or more) ways that you may be called to respond to this week's scriptures—

- in your relationship with God
- with family and friends
- at work, school, or church
- in the broader community

November 11, 2007

THIRTY-SECOND SUNDAY IN ORDINARY TIME

Today's Focus: Love's Hungers

Life has a way of feeding our hunger for relationships. Whatever shape or hue they may take, in one way or another our relationships seem to feed the deepest part of our being.

FIRST READING
2 Maccabees 7: 1–2, 9–14

It happened that seven brothers with their mother were arrested and tortured with whips and scourges by the king, to force them to eat pork in violation of God's law. One of the brothers, speaking for the others, said: "What do you expect to achieve by questioning us? We are ready to die rather than transgress the laws of our ancestors."

At the point of death he said: "You accursed fiend, you are depriving us of this present life, but the King of the world will raise us up to live again forever. It is for his laws that we are dying."

After him the third suffered their cruel sport. He put out his tongue at once when told to do so, and bravely held out his hands, as he spoke these noble words: "It was from Heaven that I received these; for the sake of his laws I disdain them; from him I hope to receive them again." Even the king and his attendants marveled at the young man's courage, because he regarded his sufferings as nothing.

After he had died, they tortured and maltreated the fourth brother in the same way. When he was near death, he said, "It is my choice to die at the hands of men with the hope God gives of being raised up by him; but for you, there will be no resurrection to life."

PSALM RESPONSE
Psalm 17:15b

Lord, when your glory appears, my joy will be full.

SECOND READING
2 Thessalonians 2:16 — 3:5

Brothers and sisters: May our Lord Jesus Christ himself and God our Father, who has loved us and given us everlasting encouragement and good hope through his grace, encourage your hearts and strengthen them in every good deed and word.

Finally, brothers and sisters, pray for us, so that the word of the Lord may speed forward and be glorified, as it did among you, and that we may be delivered from perverse and wicked people, for not all have faith. But the Lord is faithful; he will strengthen you and guard you from the evil one. We are confident of you in the Lord that what we instruct you, you are doing and will continue to do. May the Lord direct your hearts to the love of God and to the endurance of Christ.

In the shorter form of the reading, the passage in brackets is omitted.

GOSPEL *Luke 20:27–38 or 20:27, 34–38*

Some Sadducees, those who deny that there is a resurrection, came forward [and put this question to Jesus, saying, "Teacher, Moses wrote for us,

If someone's brother dies leaving a wife but no child,
his brother must take the wife
and raise up descendants for his brother.

Now there were seven brothers; the first married a woman but died childless. Then the second and the third married her, and likewise all the seven died childless. Finally the woman also died. Now at the resurrection whose wife will that woman be? For all seven had been married to her."] Jesus said to them, "The children of this age marry and remarry; but those who are deemed worthy to attain to the coming age and to the resurrection of the dead neither marry nor are given in marriage. They can no longer die, for they are like angels; and they are the children of God because they are the ones who will rise. That the dead will rise even Moses made known in the passage about the bush, when he called out 'Lord,' the God of Abraham, the God of Isaac, and the God of Jacob; and he is not God of the dead, but of the living, for to him all are alive."

Understanding the Word

Today's reading from the Gospel of Luke has the only mention of the Sadducees in this Gospel. The Sadducees were the wealthy aristocracy. In religious matters they accepted only the first five books of the Old Testament, rejected the oral tradition of the Pharisees, and did not believe in angels or the resurrection of the dead.

The Sadducees use the levirate (brother-in-law) marriage law to bait their snare. "When brothers live together and one of them dies without a son, the widow of the deceased shall not marry anyone outside the family; but her husband's brother shall go to her and perform the duty of a brother-in-law by marrying her" (Deuteronomy 25:5). The Sadducees push this to a ridiculous extreme by proposing a case in which a woman ends up marrying seven brothers. They then ask Jesus, "Now at the resurrection whose wife will that woman be?" (Luke 20:33).

Jesus responds by pointing out that in the coming age there is no marriage. Persons whom God judges worthy will be "the children of God because they are the ones who will rise" (20:36). Jesus then appeals to the Pentateuch and to Moses, both accepted by the Sadducees, to prove that there is resurrection. In the burning bush God revealed to Moses, "I am . . . the God of Abraham, the God of Isaac, the God of Jacob" (Exodus 3:6). Jesus adds, "He is not God of the dead, but of the living, for to him all are alive" (Luke 20:38). That last phrase, proper to Luke, may well depend on a text from the apocryphal Fourth Book of Maccabees: "They [the martyrs] believe that they, like the patriarchs Abraham and Isaac and Jacob, do not die to God, but live to God" (4 Maccabees 7:19).

Belief in resurrection of the body and retribution for evil first appears in the Old Testament period some two hundred years before the birth of the Lord. The book of Daniel, written at the time of the persecution of Antiochus Epiphanes (167–164 BC), says, "Many of those who sleep / in the dust of the earth shall awake; / some shall live forever, / others shall be an everlasting horror and disgrace" (Daniel 12:2).

Reflecting on the Word

We have many hungers in life, and sometimes we can overindulge in response to them. Still, one that never goes away is our hunger to be connected. We desperately shun living in isolation. For many it is marriage that feeds that hunger, but so do family or friendships or the simple attention one finds in a community of faith or a collection of back yards. They all seem to feed our yearning for deep life, even when we are inattentive or preoccupied. A person of faith might even say that these communities are God being faithful to us.

This week's Gospel is one that turns the tables on us. It snares us in our own curiosity about what heaven will be like, and whether we will know the ones we love and be with our spouses, and what if we've been married seven times? And that's just where Jesus turns the tables and says it's about relationships and not about bodies to be with; it's about our deepest hungers to be united, even beyond marriage and friends and neighbors and communities of any sort. That's what resurrection is about, Jesus replies, and then reminds us one more time (as if we'd been deaf all the other times) that God has promised it and God is faithful. God "is not God of the dead, but of the living, for to him all are alive," is how Luke has Jesus saying it (Luke 20:38). In other words, all of our relationships of loving and caring, especially those of marriage, are but hints of real and full life, and the best is yet to come. So what you've found in marriage, even if you've been married seven times, is just the beginning.

CONSIDER/ DISCUSS:

- Why do you suppose we are so often dissatisfied with the relationships we have? What is it that we hunger for?
- Make a list of all the relationships you treasure. Then sit with the list and relish those relationships the way you might sit with a bowl of ripe red cherries.

Responding to the Word

As we go through life we'd like to know just whom we are going to spend eternity with and what it's going to be like. The truth is that none of us knows. Maybe the best we can do at this time is love those around us now, and let God take care of our future.

Spend a few minutes in quiet prayer. Ask God to show you one (or more) ways that you may be called to respond to this week's scriptures—

- in your relationship with God
- with family and friends
- at work, school, or church
- in the broader community

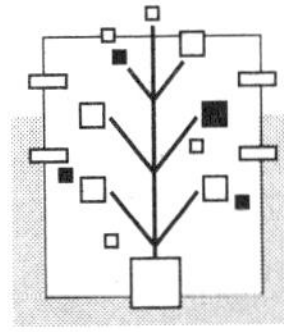

November 18, 2007

THIRTY-THIRD SUNDAY IN ORDINARY TIME

Today's Focus: The Times They Are A-Changing

Worlds change. The time comes for all of us when we recognize that life is no longer the same. Our world is different, and all that once was is no more.

FIRST READING
Malachi 3: 19–20a

Lo, the day is coming, blazing like an oven,
when all the proud and all evildoers will be stubble,
and the day that is coming will set them on fire,
leaving them neither root nor branch,
says the LORD of hosts.
But for you who fear my name, there will arise
the sun of justice with its healing rays.

PSALM RESPONSE
Psalm 98:9

The Lord comes to rule the earth with justice.

SECOND READING
2 Thessalonians 3: 7–12

Brothers and sisters: You know how one must imitate us. For we did not act in a disorderly way among you, nor did we eat food received free from anyone. On the contrary, in toil and drudgery, night and day we worked, so as not to burden any of you. Not that we do not have the right. Rather, we wanted to present ourselves as a model for you, so that you might imitate us. In fact, when we were with you, we instructed you that if anyone was unwilling to work, neither should that one eat. We hear that some are conducting themselves among you in a disorderly way, by not keeping busy but minding the business of others. Such people we instruct and urge in the Lord Jesus Christ to work quietly and to eat their own food.

GOSPEL
Luke 21:5–19

While some people were speaking about how the temple was adorned with costly stones and votive offerings, Jesus said, "All that you see here—the days will come when there will not be left a stone upon another stone that will not be thrown down."

Then they asked him, "Teacher, when will this happen? And what sign will there be when all these things are about to happen?" He answered, "See that you not be deceived, for many will come in my name, saying, 'I am he,' and 'The time has come.' Do not follow them! When you hear of wars and insurrections, do not be terrified; for such things must happen first, but it will not immediately be the end." Then he said to them, "Nation will rise against nation, and kingdom against kingdom. There will be powerful earthquakes, famines, and plagues from place to place; and awesome sights and mighty signs will come from the sky.

"Before all this happens, however, they will seize and persecute you, they will hand you over to the synagogues and to prisons, and they will have you led before kings and governors because of my name. It will lead to your giving testimony. Remember, you are not to prepare your defense beforehand, for I myself shall give you a wisdom in speaking that all your adversaries will be powerless to resist or refute. You will even be handed over by parents, brothers, relatives, and friends, and they will put some of you to death. You will be hated by all because of my name, but not a hair on your head will be destroyed. By your perseverance you will secure your lives."

Understanding the Word

Jeremiah stands at the gate of the temple in the face of an imminent threat from Babylon. God says through the prophet, "Only if you thoroughly reform your ways and your deeds . . . will I remain with you in this place, in the land which I gave your fathers long ago and forever" (Jeremiah 7:5, 7). The prophet's words were not heeded and the Babylonians in 587–586 BC destroyed Jerusalem and the temple.

Jesus is in the temple in today's Gospel, also with a prophetic oracle about the destruction of both the temple and the city of Jerusalem. His discourse is eschatological, that is, it discusses the last things, the *eschata* of Jerusalem and the temple. He also uses apocalyptic language to bring comfort to his followers, an important purpose of apocalyptic writings. He promises to be with them in adversity, even sharing his wisdom to enable refutation of enemies, which can include family members and friends (Luke 21:16) as well as "kings and governors" (21:12).

Jesus warns his followers not to be misled or terrified by false prophets claiming to be the Messiah. There will be some terrifying signs in nature together with political upheavals before the city and temple are destroyed. Jesus instructs his disciples that they will be persecuted, imprisoned, even killed "because of my name" (21:17). But he also promises to give them his "wisdom in speaking that all your adversaries will be powerless to resist or refute" (21:15).

These predictions are carried out in the pages of Luke's second volume, the Acts of the Apostles. The deacon Stephen is an excellent example. His enemies could not refute his long exposition in favor of Christianity by examining Old Testament history. Instead they stoned him to death because of his strong loyalty to Jesus. Christ promises at the end of today's Gospel, "By your perseverance you will secure your lives" (21:19). Fidelity to Jesus may lead to loss of life, as it did for Stephen and the apostle James (Acts12:1–2). True discipleship, however, will assure everlasting life with the Lord, who also died because of his dedication to the Father and his love for all God's children.

Reflecting on the Word

Worlds do change. They come and they go. One day we simply stop climbing up on our mother's or father's lap. Or we quit reading comic books, or put away our Barbies®, or we begin to notice beauty. It happens more than once in a lifetime. We pass the exam and get our driver's license, and in a moment all of childhood's boundaries crumble. We graduate from school and our days become our own, sometimes frighteningly so. We move away from home and realize we can no longer return, not to the way it once was. And while we think all those moments are of our own doing, in truth they are not, none of them. They come upon us as does November out of autumn, and frequently just as bleak. The temples of our lives that we've adorned not only with precious stones but also with precious memories and treasured ways are always being torn down without one stone left upon another. And no one ever asks our permission.

The new worlds we fear the most, however, are not the ones that change our outer landscapes so much as the ones that can reshape our inner landscapes. For believers, for those who live by the ways of Jesus, it is faith that offers us the willingness to trust and the courage to continue on. Jesus' vision can become the one still point in our ever-changing world, or the one source of life and love when all else is collapsing.

CONSIDER/ DISCUSS:

- Do you believe it is God who changes our worlds, or God who changes us when our worlds pass; or do you believe that we do our own adapting?
- Which world is currently ending for you?

Responding to the Word

Faith does not keep our worlds protected and whole. It does instill in us patient endurance by which, the Gospel reminds us, we will save our lives.

Spend a few minutes in quiet prayer. Ask God to show you one (or more) ways that you may be called to respond to this week's scriptures—

- in your relationship with God
- with family and friends
- at work, school, or church
- in the broader community

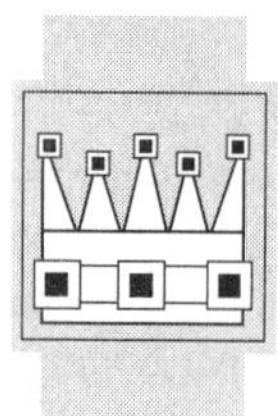

November 25, 2007

THE SOLEMNITY OF OUR LORD JESUS CHRIST THE KING

Today's Focus: The Temptation to Be King

Much of life is given to us without our asking, so much so that we're tempted to think of it all as happenstance, free to be wished away. Yet it may all be part of the process of preparing us for our life's specific task, or even the essence of our life's calling.

FIRST READING
2 Samuel 5:1–3

In those days, all the tribes of Israel came to David in Hebron and said: "Here we are, your bone and your flesh. In days past, when Saul was our king, it was you who led the Israelites out and brought them back. And the LORD said to you, 'You shall shepherd my people Israel and shall be commander of Israel.' " When all the elders of Israel came to David in Hebron, King David made an agreement with them there before the LORD, and they anointed him king of Israel.

PSALM RESPONSE
Psalm 122:1

Let us go rejoicing to the house of the Lord.

SECOND READING
Colossians 1: 12–20

Brothers and sisters: Let us give thanks to the Father, who has made you fit to share in the inheritance of the holy ones in light. He delivered us from the power of darkness and transferred us to the kingdom of his beloved Son, in whom we have redemption, the forgiveness of sins.

He is the image of the invisible God,
    the firstborn of all creation.
For in him were created all things in heaven and on earth,
    the visible and the invisible,
    whether thrones or dominions or principalities or powers;
    all things were created through him and for him.
He is before all things,
    and in him all things hold together.
He is the head of the body, the church.
He is the beginning, the firstborn from the dead,
    that in all things he himself might be preeminent.
For in him all the fullness was pleased to dwell,
    and through him to reconcile all things for him,
    making peace by the blood of his cross
    through him, whether those on earth or those in heaven.

GOSPEL
Luke 23:35–43

The rulers sneered at Jesus and said, "He saved others, let him save himself if he is the chosen one, the Christ of God." Even the soldiers jeered at him. As they approached to offer him wine they called out, "If you are King of the Jews, save yourself." Above him there was an inscription that read, "This is the King of the Jews."

Now one of the criminals hanging there reviled Jesus, saying, "Are you not the Christ? Save yourself and us." The other, however, rebuking him, said in reply, "Have you no fear of God, for you are subject to the same condemnation? And indeed, we have been condemned justly, for the sentence we received corresponds to our crimes, but this man has done nothing criminal." Then he said, "Jesus, remember me when you come into your kingdom." He replied to him, "Amen, I say to you, today you will be with me in Paradise."

Understanding the Word

The kingship of Jesus Christ is a theme carried forward from the Old Testament. "Christ" means "Messiah" or "Anointed." Jesus is the "Son of David," a direct descendant of the "anointed king of Israel" (2 Samuel 5:1–3). "Son of David" was a standard title for the Messiah in the time of Jesus. The blind beggar cries out to him as one petitions a king, "Jesus, Son of David, have pity on me!" (Luke 18:38).

The reading from the letter to the Colossians is one of the great hymns honoring Jesus Christ. His divine kingship is professed in such titles as "image of the invisible God" and "firstborn of all creation" (Colossians 1:15). He is deserving of the title "king" because of his salvific death for all persons. He is "the firstborn from the dead" (1:18). He will "reconcile all things . . . making peace by the blood of his cross" (1:20).

Salvation is a principal theme in the Gospel of Luke and "savior" is an important title for Jesus. On Christmas Eve the angel said, "Today in the city of David a savior has been born for you who is Messiah and Lord" (Luke 2:11). In today's reading one of the criminals crucified with Jesus calls out, "Are you not the Christ? Save yourself and us" (23:39). The Christian reader realizes that even though the words are spoken to mock Jesus, Christ will in fact become the savior of all. The other criminal asks for mercy, "Jesus, remember me when you come into your kingdom" (23:42).

A key point throughout Luke's Gospel is the teaching of Jesus that greatness in the kingdom is determined by service to others. At the Last Supper Jesus insisted, "[L]et the greatest among you be as the youngest, and the leader as the servant" (22:26). Jesus deserves to be called "king" because, as Savior, he takes care of the one need we all have that has eternal repercussions, namely forgiveness of our sins. He is both King and Savior. Colossians gives thanks for the Father who has "transferred us to the kingdom of his beloved Son, in whom we have redemption, the forgiveness of sins." (Colossians 1:13–14).

Reflecting on the Word

Our life's vocation is more often given to us than chosen or wished into being, whether it be the needs of parenting or the labors we take on each day, or even the vocation of simply being a child. The challenge at every age seems to be to live life as it calls us and not to wish it into oblivion, as if such wishes could be the ticket to a new and different rollercoaster, one more exciting or for others perhaps more tame.

So when we ask our children, "What would you like to be when you grow up?" it may be more nurturing to ask, "What do you think life would like you to be?" And when we ask young adults, "What are you going to do with your life?" it may be more helpful to invite them to consider, "What do you suppose life is going to do with you?" Different answers may drift into our awareness when we change the wording of our questions.

The fact is we can spend too much time wishing and trying to be something other than what life/God wants us to be. It is a great temptation simply because often it looks more glamorous or less painful. It was also the temptation of Jesus, as Luke's Gospel tells the tale. The religious leaders sneered, "He saved others, let him save himself" (Luke 23:35). And the soldiers jeered, "Save yourself!" (23:37). And one of the criminals ridiculed him and cried out, "Save yourself and us" (23:39). For Jesus it became the temptation to choose a calling other than the one given—it was the temptation to save himself. If you and I call him king, it is because he was faithful to his calling, not to save himself but to save us.

CONSIDER/ DISCUSS:

- What aspect of God's current vocation for you are you tempted to abandon?
- As you look upon your future, what do you suppose life is going to do with you?

Responding to the Word

We should be wary of the foolishness of wishing our lives away, of expending so much energy on the future that today passes wasted and unlived. The danger is that we might end up ignoring God's unfolding wisdom.

Spend a few minutes in quiet prayer. Ask God to show you one (or more) ways that you may be called to respond to this week's scriptures—

- in your relationship with God
- with family and friends
- at work, school, or church
- in the broader community

About the Authors

Msgr. Ralph Kuehner, a priest of the Archdiocese of Washington, has a licentiate in theology and in sacred scripture. He taught scripture and biblical Greek at the Josephinum College (Columbus, Ohio) and an advanced course in Koine Greek at Catholic University. He also did extensive scripture teaching in the archdiocesan permanent diaconate program. Since coming to Washington in 1967, he was a pastor for seventeen years. Msgr. Kuehner was a founder and continuing member of the Interfaith Conference of Metropolitan Washington, which brings together nine faith traditions. Social concerns has been an important ministry for him. He twice served as director of the archdicesan office dealing with social concerns (1970–1978 and 1996–2002). Msgr. Kuehner helped establish and/or develop programs for the poor, the homeless, migrants, the elderly, victims of discrimination, and family caregivers.

About the Authors

Rev. Joseph J. Juknialis is a priest of the Archdiocese of Milwaukee. Presently he is pastor of Shepherd of the Hills parish in Eden, Wisconsin, as well as Director of the Preaching Institute at Saint Francis Seminary. Ordained in 1969, he has spent the greater portion of his time in parish ministry. Over the years he has written and published a number of collections of stories for use in the classroom and in prayer settings. More recently his writings have focused on reflections for personal spirituality and prayer. In addition he writes a monthly reflection on the Sunday scriptures for the Catholic Herald, the Catholic newspaper for the Archdiocese of Milwaukee.

Notes

Notes

Notes

Notes

Notes